Biographies of Immortals

Legends of China

Special Edition

Including 3 Essays:

China and the Manchus

By Herbert A. Giles

Leaves From My Chinese Scrapbook

By Frederic H. Balfour

&

Biographies of Immortals

By Lionel Giles

El Paso Norte Press
Special Edition Books

Biographies of Immortals – Legends of China – Special Edition
By Herbert A. Giles, Frederic H. Balfour and Lionel Giles

Edited by Shawn Conners

First Edition – February 2010

Published by
EL Paso Norte Press
El Paso, Texas

ISBN 1-934255-30-0
ISBN13: 978-1-934255-30-8

Printed in the United States of America

PREFACE

Herbert Giles was a British diplomat and sinologist, educated at Charterhouse. He modified a Mandarin Chinese Romanization system earlier established by Thomas Wade, resulting in the widely known Wade-Giles Chinese transliteration system. Among his prolific works were translations of Confucius, Chuang Tzu, Lao Tzu, and the first widely published Chinese-English dictionary.

China and the Manchus is an attempt to present periods of history, as learned by oral tradition, as well as the limited historical information about China which was available to Western scholars in the 19th century. Presenting this essay first is done to help place the reader into the historical time periods from which many of the ancient Chinese legends have sprung.

Frederic Balfour was a British expatriate essayist and journalist, living in Shanghai. His letters about famine conditions in China were highly regarded, as little credible news regularly made it out of China during this period. Many of these letters appeared in *Harper's Magazine*. For most of his time in China, Balfour worked as editor-in-chief for *North China Daily News*, *The Shanghai Evening Courier*, and *The Celestial Empire* newspapers.

Leaves From My Chinese Scrapbook is a collection of stories, recollections, notes and assorted biographies which Balfour put together as he was completing his work on the groundbreaking *Taoist Texts* in 1884. Much of what is known about the life of Lao Tzu is drawn from *Leaves from My Chinese Scrapbook*.

Lionel Giles was a Victorian scholar, translator and the son of Herbert Giles. Lionel Giles served as an assistant curator at the British Museum. In this capacity he had access to many arcane ancient documents, which he spent the later part of his life transcribing and publishing. While primarily known for the first successful Western translation of *The Art of War* by Sun Tzu and *The Analects* of Confucius, Lionel Giles was a true Taoist at heart, and spent most of his life, along with his father, translating much of the source material used in the book which has come to be known today as the *Tao Te Ching*.

Biographies of Immortals was the first attempt by a Western scholar to translate the ancient Chinese book of *The Liexian Zhuan*. Lionel Giles was never able to finish completely transcribing the scrolls, but what has been preserved provides a fascinating glimpse into many historical legends of China. These accounts are presented in order of chronology, along with some brief analysis and comparisons.

Early transcription from Chinese characters into English words by sinologists such as Herbert Giles, Lionel Giles and Frederic Balfour has given way to newer, more accurate methods of transliteration, with some breathtaking results. Reading the Tao Te Ching today is a much more articulate spiritual exploration than reading similar transcriptions from the *Taoists Texts* written in 1884.

Similarly, while the teachings of Confucius have been presented in a more literate form in modern times than were originally transcribed by Lionel Giles in the early 20th century, it is important to remember that Confucius is believed to have traveled from village to village, singing many of the proverbs we have come to know, much like a bard or wandering minstrel in Western tradition. Attempts by some modern scholars to elevate the proverbial nature of many of these legendary figures, stories and anecdotes to the status of sublime literature often result in a loss of the simple humor, wisdom and universal resonance of many of the themes that run throughout the Chinese classics.

For Western students of classical Chinese texts such as the *Tao Te Ching*, *The Art of War*, *The Liexian Zhuan*, or *The Analects* of Confucius, these three essays provide valuable background, context and history for many of the legendary figures which are still prevalent in popular world culture. Being passed down from generation to generation, these stories are easily accessible, and not limited to scholars of ancient Chinese texts. Even casual modern readers will recognize the legendary figures of Lao Tzu, Confucius, and the Eight Immortals of China.

Table of Contents

Table of Contents (cont'd)

Book 3: ***Biographies of Immortals*** by Lionel Giles

China and the Manchus

By

Herbert A. Giles

CHAPTER 1 – THE NÜ-CHÊNS AND KITANS

The Manchus are descended from a branch of certain wild Tungusic nomads, who were known in the ninth century as the Nü-chêns, a name which has been said to mean "west of the sea." The cradle of their race lay at the base of the Ever-White Mountains, due north of Korea, and was fertilized by the head waters of the Yalu River.

In an illustrated Chinese work of the fourteenth century, of which the Cambridge University Library possesses the only known copy, we read that they reached this spot, originally the home of the Su-shên tribe, as fugitives from Korea; further, that careless of death and prizing valor only, they carried naked knives about their persons, never parting from them by day or night, and that they were as "poisonous" as wolves or tigers. They also tattooed their faces, and at marriage their mouths. By the close of the ninth century the Nü-chêns had become subject to the neighboring Kitans, then under the rule of the vigorous Kitan chieftain, Opaochi, who, in 907, proclaimed himself Emperor of an independent kingdom with the dynastic title of Liao, said to mean "iron," and who at once entered upon that long course of aggression against China and encroachment upon her territory which was to result in the practical division of the empire between the two powers, with the Yellow River as boundary, K`ai-fêng as the Chinese capital, and Peking, now for the first time raised to the status of a metropolis, as the Kitan capital. Hitherto, the Kitans had recognized China as their suzerain; they are first mentioned in Chinese history in A.D. 468, when they sent ambassadors to court, with tribute.

Turning now to China, the famous House of Sung, the early years of which were so full of promise of national prosperity, and which is deservedly associated with one of the two most brilliant periods in Chinese literature, was founded in 960. Korea was then forced, in order to protect herself from the encroachments of China, to accept the hated supremacy of the Kitans; but being promptly called upon to surrender large tracts of territory, she suddenly entered into an alliance with the Nü-chêns, who were also ready to revolt, and who sent an army to the assistance of their new friends. The Nü-chên and Korean armies, acting in concert, inflicted a severe defeat on the Kitans, and from this victory may be dated the beginning of the Nü-chên power. China had indeed already sent an embassy to the Nü-chêns, suggesting an alliance and also a combination with Korea, by which means the aggression of the Kitans might easily be checked; but during the eleventh century Korea became alienated from the Nü-chêns, and even went so far as to advise China to join with the Kitans in crushing the Nü-chêns. China, no doubt, would have been glad to get rid of both these troublesome neighbors, especially the Kitans, who were gradually filching territory from the empire, and driving the Chinese out of the southern portion of the province of Chihli.

For a long period China weakly allowed herself to be blackmailed by the Kitans, who, in return for a large money subsidy and valuable supplies of silk, forwarded a quite insignificant amount of local produce, which was called "tribute" by the Chinese court.

Early in the twelfth century, the Kitan monarch paid a visit to the Sungari River, for the purpose of fishing, and was duly received by the chiefs of the Nü-chên tribes in that district. On this occasion the Kitan Emperor, who had taken perhaps more liquor than was good for him, ordered the younger men of the company to get up and dance before him. This command was ignored by the son of one of the chiefs, named Akutêng (sometimes, but wrongly, written *Akuta*), and it was suggested to the Emperor that he should devise means for putting out of the way so uncompromising a spirit. No notice, however, was taken of the affair at the moment; and that night Akutêng, with a band of followers, disappeared from the scene. Making his way eastward, across the Sungari, he started a movement which may be said to have culminated five hundred years later in the conquest of China by the Manchus. In 1114 he began to act on the offensive, and succeeded in inflicting a severe defeat on the Kitans. By 1115 he had so far advanced towards the foundation of an independent kingdom that he actually assumed the title of Emperor. Thus was presented the rare spectacle of three contemporary rulers, each of whom claimed a title which, according to the Chinese theory, could only belong to one. The style he chose for his dynasty was Chin (also read *Kin*), which means "gold," and which some say was intended to mark a superiority over Liao (= iron), that of the Kitans, on the ground that gold is not, like iron, a prey to rust. Others, however, trace the origin of the term to the fact that gold was found in the Nü-chên territory.

A small point which has given rise to some confusion, may fitly be mentioned here. The tribe of Tartars hitherto spoken of as Nü-chêns, and henceforth known in history as the "Golden Dynasty," in 1035 changed the word *chên* for *chih*, and were called Nü-chih Tartars. They did this because at that date the word *chên* was part of the personal name of the reigning Kitan Emperor, and therefore taboo. The necessity for such change would of course cease with their emancipation from Kitan rule, and the old name would be revived; it will accordingly be continued in the following pages.

The victories of Akutêng over the Kitans were most welcome to the Chinese Emperor, who saw his late oppressors humbled to the dust by the victorious Nü-chêns; and in 1120 a treaty of alliance was signed by the two powers against the common enemy. The upshot of this move was that the Kitans were severely defeated in all directions, and their chief cities fell into the hands of the Nü-chêns, who finally succeeded, in 1122, in taking Peking by assault, the Kitan Emperor having already sought safety in flight. When, however, the time came for an equitable settlement of territory between China and the victorious Nü-chêns, the Chinese Emperor discovered that the Nü-chêns, inasmuch as they had done most of the fighting, were determined to have the lion's share of the reward; in fact, the yoke imposed by the latter proved if anything more burdensome than that of the dreaded Kitans. More territory was taken by the Nü-chêns, and even larger levies of money were exacted, while the same old farce of worthless tribute was carried on as before.

In 1123, Akutêng died, and was canonized as the first Emperor of the Chin, or Golden Dynasty. He was succeeded by a brother; and two years later, the last Emperor of the Kitans was captured and relegated to private life, thus bringing the dynasty to an end.

The new Emperor of the Nü-chêns spent the rest of his life in one long struggle with China. In 1126, the Sung capital, the modern K`ai-fêng Fu in Honan, was twice besieged: on the first occasion for thirty-three days, when a heavy ransom was exacted and some territory was ceded; on the second occasion for forty days, when it fell, and was given up to pillage. In 1127, the feeble Chinese Emperor was seized and carried off, and by 1129 the whole of China north of the Yang-tsze was in the hands of the Nü-chêns. The younger brother of the banished Emperor was proclaimed by the Chinese at Nanking, and managed to set up what is known as the southern Sung dynasty; but the Nü-chêns gave him no rest, driving him first out of Nanking, and then out of Hangchow, where he had once more established a capital. Ultimately, there was peace of a more or less permanent character, chiefly due to the genius of a notable Chinese general of the day; and the Nü-chêns had to accept the Yang-tsze as the dividing line between the two powers.

The next seventy years were freely marked by raids, first of one side and then of the other; but by the close of the twelfth century the Mongols were pressing the Nü-chêns from the north, and the southern Sungs were seizing the opportunity to attack their old enemies from the south. Finally, in 1234, the independence of the Golden Dynasty of Nü-chêns was extinguished by Ogotai, third son of the great Genghis Khan, with the aid of the southern Sungs, who were themselves in turn wiped out by Kublai Khan, the first Mongol Emperor to rule over a united China.

The name of this wandering people, whose territory covers such a huge space on the map, has been variously derived from (1) *moengel,* celestial, (2) *mong,* brave, and (3) *munku,* silver, the last mentioned being favored by some because of its relation to the iron and golden dynasties of the Kitans and Nü-chêns respectively.

Three centuries and a half must now pass away before entering upon the next act of the Manchu drama. The Nü-chêns had been scotched, but not killed, by their Mongol conquerors, who, one hundred and thirty-four years later (1368), were themselves driven out of China, a pure native dynasty being re-established under the style of Ming, "Bright." During the ensuing two hundred years the Nü-chêns were scarcely heard of, the House of Ming being busily occupied in other directions. Their warlike spirit, however, found scope and nourishment in the expeditions organized against Japan and Tan-lo, or Quelpart, as named by the Dutch, a large island to the south of the Korean peninsula; while on the other hand the various tribes scattered over a portion of the territory known to Europeans as Manchuria, availed themselves of long immunity from attack by the Chinese to advance in civilization and prosperity. It may be noted here that "Manchuria" is unknown to the Chinese or to the Manchus themselves as a geographical expression. The present extensive home of the Manchus is usually spoken of as the Three Eastern Provinces, namely, (1) Shêng-king, or Liao-tung, or Kuan-tung, (2) Kirin, and (3) Heilungchiang or Tsitsihar.

Among the numerous small independent communities above mentioned, which traced their ancestry to the Nü-chêns of old, one of the smallest, the members of which inhabited a tract of territory due east of what is now the city of Mukden, and were shortly to call themselves Manchus,—the origin of the name is not known,—produced, in 1559, a young hero who altered the course of Chinese history to such an extent that for nearly three hundred years his descendants sat on the throne of China, and ruled over what was for a great portion of the time the largest empire on earth. Nurhachu, the real founder of the Manchu power, was born in 1559, from a virile stock, and was soon recognized to be an extraordinary child. We need not linger over his dragon face, his phoenix eye, or even over his large, drooping ears, which have always been associated by the Chinese with intellectual ability. He first came into prominence in 1583, when, at twenty-four years of age, he took up arms, at the head of only one hundred and thirty men, in connection with the treacherous murder by a rival chieftain of his father and grandfather, who had ruled over a petty principality of almost infinitesimal extent; and he finally succeeded three years later in securing from the Chinese, who had been arrayed against him, not only the surrender of the murderer, but also a sum of money and some robes of honor. He was further successful in negotiating a treaty, under the terms of which Manchu furs could be exchanged at certain points for such Chinese commodities as cotton, sugar, and grain.

In 1587, Nurhachu built a walled city, and established an administration in his tiny principality, the even-handed justice and purity of which soon attracted a large number of settlers, and before very long he had succeeded in amalgamating five Manchu States under his personal rule. Extension of territory by annexation after victories over neighboring States followed as a matter of course, the result being that his growing power came to be regarded with suspicion, and even dread. At length, a joint attempt on the part of seven States, aided by two Mongol chieftains, was made to crush him; but, although numerical superiority was overpoweringly against him, he managed to turn the enemy's attack into a rout, killed four thousand men, and captured three thousand horses, besides other booty. Following up this victory by further annexations, he now began to present a bold front to the Chinese, declaring himself independent, and refusing any longer to pay tribute. In 1604, he built himself a new capital, Hingking, which he placed not very far east of the modern Mukden, and there he received envoys from the Mongolian chieftains, sent to congratulate him on his triumph.

At this period the Manchus, whose spoken words were polysyllabic, and not monosyllabic like Chinese, had no written language beyond certain rude attempts at alphabetic writing, formed from Chinese characters, and found to be of little practical value. The necessity for something more convenient soon appealed to the prescient and active mind of Nurhachu; accordingly, in 1599, he gave orders to two learned scholars to prepare a suitable script for his rapidly increasing subjects. This they accomplished by basing the new script upon Mongol, which had been invented in 1269, by Baschpa, or 'Phagspa, a Tibetan lama, acting under the direction of Kublai Khan. Baschpa had based his script upon the written language of the Ouigours, who were descendants of the Hsiung-nu, or Huns. The Ouigours, known by that name since the year 629, were once the ruling race in the regions which now form the khanates of Khiva and Bokhara, and had been the first of the tribes of Central

Asia to have a script of their own. This they formed from the Estrangelo Syraic of the Nestorians, who appeared in China in the early part of the seventh century. The Manchu written language, therefore, is lineally descended from Syraic; indeed, the family likeness of both Manchu and Mongol to the parent stem is quite obvious, except that these two scripts, evidently influenced by Chinese, are written vertically, though, unlike Chinese, they are read from left to right. Thirty-three years later various improvements were introduced, leaving the Manchu script precisely as we find it at the present day.

In 1613, Nurhachu had gathered about him an army of some forty thousand men; and by a series of raids in various directions, he further gradually succeeded in extending considerably the boundaries of his kingdom. There now remained but one large and important State, towards the annexation of which he directed all his efforts. After elaborate preparations which extended over more than two years, at the beginning of which (1616) the term Manchu (etymology unknown) was definitively adopted as a national title, Nurhachu, in 1618, drew up a list of grievances against the Chinese, under which he declared that his people had been and were still suffering, and solemnly committed it to the flames,—a recognized method of communication with the spirits of heaven and earth. This document consisted of seven clauses, and was addressed to the Emperor of China; it was, in fact, a declaration of war.

The Chinese, who were fast becoming aware that a dangerous enemy had arisen, and that their own territory would be the next to be threatened, at length decided to oppose any further progress on the part of Narhachu; and with this view dispatched an army of two hundred thousand men against him. These troops, many of whom were physically unfit, were divided on arrival at Mukden into four bodies, each with some separate aim, the achievement of which was to conduce to the speedy disruption of Nurhachu's power. The issue of this move was certainly not expected on either side. In a word, Nurhachu defeated his Chinese antagonists in detail, finally inflicting such a crushing blow that he was left completely master of the situation, and before very long had realized the chief object of his ambition, namely, the reunion under one rule of those states into which the Golden Dynasty had been broken up when it collapsed before the Mongols in 1234.

CHAPTER 2 – THE FALL OF THE MINGS

It is almost a conventionalism to attribute the fall of a Chinese dynasty to the malign influence of eunuchs. The Imperial court was undoubtedly at this date entirely in the hands of eunuchs, who occupied all kinds of lucrative posts for which they were quite unfitted, and even accompanied the army, nominally as officials, but really as spies upon the generals in command. One of the most notorious of these was Wei Chung-hsien, whose career may be taken as typical of his class. He was a native of Sun-ning in Chihli, of profligate character, who made himself a eunuch, and changed his name to Li Chin-chung. Entering the palace, he managed to get into the service of the mother of the future Emperor, posthumously canonized as Hsi Tsung, and became the paramour of that weak monarch's wet-nurse. The pair gained the Emperor's affection to an extraordinary degree, and Wei, an ignorant brute, was the real ruler of China during the reign of Hsi Tsung. He always took care to present memorials and other State papers when his Majesty was engrossed in carpentry, and the Emperor would pretend to know all about the question, and tell Wei to deal with it. Aided by unworthy censors, a body of officials who are supposed to be the "eyes and ears" of the monarch, and privileged to censure him for misgovernment, he gradually drove all loyal men from office, and put his opponents to cruel and ignominious deaths. He persuaded Hsi Tsung to enroll a division of eunuch troops, ten thousand strong, armed with muskets; while, by causing the Empress to have a miscarriage, his paramour cleared his way to the throne. Many officials espoused his cause, and the infatuated sovereign never wearied of loading him with favors. In 1626, temples were erected to him in all the provinces except Fuhkien, his image received Imperial honors, and he was styled Nine Thousand Years, i.e. only one thousand less than the Emperor himself, the Chinese term in the latter case being *wan sui*, which has been adopted by the Japanese as *banzai*. All successes were ascribed to his influence, a Grand Secretary declaring that his virtue had actually caused the appearance of a "unicorn" in Shantung. In 1627, he was likened in a memorial to Confucius, and it was decreed that he should be worshipped with the Sage in the

Imperial Academy. His hopes were overthrown by the death of Hsi Tsung, whose successor promptly dismissed him. He hanged himself to escape trial, and his corpse was disembowelled. His paramour was executed, and in 1629, nearly three hundred persons were convicted and sentenced to varying penalties for being connected with his schemes.

Jobbery and corruption were rife; and at the present juncture these agencies were successfully employed to affect the recall of a really able general who had been sent from Peking to recover lost ground, and prevent further encroachments by the Manchus. For a time, Nurhachu had been held in check by his skilful dispositions of troops, Mukden was strongly fortified, and confidence generally was restored; but the fatal policy of the new general rapidly alienated the Chinese inhabitants, and caused them to enter secretly into communication with the Manchus. It was thus that in 1621 Nurhachu was in a position to advance upon Mukden. Encamping within a mile or two of the city, he sent forward a reconnoitring party, which was immediately attacked by the Chinese commandant at the head of a large force. The former fled, and the latter pursued, only to fall into the inevitable ambush; and the Chinese troops, on retiring in their turn, found that the bridge across the moat had been destroyed by traitors in their own camp, so that they were unable to re-enter the city. Thus Mukden fell, the prelude to a series of further victories, one of which was the rout of an army sent to retake Mukden, and the chief of which was the capture of Liaoyang, now remembered in connection with the Russo-Japanese war. In many of these engagements the Manchus, whose chief weapon was the long bow, which they used with deadly effect, found themselves opposed by artillery, the use of which had been taught to the Chinese by Adam Schaal, the Jesuit father. The supply of powder, however, had a way of running short, and at once the pronounced superiority of the Manchu archers prevailed.

Other cities now began to tender a voluntary submission, and many Chinese took to shaving the head and wearing the queue, in acknowledgment of their allegiance to the Manchus. All, however, was not yet over, for the growing Manchu power was still subjected to frequent attacks from Chinese arms in directions as far as possible removed from points where Manchu troops were concentrated. Meanwhile Nurhachu gradually extended his borders eastward, until in 1625, the year in which he placed his capital at Mukden, his frontiers reached to the sea on the east and to the river Amur on the north, the important city of Ning-yüan being almost the only possession remaining to the Chinese beyond the Great Wall. The explanation of this is as follows.

An incompetent general, as above mentioned, had been sent at the instance of the eunuchs to supersede an officer who had been holding his own with considerable success, but who was not a *persona grata* at court. The new general at once decided that no territory outside the Great Wall was to be held against the Manchus, and gave orders for the immediate retirement of all troops and Chinese residents generally. To this command the civil governor of Ning-yüan, and the military commandant, sent an indignant protest, writing out an oath with their blood that they would never surrender the city. Nurhachu seized the opportunity, and delivered a violent attack, with which he seemed to be making some progress, until at length artillery was brought into play. The havoc caused by the guns at close quarters was terrific, and the Manchus fled. This defeat was a blow from which Nurhachu never recovered; his chagrin brought on a serious illness, and he died in 1626, aged sixty-eight. Later on, when his descendants were sitting upon the throne of China, he was canonized as T`ai Tsu, the Great Ancestor, the representatives of the four preceding generations of his family being canonized as Princes.

Nurhachu was succeeded by his fourth son, Abkhai, then thirty-four years of age, and a tried warrior. His reign began with a correspondence between himself and the governor who had been the successful defender of Ning-yüan, in which some attempt was made to conclude a treaty of peace. The Chinese on their side demanded the return of all captured cities and territory; while the Manchus, who refused to consider any such terms, suggested that China should pay them a huge subsidy in money, silk, etc., in return for which they offered but a moderate supply of furs, and something over half a ton of ginseng (*Panax repens*), the famous forked root said to resemble the human body, and much valued by the Chinese as a strengthening medicine. This, of course, was a case of "giving too little and asking too much," and the negotiations came to nothing. In 1629, Abkhai, who by this time was master of Korea, marched upon Peking, at the head of a large army, and encamped within a few miles from its walls; but he was unable to capture the city, and had finally to retire. The next few years were devoted by the Manchus, who now began to possess artillery of their own casting, to the conquest of Mongolia, in the hope of thus securing an easy passage for their armies into China. An offer of peace was now made by the Chinese Emperor, for reasons shortly to be stated; but the Manchu terms were too severe, and hostilities were resumed, the Manchus chiefly occupying themselves in devastating the country round Peking, their numbers being constantly swelled by a stream of deserters from the Chinese ranks. In 1643, Abkhai died; he was succeeded by his ninth son, a boy of five, and was later on canonized as T`ai Tsung, the Great Forefather. By 1635, he had already begun to style himself Emperor of China, and had established a system of public examinations. The name of the dynasty had been "Manchu" ever since 1616; twenty years later he translated this term into the Chinese word *Ch`ing* (or Ts`ing), which means "pure"; and as the Great Pure Dynasty it will be remembered in history. Other important enactments of his reign were prohibitions against the use of tobacco, which had been recently introduced into Manchuria from Japan, through Korea; against the Chinese fashion of dress and of wearing the hair; and against the practice of binding the feet of girls. All except the first of these were directed towards the complete denationalization of the Chinese who had accepted his rule, and whose numbers were increasing daily.

So far, the Manchus seem to have been little influenced by religious beliefs or scruples, except of a very primitive kind; but when they came into closer contact with the Chinese, Buddhism began to spread its charms, and not in vain, though strongly opposed by Abkhai himself.

In 1635 the Manchus had effected the conquest of Mongolia, aided to a great extent by frequent defections of large bodies of Mongols who had been exasperated by their own ill-treatment at the hands of the Chinese. Among some ancient Mongolian archives there has recently been discovered a document, dated 1636, under which the Mongol chiefs recognized the suzerainty of the Manchu Emperor. It was, however, stipulated that, in the event of the fall of the dynasty, all the laws existing previously to this date should again come into force.

A brief review of Chinese history during the later years of Manchu progress, as described above, discloses a state of things such as will always be found to prevail towards the close of an outworn dynasty. Almost from the day when, in 1628, the last Emperor of the Ming Dynasty ascended the throne, national grievances began to pass from a simmering and more or less latent condition to a state of open and acute hostility. The exactions and tyranny of the eunuchs had led to increased taxation and general discontent; and the horrors of famine now enhanced the gravity of the situation. Local outbreaks were common, and were with difficulty suppressed. The most capable among Chinese generals of the period, Wu San-kuei, shortly to play a leading part in the dynastic drama, was far away, employed in resisting the invasions of the Manchus, when a very serious rebellion, which had been in preparation for some years, at length burst violently forth.

Li Tz{u}-ch`êng was a native of Shensi, who, before he was twenty years old, had succeeded his father as village beadle. The famine of 1627 had brought him into trouble over the land-tax, and in 1629 he turned brigand, but without conspicuous success during the following ten years. In 1640, he headed a small gang of desperadoes, and overrunning parts of Hupeh and Honan, was soon in command of a large army. He was joined by a female bandit, formerly a courtesan, who advised him to avoid slaughter and to try to win the hearts of the people. In 1642, after several attempts to capture the city of K`ai-fêng, during one of which his left eye was destroyed by an arrow, he at length succeeded, chiefly in consequence of a sudden rise of the Yellow River, the waters of which rushed through a canal originally intended to fill the city moat and flood out the rebels. The rise of the river, however, was so rapid and so unusually high that the city itself was flooded, and an enormous number of the inhabitants perished, the rest seeking safety in flight to higher ground.

By 1744, Li Tz{u}-ch`êng had reduced the whole of the province of Shensi; whereupon he began to advance on Peking, proclaiming himself first Emperor of the Great Shun Dynasty, the term *shun* implying harmony between rulers and ruled. Terror reigned at the Chinese court, especially as meteorological and other portents appeared in unusually large numbers, as though to justify the panic. The Emperor was in despair; the exchequer was empty, and there was no money to pay the troops, who, in any case, were too few to man the city walls. Each of the Ministers of State was anxious only to secure his own safety. Li Tz{u}-ch`êng's advance was scarcely opposed, the eunuch commanders of cities and passes hastening to surrender them and save their own lives. For, in case of immediate surrender, no injury was done by Li to life or property, and even after a short resistance only a few lives were exacted as penalty; but a more obstinate defense was punished by burning and looting and universal slaughter.

The Emperor was now advised to send for Wu San-kuei; but that step meant the end of further resistance to the invading Manchus on the east, and for some time he would not consent. Meanwhile, he issued an Imperial proclamation, such as is usual on these occasions, announcing that all the troubles which had come upon the empire were due to his own incompetence and unworthiness, as confirmed by the droughts, famines, and other signs of divine wrath, of recent occurrence; that the administration was to be reformed, and only virtuous and capable officials would be employed. The near approach, however, of Li's army at length caused the Emperor to realize that it was Wu San-kuei or nothing, and belated messengers were dispatched to summon him to the defense of the capital. Long before he could possibly arrive, a gate of the southern city of Peking was treacherously opened by the eunuch in charge of it, and the next thing the Emperor saw was his capital in flames. He then summoned the Empress and the court ladies, and bade them each provide for her own safety. He sent his three sons into hiding, and actually killed with his own hand several of his favorites, rather than let them fall into the hands of the One-Eyed Rebel. He attempted the same by his daughter, a young girl, covering his face with the sleeve of his robe; but in his agony of mind he failed in his blow, and only succeeded in cutting off an arm, leaving the unfortunate princess to be dispatched later on by the Empress. After this, in concert with a trusted eunuch and a few attendants, he disguised himself, and made an attempt to escape from the city by night; but they found the gates closed, and the guard refused to allow them to pass. Returning to the palace in the early morning, the Emperor caused the great bell to be rung as usual to summon the officers of government to audience; but no one came. He then retired, with his faithful eunuch, to a kiosque, on what is known as the Coal Hill, in the palace grounds, and there wrote a last decree on the lapel of his coat:—"I, poor in virtue and of contemptible personality, have incurred the wrath of God on high. My Ministers have deceived me. I am ashamed to meet my ancestors; and therefore I myself take off my crown, and with my hair covering my face, await dismemberment at the hands of the rebels. Do not hurt a single one of my people!" Emperor and eunuch then committed suicide by hanging themselves, and the Great Ming Dynasty was brought to an end.

Li Tz{u}-ch`êng made a grand official entry into Peking, upon which many of the palace ladies committed suicide. The bodies of the two Empresses were discovered, and the late Emperor's sons were captured and kindly treated; but of the Emperor himself there was for some time no trace. At length his body was found, and was encoffined, together with those of the Empresses, by order of Li Tz{u}-ch`êng, by-and-by to receive fit and proper burial at the hands of the Manchus.

Li Tz{u}-ch`êng further possessed himself of the persons of Wu San-kuei's father and affianced bride, the latter of whom, a very beautiful girl, he intended to keep for himself. He next sent off a letter to Wu San-kuei, offering an alliance against the Manchus, which was fortified by another letter from Wu San-kuei's father, urging his son to fall in which Li's wishes, especially as his own life would be dependent upon the success of the missions. Wu San-kuei had already started on his way to relieve the capital when he heard of the events above recorded; and it seems probable that he would have yielded to circumstances and persuasion but for the fact that Li had seized the girl he intended to marry. This decided him; he retraced his steps, shaved his head after the required style, and joined the Manchus.

It was not very long before Li Tz{u}-ch`êng's army was in full pursuit, with the twofold object of destroying Wu San-kuei and recovering Chinese territory already occupied by the Manchus. In the battle which ensued, all these hopes were dashed; Li sustained a crushing defeat, and fled to Peking. There he put to death the Ming princes who were in his hands, and completely exterminated Wu San-kuei's family, with the exception of the girl above mentioned, whom he carried off after having looted and burnt the palace and other public buildings. Now was the opportunity of the Manchus; and with the connivance and loyal aid of Wu San-kuei, the Great Ch`ing Dynasty was established.

Li Tz{u}-ch`êng, who had officially mounted the Dragon Throne as Emperor of China nine days after his capture of Peking, was now hotly pursued by Wu San-kuei, who had the good fortune to recover from the rebels the girl, who had been taken with them in their flight, and whom he then married. Li Tz{u}-ch`êng retreated westwards; and after two vain attempts to check his pursuers, his army began to melt away. Driven south, he held Wu-ch`ang for a time; but ultimately he fled down the Yang-tsze, and was slain by local militia in Hupeh.
Li was a born soldier. Even hostile writers admit that his army was wonderfully well disciplined, and that he put a stop to the hideous atrocities which had made his name a terror in the empire, just so soon as he found that he could accomplish his ends by milder means. His men were obliged to march light, very little baggage being allowed; his horses were most carefully looked after. He himself was by nature calm and cold, and his manner of life was frugal and abstemious.

CHAPTER 3—SHUN CHIH

The back of the rebellion was now broken; but an alien race, called in to drive out the rebels, found themselves in command of the situation. Wu San-kuei had therefore no alternative but to acknowledge the Manchus definitely as the new rulers of China, and to obtain the best possible terms for his country. Ever since the defeat of Li by the combined forces of Chinese and Manchus, it had been perfectly well understood that the latter were to be supported in their bid for Imperial power, and the conditions under which the throne was to be transferred were as follows:—(1) No Chinese women were to be taken into the Imperial seraglio; (2) the Senior Classic at the great triennial examination, on the results of which successful candidates were drafted into the public service, was never to be a Manchu; (3) Chinese men were to adopt the Manchu dress, shaving the front part of the head and plaiting the back hair into a queue, but they were to be allowed burial in the costume of the Mings; (4) Chinese women were not to adopt the Manchu dress, nor to cease to compress their feet, in accordance with ancient custom.

Wu San-kuei was loaded with honors, among others with a triple-eyed peacock's feather, a decoration introduced, together with the "button" at the top of the hat, by the Manchus, and classed as single-, double-, and triple-eyed, according to merit. A few years later, his son married the sister of the Emperor; and a few years later still, he was appointed one of three feudatory princes, his rule extending over the huge provinces of Yünnan and Ss{u}ch`uan. There we shall meet him again.

The new Emperor, the ninth son of Abkhai, best known by his year-title as Shun Chih (favorable sway), was a child of seven when he was placed upon the throne in 1644, under the regency of an uncle; and by the time he was twelve years old, the uncle had died, leaving him to his own resources. Before his early death, the regent had already done some excellent work on behalf of his nephew. He had curtailed the privileges of the eunuchs to such an extent that for a hundred and fifty years to come,—so long, in fact, as the empire was in the hands of wise rulers,—their malign influence was inappreciable in court circles and politics generally. He left Chinese officials in control of the civil administration, keeping closely to the lines of the system which had obtained under the previous dynasty; he did not hastily press for the universal adoption of Manchu costume; and he even caused sacrificial ceremonies to be performed at the mausolea of the Ming Emperors. One new rule of considerable importance seems to have been introduced by the Manchus, namely, that no official should be allowed to hold office within the boundaries of his own province. Ostensibly a check on corrupt practices, it is probable that this rule had a more far-reaching political purport. The members of the Han-lin College presented an address praying him (1) to prepare a list of all worthy men; (2) to search out such of these as might be in hiding; (3) to exterminate all rebels; (4) to proclaim an amnesty; (5) to establish peace; (6) to disband the army, and (7) to punish corrupt officials.

The advice conveyed in the second clause of the above was speedily acted upon, and a number of capable men were secured for the government service. At the same time, with a view to the full technical establishment of the dynasty, the Imperial ancestors were canonized, and an ancestral shrine was duly constituted. The general outlook would now appear to have been satisfactory from the point of view of Manchu interests; but from lack of means of communication, China had in those days almost the connotation of space infinite, and events of the highest importance, involving nothing less than the change of a dynasty, could be carried through in one portion of the empire before their imminence had been more than whispered in another. No sooner was Peking taken by the One-Eyed Rebel, than a number of officials fled southwards and took refuge in Nanking, where they set up a grandson of the last Emperor but one of the Ming Dynasty, who was now the rightful heir to the throne. The rapidly growing power of the Manchus had been lost sight of, if indeed it had ever been thoroughly realized, and it seemed quite natural that the representative of the House of Ming should be put forward to resist the rebels.

This monarch, however, was quite unequal to the fate which had befallen him; and, before long, both he himself and his capital were in the hands of the Manchus. Other claimants to the throne appeared in various places; notably, one at Hangchow and another at Foochow, each of whom looked upon the other as a usurper. The former was soon disposed of, but the latter gradually established his rule over a wide area, and for a long time kept the Manchus at bay, so hateful was the thought of an alien domination to the people of the province in question. Towards the close of 1646, he too had been captured, and the work of pacification went on, the penalty of death now being exacted in the case of officials who refused to shave the head and wear the queue. Two more Emperors, both of Imperial Ming blood, were next proclaimed in Canton, one of whom strangled himself on the advance of the Manchus, while the other disappeared. A large number of loyal officials, rather than shave the front part of the head and wear the Manchu queue, voluntarily shaved the whole head, and sought sanctuary in monasteries, where they joined the Buddhist priesthood.

One more early attempt to re-establish the Mings must be noticed. The fourth son of a grandson of the Ming Emperor Wan Li (died 1620) was in 1646 proclaimed Emperor at Nan-yang in Honan. For a number of years of bloody warfare he managed to hold out; but gradually he was forced to retire, first to Fuhkien and Kuangtung, and then into Kueichou and Yünnan, from which he was finally expelled by Wu San-kuei. He next fled to Burma, where in 1661 he was handed over to Wu San-kuei, who had followed in pursuit; and he finally strangled himself in the capital of Yünnan. He is said to have been a Christian, as also many of his adherents, in consequence of which, the Jesuit father, A. Koffler, bestowed upon him the title of the Constantine of China. In view of the general character for ferocity with which the Manchus are usually credited, it is pleasant to be able to record that when the official history of the Ming Dynasty came to be written, a Chinese scholar of the day, sitting on the historical commission, pleaded that three of the princes above mentioned, who were veritable scions of the Imperial stock, should be entered as "brave men" and not as "rebels," and that the Emperor, to whose reign we are now coming, graciously granted his request.

In the year 1661 Shun Chih, the first actual Emperor of the Ch`ing dynasty, "became a guest on high." He does not rank as one of China's great monarchs, but his kindly character as a man, and his magnanimity as a ruler, were extolled by his contemporaries. He treated the Catholic missionaries with favor. The Dutch and Russian embassies to his court in 1656 found there envoys from the Great Mogul, from the Western Tartars, and from the Dalai Lama. China, in the days when her civilization towered above that of most countries on the globe, and when her strength commanded the respect of all nations, great and small, was quite accustomed to receive embassies from foreign parts; the first recorded instance being that of "An-tun" = Marcus Aurelius *Anton*inus, which reached China in A.D. 166. But because the tribute offered in this case contained no jewels, consisting merely of ivory, rhinoceros-horn, tortoiseshell, etc., which had been picked up in Annam, some have regarded it merely as a trading enterprise, and not really an embassy from the Roman Emperor; Chinese writers, on the other hand, suggest that the envoys sold the valuable jewels and bought a trumpery collection of tribute articles on the journey.

By the end of Shun Chih's reign, the Manchus, once a petty tribe of hardy bowmen, far beyond the outskirts of the empire, were in undoubted possession of all China, of Manchuria, of Korea, of most of Mongolia, and even of the island of Formosa. How this island, discovered by the Chinese only in 1430, became Manchu property, is a story not altogether without romance.

The leader of a large fleet of junks, traders or pirates as occasion served, known to the Portuguese of the day as Iquon, was compelled to place his services at the command of the last sovereign of the Ming dynasty, in whose cause he fought against the Manchu invaders along the coasts of Fuhkien and Kuangtung. In 1628 he tendered his submission to the Manchus, and for a time was well treated, and cleared the seas of other pirates. Gradually, however, he became too powerful, and it was deemed necessary to restrain him by force. He was finally induced to surrender to the Manchu general in Fuhkien; and having been made a prisoner, was sent to Peking, with two of his sons by a Japanese wife, together with other of his adherents, all of whom were executed upon arrival. Another son, familiar to foreigners under the name of Koxinga, a Portuguese corruption of his title, had remained behind with the fleet when his father surrendered, and he, determined to avenge his father's treacherous death, declared an implacable war against the Manchus. His piratical attacks on the coast of China had long been a terror to the inhabitants; to such an extent, indeed, that the populations of no fewer than eighty townships had been forced to remove inland. Then Formosa, upon which the Dutch had begun to form colonies in 1634, and where substantial portions of their forts are still to be seen, attracted his piratical eye. He attacked the Dutch, and succeeded in driving them out with great slaughter, thus possessing himself of the island; but gradually his followers began to drop off, in submission to the new dynasty, and at length he himself was reported to Peking as dead. In 1874, partly on the ground that he was really a supporter of the Ming dynasty and not a rebel, and partly on the ground that "he had founded in the midst of the waters a dominion which he had transmitted to his descendants, and which was by them surrendered to the Imperial sway,"—a memorial was presented to the throne, asking that his spirit might be canonized as the guardian angel of Formosa, and that a shrine might be built in his honor. The request was granted.

Consolidation of the empire thus won by the sword was carried out as follows. In addition to the large Manchu garrison at Peking, smaller garrisons were established at nine of the provincial capitals, and at ten other important points in the provinces. The Manchu commandant of each of the nine garrisons above mentioned, familiar to foreigners as the Tartar General, was so placed in order to act as a check upon the civil Governor or Viceroy, of whom he, strictly speaking, took precedence, though in practice their ranks have always been regarded as equal. With the empire at peace, the post of Tartar General has always been a sinecure, and altogether out of comparison with that of the Viceroy and his responsibilities; but in the case of a Viceroy suspected of disloyalty and collusion with rebels, the swift opportunity of the Tartar General was the great safeguard of the dynasty, further strengthened as he was by the regulation which gave to him the custody of the keys to the city gates. Those garrisons, the soldiers of which were accompanied by their wives and families, were from the first intended to be permanent institutions; and there until quite recently were to be found the descendants of the original drafts, not allowed to intermarry with their Chinese neighbors, but otherwise influenced to such an extent that their Manchu characteristics had almost entirely disappeared. In one direction the Manchus made a curious concession which, though entirely sentimental, was nevertheless well calculated to appeal to a proud though unconquered people. A rule was established under which every Manchu high official, when memorializing the throne, was to speak of himself to the Emperor as "your Majesty's slave," whereas the term accepted from every Chinese high official was simply "your Majesty's servant." During the early years of Manchu rule, proficiency in archery was as much insisted on as in the days of Edward III with us; and even down to a few years ago Manchu Bannermen, as they came to be called, might be seen everywhere diligently practicing the art—actually one of the six fine arts of China—by the aid of which their ancestors had passed from the state of a petty tribal community to possession of the greatest empire in the world.

The term Bannerman, it may here be explained, is applied to all Manchus in reference to their organization under one or other of eight banners of different color and design; besides which, there are also eight banners for Mongolians, and eight more for the descendants of those Chinese who sided with the Manchus against the Mings, and thus helped to establish the Great Pure dynasty.

One of the first cares to the authorities of a newly-established dynasty in China is to provide the country with a properly authorized Penal Code, and this has usually been accomplished by accepting as basis the code of the preceding rulers, and making such changes or modifications as may be demanded by the spirit of the times. It is generally understood that such was the method adopted under the first Manchu Emperor. The code of the Mings was carefully examined, its severities were softened, and various additions and alterations were made; the result being a legal instrument which has received almost unqualified admiration from eminent Western lawyers. It has, however, been stated that the true source of the Manchu code must be looked for in the code of the T`ang dynasty (A.D. 618-905); possibly both codes were used. Within the compass of historical times, the country has never been without one, the first code having been drawn up by a distinguished statesman so far back as 525 B.C. In any case, at the beginning of the reign of Shun Chih a code was issued, which contained only certain fundamental and unalterable laws for the empire, with an Imperial preface, nominally from the hand of the Emperor himself. The next step was to supply any necessary additions and modifications; and as time went on these were further amended or enlarged by Imperial decrees, founded upon current events,—a process which has been going on down to the present day. The code therefore consists of two parts: (1) immutable laws more or less embodying great principles beyond the reach of revisions, and (2) a body of case-law which, since 1746, has been subject to revision every five years. With the publication of the Penal Code, the legal responsibilities of the new Emperor began and ended. There is not, and never has been, anything in China of the nature of civil law, beyond local custom and the application of common sense.

Towards the close of this reign, intercourse with China brought about an economic revolution in the West, especially in England, the importance of which it is difficult to realize sufficiently at this distant date. A new drink was put on the breakfast-table, destined to displace completely the quart of ale with which even Lady Jane Grey is said to have washed down her morning bacon. It is mentioned by Pepys, under the year 1660, as "tee (a China drink)," which he says he had never tasted before. Two centuries later, the export of tea from China had reached huge proportions, no less an amount than one hundred million *lb.* having been exported in one season from Foochow alone.

CHAPTER 4 – K`ANG HSI

The Emperor Shun Chih was succeeded by his third son, known by his year-title as K`ang Hsi (lasting prosperity), who was only eight years old at the time of his accession. Twelve years later the new monarch took up the reins of government, and soon began to make his influence felt. Fairly tall and well proportioned, he loved all manly exercises, and devoted three months annually to hunting. Large bright eyes lighted up his face, which was pitted with small-pox. Contemporary observers vie with one another in praising his wit, understanding, and liberality of mind. He was not twenty when the three feudatory princes broke into open rebellion. Of these, Wu San-kuei, the virtual founder of the dynasty, who had been appointed in 1659, was the chief; and it was at his instigation that his colleagues who ruled in Kuangtung and Fuhkien determined to throw off their allegiance and set up independent sovereignties. Within a few months, K`ang Hsi found vast portions of the empire slipping from his grasp; but though at one moment only the provinces of Chihli, Honan, and Shantung were left to him in peaceable possession, he never lost heart. The resources of Wu San-kuei were ultimately found to be insufficient for the struggle, the issue of which was determined partly by his death in 1678, and partly by the powerful artillery manufactured for the Imperial forces by the Jesuit missionaries, who were then in high favor at court. The capital city of Yünnan was taken by assault in 1681, upon which Wu San-kuei's son committed suicide, and the rebellion collapsed. From that date the Manchus decided that there should be no more "princes" among their Chinese subjects, and the rule has been observed until the present day.

Under the Emperor K`ang Hsi a re-arrangement of the empire was planned and carried out; that is to say, whereas during the Mongol dynasty there had only been thirteen provinces, increased to fifteen by the Mings, there was now a further increase of three, thus constituting what is known as the Eighteen Provinces, or China Proper. To effect this, the old province of Kiangsan was divided into the modern Anhui and Kiangsu; Kansuh was carved out of Shensi; and

Hukuang was separated into Hupeh and Hunan. Formosa, which was finally reconquered in 1683, was made part of the province of Fuhkien, and so remained for some two hundred years, when it was erected into an independent province. Thus, for a time China Proper consisted of nineteen provinces, until the more familiar "eighteen" was recently restored by the transfer of Formosa to Japan. In addition to the above, the eastern territory, originally inhabited by the Manchus, was divided into the three provinces already mentioned, all of which were at first organized upon a purely military basis; but of late years the administration of the southernmost province, in which stands Mukden, the Manchu capital, has been brought more into line with that of China Proper.

In 1677 the East India Company established an agency at Amoy, which, though withdrawn in 1681, was re-established in 1685. The first treaty with Russia was negotiated in 1679, but less than ten years later a further treaty was found necessary, under which it was agreed that the river Amur was to be the boundary-line between the two dominions, the Russians giving up possession of both banks. Thus Ya-k`o-sa, or Albazin, was ceded by Russia to China, and some of the inhabitants, who appear to have been either pure Russians or half-castes, were sent as prisoners to Peking, where religious instruction was provided for them according to the rules of the orthodox church. All the descendants of these Albazins probably perished in the destruction of the Russian college during the siege of the Legations in 1900. Punitive expeditions against Galdan and Arabtan carried the frontiers of the empire to the borders of Khokand and Badakshan, and to the confines of Tibet.

Galdan was a khan of the Kalmucks, who succeeded in establishing his rule through nearly the whole of Turkestan, after attaining his position by the murder of a brother. He attacked the Khalkas, and thus incurred the resentment of K`ang Hsi, whose subjects they were; and in order to strengthen his power, he applied to the Dalai Lama for ordination, but was refused. He then feigned conversion to Mahometanism, though without attracting Mahometan sympathies. In 1689 the Emperor in person led an army against him, crossing the deadly desert of Gobi for this purpose. Finally, after a further expedition and a decisive defeat in 1693, Galdan became a fugitive, and died three years afterwards. He was succeeded as khan by his nephew, Arabtan, who soon took up the offensive against China. He invaded Tibet, and pillaged the monasteries as far as Lhasa; but was ultimately driven back by a Manchu army to Sungaria, where he was murdered in 1727.

The question of the calendar early attracted attention under the reign of K`ang Hsi. After the capture of Peking in 1644, the Manchus had employed the Jesuit Father, Schaal, upon the Astronomical Board, an appointment which, owing to the jealousies aroused, very nearly cost him his life. What he taught was hardly superior to the astronomy then in vogue, which had been inherited from the Mongols, being nothing more than the old Ptolemaic system, already discarded in Europe. In 1669, a Flemish Jesuit Father from Courtrai, named Verbiest, was placed upon the Board, and was entrusted with the correction of the calendar according to more recent investigations.

Christianity was officially recognized in 1692, and an Imperial edict was issued ordering its toleration throughout the empire. The discovery of the Nestorian tablet in 1625 had given a considerable impulse, in spite of its heretical associations, to Christian propagandism; and it was estimated that in 1627 there were no fewer than thirteen thousand converts, many of whom were highly placed officials, and even members of the Imperial family. An important question, however, now came to a head, and completely put an end to the hope that China under the Manchus might embrace the Roman Catholic faith. The question was this: May converts to Christianity continue the worship of ancestors? Ricci, the famous Jesuit, who died in 1610, and who is the only foreigner mentioned by name in the dynastic histories of China, was inclined to regard worship of ancestors more as a civil than a religious rite. He probably foresaw, as indeed time has shown, that ancestral worship would prove to be an insuperable obstacle to many inquirers, if they were called upon to discard it once and for all; at the same time, he must have known that an invocation to spirits, coupled with the hope of obtaining some benefit therefrom, is *worship* pure and simple, and cannot be explained away as an unmeaning ceremony.

Against the Jesuits in this matter were arrayed the Dominicans and Franciscans; and the two parties fought the question before several Popes, sometimes one side carrying its point, and sometimes the other. At length, in 1698, a fresh petition was forwarded by the Jesuit order in China, asking the Pope to sanction the practice of this rite by native Christians, and also praying that the Chinese language might be used in the celebration of mass. K`ang Hsi supported the Jesuits in the view that ancestral worship was a harmless ceremony; but after much wrangling, and the dispatch of a Legate to the Manchu court, the Pope decided against the Jesuits and their Imperial ally. This was too much for the pride of K`ang Hsi, and he forthwith declared that in future he would only allow facilities for preaching to those priests who shared his view. In 1716, an edict was issued, banishing all missionaries unless excepted as above. The Emperor had indeed been annoyed by another ecclesiastical squabble, on a minor scale of importance, which had been raging almost simultaneously round the choice of an appropriate Chinese term for God. The term approved, if not suggested, by K`ang Hsi, and indisputably the right one, as shown by recent research, was set aside by the Pope in 1704 in favor of one which was supposed for a long time to have been coined for the purpose, but which had really been applied for many centuries previously to one of the eight spirits of ancient mythology.

In addition to his military campaigns, K`ang Hsi carried out several journeys of considerable length, and managed to see something of the empire beyond the walls of Peking. He climbed the famous mountain, T`ai-shan, in Shantung, the summit of which had been reached in 219 B.C. by the famous First Emperor, burner of the books and part builder of the Great Wall, and where a century later another Emperor had instituted the mysterious worship of Heaven and Earth. The ascent of T`ai-shan had been previously accomplished by only six Emperors in all, the last of whom went up in the year 1008; since K`ang Hsi no further Imperial attempts have been made, so that his will close the list in connection with the Manchu dynasty. It was on this occasion too that he visited the tomb of Confucius, also in Shantung.

The vagaries of the Yellow River, named "China's Sorrow" by a later Emperor, were always a source of great anxiety to K`ang Hsi; so much so that he paid a personal visit to the scene, and went carefully into the various plans for keeping the waters to a given course. Besides causing frequently recurring floods, with immense loss of life and property, this river has a way of changing unexpectedly its bed; so lately as 1856, it turned off at right angles near the city of K`ai-fêng, in Honan, and instead of emptying itself into the Yellow Sea about latitude 34°, found a new outlet in the Gulf of Peichili, latitude 38°.

K`ang Hsi several times visited Hangchow, returning to Tientsin by the Grand Canal, a distance of six hundred and ninety miles. This canal, it will be remembered, was designed and executed under Kublai Khan in the thirteenth century, and helped to form an almost unbroken line of water communication between Peking and Canton. At Hangchow, during one visit, he held an examination of all the (so-called) B.A.'s and M.A.'s, especially to test their poetical skill; and he also did the same at Soochow and Nanking, taking the opportunity, while at Nanking, to visit the mausoleum of the founder of the Ming dynasty, who lies buried nearby, and whose descendants had been displaced by the Manchus. Happily for K`ang Hsi's complacency, the book of fate is hidden from Emperors, as well as from subjects, –

All but the page prescribed, their present state and he was unable to foresee another visit paid to that mausoleum two hundred and seven years later, under very different conditions, to which we shall come in due course.

The census has always been an important institution in China. Without going back so far as the legendary golden age, the statistics of which have been invented by enthusiasts, we may accept unhesitatingly such records as we find subsequent to the Christian era, on the understanding that these returns are merely approximate. They could hardly be otherwise, inasmuch as the Chinese count families and not heads, roughly allowing five souls to each household. This plan yields a total of rather over fifty millions for the year A.D. 156, and one hundred and five millions for the fortieth year of the reign of K`ang Hsi, 1701.

No record of this Emperor, however brief, could fail to notice the literary side of his character, and his extraordinary achievements in this direction. It is almost paradoxical, though absolutely true, that two Manchu Emperors, sprung from a race which but a few decades before had little thought for anything beyond war and the chase, and which had not even a written language of its own, should have conferred more benefits upon the student of literature than all the rest of China's Emperors put together. The literature in question is, of course, Chinese literature. Manchu was the court language, spoken as well as written, for many years after 1644, and down to quite recent times all official documents were in duplicate, one copy in Chinese and one in Manchu; but a Manchu literature can hardly be said to exist, beyond translations of all the most important Chinese works. The Manchu dynasty is an admirable illustration of the old story: conquerors taken captive by the conquered.

At this moment, the term "K`ang Tsi" is daily on the lips of every student of the Chinese language, native or foreign, throughout the empire. This is due to the fact that the Emperor caused to be produced under his own personal superintendence, on a more extensive scale and a more systematic plan than any previous work of the kind, a lexicon of the Chinese language, containing over forty thousand characters, with numerous illustrative phrases chronologically arranged, the spelling of each character according to the method introduced by Buddhist teachers and first used in the third century, the tones, various readings, etc., etc., altogether a great work and still without a rival at the present day.

It would be tedious even to enumerate all the various literary undertakings conceived and carried out under the direction of K`ang Hsi; but there are two works in particular which cannot be passed over. One of these is the huge illustrated encyclopedia in which everything which has ever been said upon each of a vast array of subjects is brought into a systematized book of reference, running to many hundred volumes, and being almost a complete library in itself. It was printed, after the death of K`ang Hsi, from movable copper types. The other is, if anything, a still more extraordinary though not such a voluminous work. It is a concordance to all literature; not of words, but of phrases. A student meeting with an unfamiliar combination of characters can turn to its pages and find every passage given, in sufficient fullness, where the phrase in question has been used by poet, historian, or essayist.

The last years of K`ang Hsi were beclouded by family troubles. For some kind of intrigue, in which magic played a prominent part, he had been compelled to degrade the Heir Apparent, and to appoint another son to the vacant post; but a year or two later, this son was found to be mentally deranged, and was placed under restraint. So things went on for several more years, the Emperor apparently unable to make up his mind as to the choice of a successor; and it was not until the last day of his life that he finally decided in favor of his fourth son. Dying in 1723, his reign had already extended beyond the Chinese cycle of sixty years, a feat which no Emperor of China, in historical times, had ever before achieved, but which was again to be accomplished, before the century was out, by his grandson.

CHAPTER 5 – YUNG CHÊNG AND CH`IEN LUNG

The fourth son of K`ang Hsi came to the throne under the year-title of Yung Chêng (harmonious rectitude). He was confronted with serious difficulties from the very first. Dissatisfaction prevailed among his numerous brothers, at least one of whom may have felt that he had a better claim to rule than his junior in the family. This feeling culminated in a plot to dethrone Yung Chêng, which was, however, discovered in time, and resulted only in the degradation of the guilty brothers. The fact that among his opponents were native Christians – some say that the Jesuits were at the bottom of all the mischief – naturally influenced the Emperor against Christianity; no fewer than three hundred churches were destroyed, and all Catholic missionaries were thenceforward obliged to live either at Peking or at Macao. In 1732 he thought of expelling them altogether; but finding that they were enthusiastic teachers of filial piety, he left them alone, merely prohibiting fresh recruits from coming to China.

These domestic troubles were followed by a serious rebellion in Kokonor, which was not fully suppressed until the next reign; also by an outbreak among the aborigines of Kueichow and Yünnan, which lasted until three years later, when the tribesmen were brought under Imperial rule.

A Portuguese envoy, named Magalhaens (or Magaillans), visited Peking in 1727, bearing presents for the Emperor; but nothing very much resulted from his mission. In 1730, in addition to terrible floods, there was a severe earthquake, which lasted ten days, and in which one hundred thousand persons are said to have lost their lives. In 1735, Yung Chêng's reign came to an end amid sounds of a further outbreak of the aborigines in Kueichow. Before his death, he named his fourth son, then only fifteen, as his successor, under the regency of two of the boy's uncles and two Grand Secretaries, one of the latter being a distinguished scholar, who was entrusted with the preparation of the history of the Ming dynasty. Yung Chêng's name has always been somewhat unfairly associated by foreigners with a bitter hostility to the Catholic priests of his day, simply because he refused to allow them a free hand in matters outside their proper sphere. Altogether, it may be said that he was a just and public-spirited ruler, anxious for his people's welfare. He hated war, and failed to carry on his father's vigorous policy in Central Asia; nevertheless, by 1730, Chinese rule extended to the Laos border, and the Shan States paid tribute. He was a man of letters, and completed some of his father's undertakings.

Yung Chêng's successor was twenty-five years of age when he came to the throne with the year-title of Ch`ien Lung (or Kien Long = enduring glory), and one of his earliest acts was to forbid the propagation of Christian doctrine, a prohibition which developed between 1746 and 1785 into active persecution of its adherents. The first ten years of this reign were spent chiefly in internal reorganization; the remainder, which covered half a century, was almost a continuous succession of wars. The aborigines of Kueichow, known as the Miao-Tz{u}, offered a determined resistance to all attempts to bring them under the regular administration; and although they were ultimately conquered, it was deemed advisable not to insist upon the adoption of the queue, and also to leave them a considerable measure of self-government. Acting under Manchu guidance, chiefs and leading tribesmen were entrusted with important executive offices; they had to keep the peace among their people, and to collect the revenue of local produce to be forwarded to Peking. These posts were hereditary. On the death of the father, the eldest son proceeded to Peking and received his appointment in person, together with his seal of office. Failing sons or their children, brothers had the right of succession.

In 1741 the population was estimated by Père Amiot, S.J., at over one hundred and fifty millions, as against twenty-one million households in 1701.

In 1753 there was trouble in Ili. After the death of Galdan II., son of Arabtan, an attempt was made by one, Amursana, to usurp the principality. He was, however, driven out, and fled to Peking, where he was favorably received by Ch`ien Lung, and an army was sent to reinstate him. With the subsequent settlement, under which he was to have only one quarter of Ili, Amursana was profoundly dissatisfied, and took the earliest opportunity of turning on his benefactors. He murdered the Manchu-Chinese garrison and all the other Chinese he could find, and proclaimed himself khan of the Eleuths. His triumph was short-lived; another army was sent from Peking, this time against him, and he fled into Russian territory, dying there soon afterwards of smallpox. This campaign was lavishly illustrated by Chinese artists, who produced a series of realistic pictures of the battles and skirmishes fought by Ch`ien Lung's victorious troops. How far these were prepared under the guidance of the Jesuit Fathers does not seem to be known. About sixty years previously, under the reign of K`ang Hsi, the Jesuits had carried out extensive surveys, and had drawn fairly accurate maps of Chinese territory, which had been sent to Paris and there engraved on copper by order of Louis XIV. In like manner, the pictures now in question were forwarded to Paris and engraved, between 1769 and 1774, by skilled draughtsmen, as may be gathered from the lettering at the foot of each; for instance—*Gravé par J. P. Le Bas, graveur du cabinet du roi* (Cambridge University Library).

Kuldja and Kashgaria were next added to the empire, and Manchu supremacy was established in Tibet. Burma and Nepal were forced to pay tribute, after a disastrous war (1766-1770) with the former country, in which a Chinese army had been almost exterminated; rebellions in Ss{u}ch`uan (1770), Shantung (1777), and Formosa (1786) were suppressed.

Early in the eighteenth century, the Turguts, a branch of the Kalmuck Tartars, unable to endure the oppressive tyranny of their rulers, trekked into Russia, and settled on the banks of the Volga. Some seventy years later, once more finding the burden of taxation too heavy, they again organized a trek upon a colossal scale. Turning their faces eastward, they spent a whole year of fearful suffering and privation in reaching the confines of Ili, a terribly diminished host. There they received a district, and were placed under the jurisdiction of a khan. This journey has been dramatically described by De Quincey in an essay entitled "Revolt of the Tartars, or Flight of the Kalmuck Khan and his people from the Russian territories to the Frontiers of China." Of this contribution to literature it is only necessary to remark that the scenes described, and especially the numbers mentioned, must be credited chiefly to the perfervid imagination of the essayist, and also to certain not very trustworthy documents sent home by Père Amiot. It is probable that about one hundred and sixty thousand Turguts set out on that long march, of whom only some seventy thousand reached their goal.

In 1781, the Dungans (or Tungans) of Shensi broke into open rebellion, which was suppressed only after huge losses to the Imperialists. These Dungans were Mahometan subjects of China, who in very early times had colonized, under the name of Gao-tchan, in Kansuh and Shensi, and subsequently spread westward into Turkestan. Some say that they were a distinct race, who, in the fifth and sixth centuries, occupied the Tian Shan range, with their capital at Harashar. The name, however, means, in the dialect of Chinese Tartary, "converts," that is, to Mahometanism, to which they were converted in the days of Timour by an Arabian adventurer. We shall hear of them again in a still more serious connection.

Eight years later there was a revolution in Cochin-China. The king fled to China, and Ch`ien Lung promptly espoused his cause, sending an army to effect his restoration. This was no sooner accomplished than the chief Minister rebelled, and, rapidly attracting large numbers to his standard, succeeded in cutting off the retreat of the Chinese force. Ch`ien Lung then sent another army, whereupon the rebel Minister submitted, and humbled himself so completely that the Emperor appointed him to be king instead of the other. After this, the Annamese continued to forward tribute, but it was deemed advisable to cease from further interference with their government.

The next trouble was initiated by the Gurkhas, who, in 1790, raided Tibet. On being defeated and pursued by a Chinese army, they gave up all the booty taken, and entered into an agreement to pay tribute once every five years.

The year 1793 was remarkable for the arrival of an English embassy under Lord Macartney, who was received in audience by the Emperor at Jehol (= hot river), an Imperial summer residence lying about a hundred miles north of Peking, beyond the Great Wall. It had been built in 1780 after the model of the palace of the Panshen Erdeni at Tashilumbo, in Tibet, when that functionary, the spiritual ruler of Tibet, as opposed to the Dalai Lama, who is the secular ruler, proceeded to Peking to be present on the seventieth anniversary of Ch`ien Lung's birthday. Two years later, the aged Emperor, who had, like his grandfather, completed his cycle of sixty years on the throne, abdicated in favor of his son, dying in retirement some four years after. These two monarchs, K`ang Hsi and Ch`ien Lung, were among the ablest, not only of Manchu rulers, but of any whose lot it has been to shape the destinies of China. Ch`ien Lung was an indefatigable administrator, a little too ready perhaps to plunge into costly military expeditions, and somewhat narrow in the policy he adopted towards the "outside barbarians" who came to trade at Canton and elsewhere, but otherwise a worthy rival of his grandfather's fame as a sovereign and patron of letters. From the long list of works, mostly on a very extensive scale, produced under his supervision, may be mentioned the new and revised editions of the Thirteen Classics of Confucianism and of the Twenty-Four Dynastic Histories. In 1772 a search was instituted under Imperial orders for all literary works worthy of preservation, and high provincial officials vied with one another in forwarding rare and important works to Peking. The result was the great descriptive Catalogue of the Imperial Library, arranged under the four heads of Classics (Confucianism), History, Philosophy, and General Literature, in which all the facts known about each work are set forth, coupled with judicious critical remarks,—an achievement which has hardly a parallel in any literature in the world.

CHAPTER 6—CHIA CH`ING

Ch`ien Lung's son, who reigned as Chia Ch`ing (high felicity—not to be confounded with Chia Ching of the Ming dynasty, 1522-1567), found himself in difficulties from the very start. The year of his accession was marked by a rising of the White Lily Society, one of the dreaded secret associations with which China is, and always has been, honeycombed. The exact origin of this particular society is not known. A White Lily Society was formed in the second century A.D. by a certain Taoist patriarch, and eighteen members were accustomed to assemble at a temple in modern Kiangsi for purposes of meditation. But this seems to have no connection with the later sect, of which we first hear in 1308, when its existence was prohibited, its shrines destroyed, and its votaries forced to return to ordinary life. Members of the fraternity were then believed to possess a knowledge of the black art; and later on, in 1622, the society was confounded by Chinese officials in Shantung with Christianity. In the present instance, it is said that no fewer than thirty thousand adherents were executed before the trouble was finally suppressed; from which statement it is easy to gather that under whatever form the White Lily Society may have been originally initiated, its activities were now of a much more serious character, and were, in fact, plainly directed against the power and authority of the Manchus.

Almost from this very date may be said to have begun that turn of the tide which was to reach its flood a hundred years afterwards. The Manchus came into power, as conquerors by force of arms, at a time when the mandate of the previous dynasty had been frittered away in corruption and misrule; and although to the Chinese eye they were nothing more than "stinking Tartars," there were not wanting many glad enough to see a change of rule at any price. Under the first Emperor, Shun Chih, there was barely time to find out what the new dynasty was going to do; then came the long and glorious reign of K`ang Hsi, followed, after the thirteen harmless years of Yung Chêng, by the equally long and equally glorious reign of Ch`ien Lung. The Chinese people, who, strictly speaking, govern themselves in the most democratic of all republics, have not the slightest objection to the Imperial tradition, which has indeed been their continuous heritage from remotest antiquity, provided that public liberties are duly safeguarded, chiefly in the sense that there shall always be equal opportunities for all. They are quick to discover the character of their rulers, and discovery in an unfavorable direction leads to an early alteration of popular thought and demeanor. At the beginning of the seventeenth century, they had tired of eunuch oppression and unjust taxation, and they naturally hailed the genuine attempt in 1662 to get rid of eunuchs altogether, coupled with the persistent attempts of K`ang Hsi, and later of Ch`ien Lung, to lighten the burdens of revenue which weighed down the energies of all. But towards the end of his reign Ch`ien Lung had become a very old man; and the gradual decay of his powers of personal supervision opened a way for the old abuses to creep in, bringing in their train the usual accompaniment of popular discontent.

The Emperor Chia Ch`ing, a worthless and dissolute ruler, never commanded the confidence of his people as his great predecessors had done, nor had he the same confidence in them. This want of mutual trust was not confined to his Chinese subjects only. In 1799, Ho-shên, a high Manchu official who had been raised by Ch`ien Lung from an obscure position to be a Minister of State and Grand Secretary, was suspected, probably without a shadow of evidence, of harboring designs upon the throne. He was seized and tried, nominally for corruption and undue familiarity, and was condemned to death, being allowed as an act of grace to commit suicide.

In 1803 the Emperor was attacked in the streets of Peking; and ten years later there was a serious outbreak organized by a secret society in Honan, known as the Society of Divine Justice, and alternatively as the White Feather Society, from the badge worn by those members who took part in the actual movement, which happened as follows. An attack upon the palace during the Emperor's absence on a visit to the Imperial tombs was arranged by the leaders, who represented a considerable body of malcontents, roused by the wrongs which their countrymen were suffering all over the empire at the hands of their Manchu rulers. By promises of large rewards and appointments to lucrative offices when the Manchus should be got rid of, the collusion of a number of the eunuchs was secured; and on a given day some four hundred rebels, disguised as villagers carrying baskets of fruit in which arms were concealed, collected about the gates of the palace. Some say that one of the leaders was betrayed, others that the eunuchs made a mistake in the date; at any rate there was a sudden rush on the part of the conspirators, the guards at the gates were overpowered, everyone who was not wearing a white feather was cut down, and the palace seemed to be at the mercy of the rebels. The latter, however, were met by a desperate resistance from the young princes, who shot down several of them, and thus alarmed the soldiers. Assistance was promptly at hand, and the rebels were all killed or captured. Immediate measures were taken to suppress the Society, of which it is said that over twenty thousand members were executed.

Not one, however, of the numerous secret societies, which from time to time have flourished in China, can compare for a moment either in numbers or organization with the formidable association known as the Heaven and Earth Society, and also as the Triad Society, or Hung League, which dates from the reign of Yung Chêng, and from first to last has had one definite aim,—the overthrow of the Manchu dynasty.

The term "Triad" signifies the harmonious union of heaven (q.d. God), earth, and man; and members of the fraternity communicate to one another the fact of membership by pointing first up to the sky, then down to the ground, and last to their own hearts. The Society was called the Hung League, because all the members adopted Hung as a surname, a word which suggests the idea of a cataclysm. By a series of lucky chances the inner working of this Society became known about fifty years ago, when a mass of manuscripts containing the history of the Society, its ritual, oaths, and secret signs, together with an elaborate set of drawings of flags and other regalia, fell into the hands of the Dutch Government at Batavia. These documents, translated by Dr. G. Schlegel, disclose an extraordinary similarity in many respects between the working of

Chinese lodges and the working of those which are more familiar to us as temples of the Ancient Order of Free and Accepted Masons. Such points of contact, however, as may be discoverable, are most probably mere coincidences; if not, and if, as is generally understood, the ritual of the European craft was concocted by Cagliostro, then it follows that he must have borrowed from the Chinese, and not the Chinese from him. The use of the square and compasses as symbols of moral rectitude, which forms such a striking feature of European masonry, finds no place in the ceremonial of the Triad Society, although recognized as such in Chinese literature from the days of Confucius, and still so employed in the every-day colloquial of China.

In 1816 Lord Amherst's embassy reached Peking. Its object was to secure some sort of arrangement under which British merchants might carry on trade after a more satisfactory manner than had been the case hitherto. The old Co-hong, a system first established in 1720, under which certain Chinese merchants at Canton became responsible to the local authorities for the behavior of the English merchants, and to the latter for all debts due to them, had been so complicated by various oppressive laws, that at one time the East India Company had threatened to stop all business. Lord Amherst, however, accomplished nothing in the direction of reform. From the date of his landing at Tientsin, he was persistently told that unless he agreed to perform the *kotow*, he could not possibly be permitted to an audience. It was probably his equally persistent refusal to do so—a ceremonial which had been excused by Ch`ien Lung in the case of Lord Macartney—that caused the Ministers to change their tactics, and to declare, on Lord Amherst's arrival at the Summer Palace, tired and wayworn, that the Emperor wished to see him immediately. Not only had the presents, of which he was the bearer, not arrived at the palace, but he and his suite, among whom were Sir George Stanton, Dr Morrison, and Sir John Davids, had not received the trunks containing their uniforms. It was therefore impossible for the ambassador to present himself before the Emperor, and he flatly refused to do so; whereupon he received orders to proceed at once to the sea-coast, and take himself off to his own country. A curious comment on this fiasco was made by Napoleon, who thought that the English Government had acted wrongly in not having ordered Lord Amherst to comply with the custom of the place he was sent to; otherwise, he should not have been sent at all. "It is my opinion that whatever is the custom of a nation, and is practiced by the first characters of that nation towards their chief, cannot degrade strangers who perform the same."

In 1820 Chia Ch`ing died, after a reign of twenty-five years, notable, if for nothing else, as marking the beginning of Manchu decadence, evidence of which is to be found in the unusually restless temper of the people, and even in such apparent trifles as the abandonment of the annual hunting excursions, always before carried out on an extensive scale, and presenting, as it were, a surviving indication of former Manchu hardihood and personal courage. He was succeeded by his second son, who was already forty years of age, and whose hitherto secluded life had ill-prepared him for the difficult problems he was shortly called upon to face.

CHAPTER 7 – TAO KUANG

Tao Kuang (glory of right principle), as he is called, from the style chosen for his reign, gave promise of being a useful and enlightened ruler; at the least a great improvement on his father. He did his best at first to purify the court, but his natural indolence stood in the way of any real reform, and with the best intentions in the world he managed to leave the empire in a still more critical condition than that in which he had found it. Five years after his accession, his troubles began in real earnest. There was a rising of the people in Kashgaria, due to criminal injustice practiced over a long spell of time on the part of the Chinese authorities. The rebels found a leader in the person of Jehangir, who claimed descent from one of the old native chiefs, formerly recognized by the Manchu Emperors, but now abolished as such. Thousands flocked to his standard; and by the time an avenging army could arrive on the scene, he was already master of the country. During the campaign which followed, his men were defeated in battle after battle; and at length he himself was taken prisoner and forwarded to Peking, where he failed to defend his conduct, and was put to death.

The next serious difficulty which confronted the Emperor was a rising, in 1832, of the wild Miao tribes of Kuangsi and Hunan, led by a man who either received or adopted the title of the Golden Dragon. At the bottom of all the trouble we find, as usually to be expected henceforward, the secret activities of the far-reaching Triad Society, which seized the occasion to foment into open rebellion the dissatisfaction of the tribesmen with the glaring injustice they were suffering at the hands of the local authorities. After some initial massacres and reprisals, a general was sent to put an end to the outbreak; but so far from doing this, he seems to have come off second best in most of the battles which ensued, and was finally driven into Kuang-tung. For this he was superseded, and two Commissioners dispatched to take charge of further operations. It occurred to these officials that possibly persuasion might succeed where violence had failed; and accordingly a proclamation was widely circulated, promising pardon and redress of wrongs to all who would at once return to their allegiance, and pointing out at the same time the futility of further resistance. The effect of this move was magical; within a few days the rebellion was over.

We are now reaching a period at which European complications began to be added to the more legitimate worries of a Manchu Emperor. Trade with the Portuguese, the Spaniards, the Dutch, and the English, had been carried on since the early years of the sixteenth century, but in a very haphazard kind of way, and under many vexatious restrictions, bribery being the only effectual means of bringing commercial ventures to a successful issue. So far back as 1680, the East India Company had received its charter, and commercial relations with Chinese merchants could be entered into by British subjects only through this channel. Such machinery answered its purpose very well for a long period; but a monopoly of the kind became out of date as time went on, and in 1834 it ceased altogether. The Company was there for the sake of trade, and for nothing else; and one of its guiding principles was avoidance of any acts which might wound Chinese susceptibilities, and tend to defeat the object of its own existence. Consequently, the directors would not allow opium to be imported in their vessels; neither were they inclined to patronize missionary efforts. It is true that Morrison's dictionary was printed at the expense of the Company, when the punishment for a native teaching a foreigner the Chinese language was death; but no pecuniary assistance was forthcoming when the same distinguished missionary attempted to translate the Bible for distribution in China.

The Manchus, who had themselves entered the country as robbers of the soil and spoliators of the people, were determined to do their best to keep out all future intruders; and it was for this reason that, suspicious of the aims of the barbarian, every possible obstacle was placed in the way of those who wished to learn to speak and read Chinese. This suspicion was very much increased in the case of missionaries, whose real object the Manchus failed to appreciate, and behind whose plea of religious propagandism they thought they detected a deep-laid scheme for territorial aggression, to culminate of course in their own overthrow; and already in 1805 an edict had been issued, strictly forbidding anyone to teach even Manchu to any foreigner.

From this date (1834), any British subject was free to engage in the trade, and the Home Government sent out Lord Napier to act as Chief Superintendent, and to enter into regular diplomatic relations with the Chinese authorities. Lord Napier, however, even though backed by a couple of frigates, was unable to gain admission to the city of Canton, and after a demonstration, the only result of which was to bring all business to a standstill, he was finally obliged in the general interest to retire. He went to Macao, a small peninsula to the extreme south-west of the Kuangtung province, famous as the residence of the poet Camoens, and there he died a month later. Macao was first occupied by the Portuguese trading with China in 1557; though there is a story that in 1517 certain Portuguese landed there under pretence of drying some tribute presents to the Emperor, which had been damaged in a storm, and proceeded to fortify their encampment, whereupon the local officials built a wall across the peninsula, shutting off further access to the mainland. It also appears that, in 1566, Macao was actually ceded to the Portuguese on condition of payment of an annual sum to China, which payment ceased after trouble between the two countries in 1849.

The next few years were employed by the successors of Lord Napier in endeavors, often wrongly directed, to establish working, if not harmonious, relations with the Chinese authorities; but no satisfactory point was reached, for the simple reason that recent events had completely confirmed the officials and the people in their old views as to the relative status of the barbarians and themselves.

It is worth noticing here that Russia, with her conterminous and ever-advancing frontier, has always been regarded somewhat differently from the oversea barbarian. She has continually during the past three centuries been the dreaded foreign bogy of the Manchus; and a few years back, when Manchus and Chinese alike fancied that their country was going to be "chopped up like a melon" and divided among western nations, a warning geographical cartoon was widely circulated in China, showing Russia in the shape of a huge bear stretching down from the north and clawing the vast areas of Mongolia and Manchuria to herself.

Now, to aggravate the already difficult situation, the opium question came suddenly to the front in an acute form. For a long time the import of opium had been strictly forbidden by the Government, and for an equally long time smuggling the drug in increasing quantities had been carried on in a most determined manner until, finally, swift vessels with armed crews, sailing under foreign flags, succeeded in terrorizing the native revenue cruisers, and so delivering their cargoes as they pleased. It appears that the Emperor Tao Kuang, who had sounded the various high authorities on the subject, was genuinely desirous of putting an end to the import of opium, and so checking the practice of opium-smoking, which was already assuming dangerous proportions; and in this he was backed up by Captain Elliot (afterwards Sir Charles Elliot), now Superintendent of Trade, an official whose vacillating policy towards the Chinese authorities did much to precipitate the disasters about to follow. After a serious riot had been provoked, in which the foreign merchants of Canton narrowly escaped with their lives, and to quell which it was necessary to call out the soldiery, the Emperor decided to put a definite stop to the opium traffic; and for this purpose he appointed one of his most distinguished servants, at that time Viceroy of Hukuang, and afterwards generally known as Commissioner Lin, a name much reverenced by the Chinese as that of a true patriot, and never mentioned even by foreigners without respect. Early in 1839, Lin took up the post of Viceroy of Kuangtung, and immediately initiated an attack which, to say the least of it, deserved a better fate.

Within a few days a peremptory order was made for the delivery of all opium in the possession of foreign merchants at Canton. This demand was resisted, but for a short time only. All the foreign merchants, together with Captain Elliot, who had gone up to Canton specially to meet the crisis, found themselves prisoners in their own houses, deprived of servants and even of food. Then Captain Elliot undertook, on behalf of his Government, to indemnify British subjects for their losses; whereupon no fewer than twenty thousand two hundred and ninety-one chests of opium were surrendered to Commissioner Lin, and the incident was regarded by the Chinese as closed. On receipt of the Emperor's instructions, the whole of this opium, for which the owners received orders on the Treasury at the rate of £120 per chest, was mixed with lime and salt water, and was entirely destroyed.

Lin's subsequent demands were so arbitrary that at length the English mercantile community retired altogether from Canton, and after a futile attempt to settle at Macao, where their presence, owing to Chinese influence with the Portuguese occupiers, was made unwelcome, they finally found a refuge at Hong Kong, then occupied only by a few fishermen's huts. Further negotiations as to the renewal of trade having fallen through, Lin gave orders for all British ships to leave China within three days, which resulted in a fight between two men-of-war and twenty-nine war-junks, in which the latter were either sunk or driven off with great loss. In June, 1840, a British fleet of seventeen men-of-war and twenty-seven troopships arrived at Hong Kong; Canton was blockaded; a port on the island of Chusan was subsequently occupied; and Lord Palmerston's letter to the Emperor was carried to Tientsin, and delivered there to the Viceroy of Chihli. Commissioner Lin was now cashiered for incompetency; but was afterwards instructed to act with the Viceroy of Chihli, who was sent down to supersede him. Further vexatious action, or rather inaction, on the part of these two at length drove Captain Elliot to an ultimatum; and as no attention was paid to this, the Bogue forts near the mouth of the Canton river were taken by the British fleet, after great slaughter of the Chinese. In January, 1841, a treaty of peace was arranged, under which the island of Hong Kong was to be ceded to England, a sum of over a million pounds was to be paid for the opium destroyed, and satisfactory concessions were to be made in the matter of official intercourse between the two nations. The Emperor refused ratification, and ordered the extermination of the barbarians to be at once proceeded with. Again the Bogue forts were captured, and Canton would have been occupied but for another promised treaty, the terms of which were accepted by Sir Henry Pottinger, who now superseded Elliot. At this juncture the British fleet sailed northwards, capturing Amoy and Ningpo, and occupying the island of Chusan. The further capture of Chapu, where munitions of war in huge quantities were destroyed, was followed by similar successes at Shanghai and Chinkiang. At the last-mentioned, a desperate resistance was offered by the Manchu garrison, who fought heroically against certain defeat, and who, when all hope was gone, committed suicide in large numbers rather than fall into the hands of the enemy, from whom, in accordance with prevailing ideas and with what would have been their own practice, they expected no quarter. The Chinese troops, as distinguished from the Manchus, behaved differently; they took to their heels before a shot had been fired. This behavior, which seems to be nothing more than arrant cowardice, is nevertheless open to a more favorable interpretation. The yoke of the Manchu dynasty was already beginning to press heavily, and these men felt that they had no particular cause to fight for, certainly not such a personal cause as then stared the Manchus in the face. The Manchu soldiers were fighting for their all: their very supremacy was at stake; while many of the Chinese troops were members of the Triad Society, the chief object of which was to get rid of the alien dynasty. It is thus, too, that we can readily explain the assistance afforded to the enemy by numerous Cantonese, and the presence of many as servants on board the vessels of our fleet; they did not help us or accompany us from any lack of patriotism, of which virtue Chinese annals have many striking examples to show, but because they were entirely out of sympathy with their rulers, and would have been glad to see them overthrown, coupled of course with the tempting pay and good treatment offered by the barbarian.

It now remained to take Nanking, and thither the fleet proceeded in August, 1842, with that purpose in view. This move the Chinese authorities promptly anticipated by offering to come to terms in a friendly way; and in a short time conditions of peace were arranged under an important instrument, known as the Treaty of Nanking. Its chief clauses provided for the opening to British trade of Canton, Amoy, Foochow, Ningpo, and Shanghai, at which all British subjects were to enjoy the rights of extraterritoriality, being subject to the jurisdiction of their own officials only; also, for the cession to

England of the island of Hong Kong, and for the payment of a lump sum of about five million pounds as compensation for loss of opium, expenses of the war, etc. All prisoners were to be released, and there was a special amnesty for such Chinese as had given their services to the British during the war. An equality of status between the officials of both nations was further conceded, and suitable rules were to be drawn up for the regulation of trade. The above treaty having been duly ratified by Tao Kuang and by Queen Victoria, it must then have seemed to British merchants that a new and prosperous era had really dawned. But they counted without the ever-present desire of the great bulk of the Chinese people to see the last of the Manchus; and the Triad Society, stimulated no doubt by the recent British successes, had already shown signs of unusual activity when, in 1850, the Emperor died, and was succeeded by his fourth son, who reigned under the title of Hsien Fêng (or Hien Fong = universal plenty).

CHAPTER 8 – HSIEN FÊNG

Hsien Fêng came to the throne at the age of nineteen, and found himself in possession of a heritage which showed evident signs of going rapidly to pieces. His father, in the opinion of many competent Chinese, had been sincerely anxious for the welfare of his country; on the other hand, he had failed to learn anything from the lessons he had received at the hands of foreigners, towards whom his attitude to the last was of the bow-wow order. On one occasion, indeed, he borrowed a classical phrase, and referring to the intrusions of the barbarian, declared roundly that he would allow no man to snore alongside of his bed. Brought up in this spirit, Hsien Fêng had already begun to exhibit an anti-foreign bias, when he found himself in the throes of a struggle which speedily reduced the European question to quite insignificant proportions.

A clever young Cantonese, named Hung Hsiu-ch`üan, from whom great things were expected, failed, in 1833, to secure the first degree at the usual public examination. Four years later, when twenty-four years of age, he made another attempt, only, however, to be once more rejected. Chagrin at this second failure brought on melancholia, and he began to see visions; and later on, while still in this depressed state of mind, he turned his attention to some Christian tracts which had been given to him on his first appearance at the examination, but which he had so far allowed to remain unread. In these he discovered what he thought were interpretations of his earlier dreams, and soon managed to persuade himself that he had been divinely chosen to bring to his countrymen a knowledge of the true God.

In one sense this would only have been reversion to a former condition, for in ancient times a simple monotheism formed the whole creed of the Chinese people; but Hung went much further, and after having become head of a Society of God, he started a sect of professing Christians, and set to work to collect followers, styling himself the Brother of Christ. Gradually, the authorities became aware of his existence, and also of the fact that he was drawing together a following on a scale which might prove dangerous to the public peace. It was then that force of circumstances changed his status from that of a religious reformer to that of a political adventurer; and almost simultaneously with the advent of Hsien Fêng to the Imperial power, the long-smouldering discontent with Manchu rule, carefully fostered by the organization of the Triad society, broke into open rebellion. A sort of holy war was proclaimed against the Manchus, stigmatized as usurpers and idolaters, who were to be displaced by a native administration, called the T`ai P`ing (great peace) Heavenly Dynasty, at the head of which Hung placed himself, with the title of "Heavenly King," in allusion to the Christian principles on which this new departure was founded.

"Our Heavenly King," so ran the rebel proclamations, "has received a divine commission to exterminate the Manchus utterly, men, women, and children, with all idolaters, and to possess the empire as its true sovereign. For the empire and everything in it is his; its mountains and rivers, its broad lands and public treasuries; you and all that you have, your family, males and females alike, from yourself to your youngest child, and your property, from your patrimonial estates to the bracelet on your infant's arm. We command the services of all, and we take everything. All who resist us are rebels and idolatrous demons, and we kill them without sparing; but whoever acknowledges our Heavenly King and exerts himself in our service shall have full reward,—due honor and station in the armies and court of the Heavenly Dynasty."

The T`ai-p`ings now got rid of the chief outward sign of allegiance to the Manchus, by ceasing to shave the forepart of the head, and allowing all their hair to grow long, from which they were often spoken of at the time—and the name still survives—as the long-haired rebels. Their early successes were phenomenal; they captured city after city, moving northwards through Kuangsi into Hunan, whence, after a severe check at Ch`ang-sha, the provincial capital, the siege of which they were forced to raise, they reached and captured, among others, the important cities of Wu-ch`ang, Kiukiang, and An-ch`ing, on the Yangtsze. The next stage was to

Nanking, a city occupying an important strategic position, and famous as the capital of the empire in the fourth and fourteenth centuries. Here the Manchu garrison offered but a feeble resistance, the only troops who fought at all being Chinese; within ten days (March, 1853) the city was in the hands of the T`ai-p`ings; all Manchus,—men, women, and children, said to number no fewer than twenty thousand,—were put to the sword; and in the same month, Hung was formally proclaimed first Emperor of the T`ai P`ing Heavenly Dynasty, Nanking from this date receiving the name of the Heavenly City. So far, the generals who had been sent to oppose his progress had affected nothing. One of these was Commissioner Lin, of opium fame, who had been banished and recalled, and was then living in retirement after having successfully held several high offices. His health was not equal to the effort, and he died on his way to take up his post.

After the further capture of Chinkiang, a feat which created a considerable panic at Shanghai, a force was detached from the main body of the T`ai-p`ings, and dispatched north for no less a purpose than the capture of Peking. Apparently a fool-hardy project, it was one that came nearer to realization than the most sanguine outsider could possibly have expected. The army reached Tientsin, which is only eighty miles from the capital; but when there, a slight reverse, together with other unexplained reasons, resulted in a return (1855) of the troops without having accomplished their object. Meanwhile, the comparative ease with which the T`ai-p`ings had set the Manchus at defiance, and continued to hold their own, encouraged various outbreaks in other parts of the empire; until at length more systematic efforts were made to put a stop to the present impossible condition of affairs.

Opportunity just now was rather on the side of the Imperialists, as the futile expedition to Peking had left the rebels in a somewhat aimless state, not quite knowing what to do next. It is true that they were busy spreading the T`ai-p`ing conception of Christianity, in establishing schools, and preparing an educational literature to meet the exigencies of the time. They achieved the latter object by building anew on the lines, but not in the spirit, of the old. Thus the

Trimetrical Classic, the famous schoolboy's handbook, a veritable guide to knowledge in which a variety of subjects are lightly touched upon, was entirely rewritten. The form, rhyming stanzas with three words to each line, was preserved; but instead of beginning with the familiar Confucian dogma that man's nature is entirely good at his birth and only becomes depraved by later environment, we find the story of the Creation, taken from the first chapter of Genesis.

By 1857, Imperialist troops were drawing close lines around the rebels, who had begun to lose rather than to gain ground. An-ch`ing and Nanking, the only two cities which remained to them, were blockaded, and the Manchu plan was simply to starve the enemy out. During this period we hear little of the Emperor, Hsien Fêng; and what we do hear is not to his advantage. He had become a confirmed debauchee, in the hands of a degraded clique, whose only contribution to the crisis was a suggested issue of paper money and debasement of the popular coinage. Among his generals, however, there was now one, whose name is still a household word all over the empire, and who initiated the first checks which led to the ultimate suppression of the rebellion. Tsêng Kuo-fan had been already employed in high offices, when, in 1853, he was first ordered to take up arms against the T`ai-p`ings. After some reverses, he entered upon a long course of victories by which the rebels were driven from most of their strongholds; and in 1859, he submitted a plan for an advance on Nanking, which was approved and ultimately carried out. Meanwhile, the plight of the besieged rebels in Nanking had become so unbearable that something had to be done. A sortie on a large scale was accordingly organized, and so successful was it that the T`ai-p`ings not only routed the besieging army, but were able to regain large tracts of territory, capturing at the same time huge stores of arms and munitions of war. These victories were in reality the death-blow to the rebel cause, for the brutal cruelty then displayed to the people at large was of such a character as to alienate completely the sympathy of thousands who might otherwise have been glad to see the end of the Manchus. Among other acts of desolation, the large and beautiful city of Soochow was burnt and looted, an outrage for which the T`ai-p`ings were held responsible, and regarding which there is a pathetic tale told by an eye-witness of the ruins; in this instance, however, if indeed in no others, the acts of vandalism in question were committed by Imperialist soldiers.

It is with the T`ai-p`ing rebellion that we associate *likin*, a tax which has for years past been the bugbear of the foreign merchant in China. The term means "thousandth-part money,' that is, the thousandth part of a *tael* or Chinese ounce of silver, say one *cash*; and it was originally applied to a tax of one *cash* per tael on all sales, said to have been voluntarily imposed on themselves by the people, as a temporary measure, with a view to make up the deficiency in the land-tax caused by the rebellion. It was to be set apart for military purposes only—hence its common name, "war-tax"; but it soon drifted into the general body of taxation, and became a serious impost on foreign trade. We first hear of it in 1852, as collected by the Governor of Shantung; to hear the last of it has long been the dream of those who wish to see the expansion of trade with China.

Tsêng Kuo-fan was now (1860) appointed Imperial War Commissioner as well as Viceroy of the Two Kiang (= provinces of Kiangsi and Kiangsu + Anhui). He had already been made a *bataru*, a kind of order instituted by the first Manchu Emperor Shun Chih, as a reward for military prowess; and had also received the Yellow Riding Jacket from the Emperor Hsien Fêng, who drew off the jacket he was himself wearing at the time, and placed it on the shoulders of the loyal and successful general. In 1861 he succeeded in recapturing An-ch`ing and other places; and with this city as his headquarters, siege was forthwith laid to Nanking.

The Imperialist forces were at this juncture greatly strengthened by the appointments, on Tsêng's recommendation, of two notable men, Tso Tsung-t`ang and Li Hung-chang, as Governors of Chehkiang and Kiangsu respectively. Assistance, too, came from another and most unexpected quarter. An American adventurer, named Ward, a man of considerable military ability, organized a small force of foreigners, which he led to such purpose against the T`ai-p`ings, that he rapidly gathered into its ranks a large if motley crowd of foreigners and Chinese, all equally bent on plunder, and with that end in view submitting to the discipline necessary to success. A long run of victories gained for this force the title of the Ever Victorious Army; until at length Ward was killed in battle. He was buried at Sungkiang, near Shanghai, a city which he had retaken from the T`ai-p`ings, and there a shrine was erected to his memory, and for a long time—perhaps even now—offerings were made to his departed spirit. An attempt was made to replace him by another American named Burgevine, who had been Ward's second in command. This man, however, was found to be incapable and was superceded; and in 1863 Major Gordon, R.E., was allowed by the British authorities to take over command of what was then an army of about five thousand men, and to act in co-operation with Tsêng Kuo-fan and Li Hung-chang. Burgevine shortly afterwards went over to the rebels with about three hundred men, and finally came to a tragic end.

Gordon's appointment to the work which will always be associated with his name, was speedily followed by disastrous results to the T`ai-p`ings. The Ever Victorious troops, who had recently been worsted in more than one encounter with their now desperate enemies, began to retrieve their reputation, greatly stimulated by the regular pay which Gordon always insisted upon. Towards the close of the year, the siege of Soochow ended in a capitulation on terms which Gordon understood to include a pardon for the eight T`ai-p`ing "princes" engaged in its defense. These eight were hurriedly decapitated by order of Li Hung-chang, and Gordon immediately resigned, after having searched that same night, so the story goes, revolver in hand, for Li Hung-chang, whose brains he had determined to blow out on the spot. The Emperor sent him a medal and a present of about £3,000, both of which he declined; and Imperial affairs would again have been in a bad way, but that Gordon, yielding to a sense of duty, agreed to resume command. Foreign interests had begun to suffer badly; trade was paralyzed; and something had to be done. Further successes under Gordon's leadership reduced the T`ai-p`ings to their last extremity. Only Nanking remained to be captured, and that was already fully invested by Tsêng Kuo-fan. Gordon therefore laid down his command, and was rewarded with the title of Provincial Commander-in-Chief, and also with the bestowal of the Yellow Riding Jacket. A month or so later (July, 1864), Nanking was carried by storm, defended bravely to the last by the only remaining "prince," the Heavenly King himself having taken poison three weeks beforehand. This prince escaped with the new king, a boy of sixteen, who had just succeeded his father; but he was soon caught and executed, having first been allowed time to write a short history of the movement from the T`ai-p`ing point of view. The boy shared his fate. The Imperial edicts of this date show clearly what a sense of relief came over the Manchu court when once it could be said definitively that the great rebellion was over. On the other hand, there were not wanting some foreigners who would have liked to see the Manchus overthrown, and who severely blamed the British Government for helping to bolster up a dynasty already in the last stage of decay; for it seems to be an indubitable fact that but for British intervention, the rebellion would ultimately have succeeded in that particular direction.

During a great part of the last eight years described above, an ordinary observer would have said that the Manchus had already sufficient troubles on hand, and would be slow to provoke further causes of anxiety. It is none the less true, however, that at one of the most critical periods of the rebellion, China was actually at war with the very power which ultimately came to the rescue. In 1856 the Viceroy of Canton, known to foreigners as Governor Yeh, a man who had gained favor at the Manchu court by his wholesale butchery of real and suspected rebels, arrested twelve Chinese sailors on board the "Arrow," a Chinese-owned vessel lying at Canton, which had been licensed at Hong Kong to sail under the British flag, and at the same time the flag was hauled down by Yeh's men. Had this been an isolated act, it is difficult to see why very grave circumstances need have followed, and perhaps Justin McCarthy's condemnation of our Consul, Mr (afterwards Sir Harry) Parkes, as "fussy," because he sent at once to Hong Kong for armed assistance, might in such case be allowed to stand unchallenged; but it must be remembered that Yeh was all the time refusing to foreigners rights which had been already conceded under treaty, and that action such as Parkes took, against an adversary such as Yeh, was absolutely necessary either to mend or end the situation. Accordingly, his action led to what was at first an awkward state of reprisals, in which some American men-of-war joined for grievances of their own; forts being attacked and occupied, the foreign houses of business at Canton being burned down, and rewards offered for foreigners' heads. In January, 1857, an attempt was actually made in Hong Kong to get rid of all foreigners at one fell stroke, in which plot there is no doubt that the local officials at Canton were deeply implicated. The bread was one day found to be poisoned with arsenic, but so heavily that little mischief was done. The only possible end to this tension was war; and by the end of the year a joint British and French force, with Lord Elgin and Baron Gros as plenipotentiaries, was on the spot. Canton was captured after a poor resistance; and Governor Yeh, whose enormous bulk made escape difficult, was captured and banished to Calcutta, where he died. On the voyage he sank into a kind of stupor, taking no interest whatever in his new surroundings; and when asked by Alabaster, who accompanied him as interpreter, why he did not read, he pointed to his stomach, the Chinese receptacle for learning, and said that there was nothing worth reading except the Confucian Canon, and that he had already got all that inside him. After his departure the government of the city was successfully directed by British and French authorities, acting in concert with two high Manchu officials.

Lord Elgin then decided to proceed forth, in the hope of being able to make satisfactory arrangements for future intercourse; but the obstructive policy of the officials on his arrival at the Peiho compelled him to attack and capture the Taku forts, and finally, to take up his residence in Tientsin. The lips, as the Chinese say, being now gone, the teeth began to feel cold; the court was in a state of panic, and within a few weeks a treaty was signed (June 26, 1858) containing, among other concessions to England, the right to have a diplomatic representative stationed in Peking, and permission to trade in the interior of China. It would naturally be supposed that Lord Elgin's mission was now ended, and indeed he went home; the Emperor, however, would not hear of ratifications of the treaty being exchanged in Peking, and in many other ways it was made plain that there was no intention of its stipulations being carried out. There was the example of Confucius, who had been captured by rebels and released on condition that he would not travel to the State of Wei. Thither, notwithstanding, he continued his route; and when asked by a disciple if it was right to violate his oath, he replied, "This was a forced oath; the spirits do not hear such."

By June, 1859, another Anglo-French force was at the mouth of the Peiho, only to find the Taku forts now strongly fortified, and the river staked and otherwise obstructed. The allied fleet, after suffering considerable damage, with much loss of life, was compelled to retire, greatly to the joy and relief of the Emperor, who at last saw the barbarian reduced to his proper status. It was on this occasion that Commander Tatnell of the U.S. navy, who was present, strictly speaking, as a spectator only, in complete violation of international law, of which luckily the Chinese knew nothing at that date, lent efficient aid by towing boat-loads of British marines into action, justifying his conduct by a saying which will always be gratefully associated with his name,—"Blood is thicker than water."

By August, 1860, thirteen thousand British troops, seven thousand French, and two thousand five hundred Cantonese coolies, were ready to make another attempt. This time there were no frontal attacks on the forts from the seaward; capture was effected, after a severe struggle, by land from the rear, a feat which was generally regarded by the Tartar soldiery as most unsportsmanlike. High Manchu officials were now hurriedly dispatched from Peking to Tientsin to stop by fair promises the further advance of the allies; but the British and French plenipotentiaries decided to move up to T`ung-chow, a dozen miles or so from the capital. It was on this march that Parkes, Loch, and others, while carrying out orders under a flag of truce, were treacherously seized by the soldiers of Sêng-ko-lin-sin, the Manchu prince and general (familiar to the British troops as "Sam Collinson"), who had just experienced a severe defeat at the taking of the Taku forts. After being treated with every indignity, the prisoners, French and English, numbering over thirty in all, were forwarded to Peking. There they were miserably tortured, and many of them succumbed; but events were moving quickly now, and relief was at hand for those for whom it was not already too late. Sêng-ko-lin-sin and his vaunted Tartar cavalry were completely routed in several encounters, and Peking lay at the mercy of the foreigner, the Emperor having fled to Jehol, where he died in less than a year. Only then did Prince Kung, a younger brother of Hsien Fêng, who had been left to bear the brunt of foreign resentment, send back, in a state too terrible for words, fourteen prisoners, less than half the original number of those so recently captured. Something in the form of a punitive act now became necessary, to mark the horror with which this atrocious treatment of prisoners by the Manchu court was regarded among the countrymen of the victims. Accordingly, orders were given to burn down the Summer Palace, appropriately condemned as being the favorite residence of the Emperor, and also the scene of the unspeakable tortures inflicted. This palace was surrounded by a beautiful pleasance lying on the slope of the western hills, about nine miles to the north-west of Peking. Yüan-ming Yüan, or the "Bright Round Garden," to give it its proper name, had been laid out by the Jesuit fathers on the plan of the Trianon at Versailles, and was packed with valuable porcelain, old bronzes, and every conceivable kind of curio, most of which were looted or destroyed by the infuriated soldiery.

The ratification of the Treaty of Tientsin (1858) was now completed, and before the end of the year the allied forces were gone, save and except garrisons at Tientsin and Taku, which were to remain until the indemnity was paid.

CHAPTER 9—T`UNG CHIH

On the death of the Emperor, a plot was concocted by eight members of the extreme anti-foreign party at Court, who claimed to have been appointed Regents, to make away with the Empress Dowager, the concubine mother, known as the Western Empress, of the five-year-old child just proclaimed under the title of Chi Hsiang (good omen), and also the late Emperor's three brothers, thus securing to themselves complete control of the administration. Prince Kung, however, managed to be "first at the fire," and in accordance with the Chinese proverb, was therefore "first with his cooking." Having got wind of the scheme, in concert with the two Empresses Dowager, who had secured possession of the Emperor, he promptly caused the conspirators to be seized. Two of them, Imperial princes, were allowed to commit suicide, and the others were either executed or banished, while Prince Kung and the two Empresses formed a joint regency for the direction of public affairs, after changing the style of the reign from Chi Hsiang to T`ung Chih (united rule).

The position of these two Empresses was a curious one. The Empress Dowager *par excellence*—for there is only one legal wife in China—had no children; a concubine had provided the heir to the throne, and had in consequence been raised to the rank of Western Empress, subordinate only to the childless Eastern Empress. Of the latter, there is nothing to be said, except that she remained a cipher to the end of her life; of the concubine, a great deal has been said, much of which is untrue. Taken from an ordinary Manchu family into the palace, she soon gained an extraordinary influence over Hsien Fêng, and began to make her voice heard in affairs of State. Always on the side of determined measures, she had counseled the Emperor to remain in Peking and face the barbarians; she is further believed to have urged the execution of Parkes and Loch, the order luckily arriving too late to be carried out. For the next three years the Regents looked anxiously for the final collapse of the T`ai-p`ings, having meanwhile to put up with the hateful presence of foreign diplomats, now firmly established within the Manchu section of the city of Peking. No sooner was the great rebellion entirely suppressed (1864), than another rising broke out. The Nien-fei, or Twist Rebels, said to have been so called because they wore as a badge turbans twisted with grease, were mounted banditti who, here to-day and gone to-morrow, for several years committed much havoc in the northern provinces of China, until finally suppressed by Tso Tsung-t`ang.

Turkestan was the next part of the empire to claim attention. A son and successor of Jehangir, ruling as vassal of China at Khokand, had been murdered by his lieutenant, Yakoob Beg, who, in 1866, had set himself up as Ameer of Kashgaria, throwing off the Manchu yoke and attracting to his standard large numbers of discontented Mahometans from all quarters. His attack upon the Dunganis, who had risen on their own account and had spread rebellion far and wide between the province of Shensi and Kuldja, caused Russia to step in and annex Kuldja before it could fall into his hands. Still, he became master of a huge territory; and in 1874 the title of Athalik Ghazi, "Champion Father," was conferred upon him by the Ameer of Bokhara. He is also spoken of as the Andijani, from Andijan, a town in Khokhand whence he and many of his followers came. Luckily for the Manchus, they were able to avail themselves of the services of a Chinese general whose extraordinary campaign on this occasion has marked him as a commander of the first order. Tso Tsung-k`ang, already distinguished by his successes against the T`ia-p`ings and the Nien-fei, began by operations, in 1869, against the Mahometans in Shensi. Fighting his way through difficulties caused by local outbreaks and mutinies in his rear, he had captured by 1873 the important city of Su-chow in Kansuh, and by 1874 his advance-guard had reached Hami. There he was forced to settle down and raise a crop in order to feed his troops, supplies being very uncertain. In 1876 Urumtsi was recovered; and in 1877, Turfan, Harashar, Yarkand, and Kashgar. At this juncture, Yakoob Beg was assassinated, after having held Kashgaria for twelve years. Khoten fell on January 2, 1878. This wonderful campaign was now over, but China had lost Kuldja. A Manchu official, named Ch`ung-hou, who was sent to St Petersburg to meet Russian diplomats on their own ground, the main object being to recover this lost territory, was condemned to death on his return for the egregious treaty he had managed to negotiate, and was only spared at the express request of Queen Victoria; he will be mentioned again shortly. His error was afterwards retrieved by a young and brilliant official, son of the great Tsêng Kuo-fan, and later a familiar figure as the Marquis Tsêng, Minister at the Court of St James's, by whom Kuldja was added once more to the Manchu empire.

The year 1868 is remarkable for a singular episode. The Regents and other high authorities in Peking decided, at whose instigation can only be surmised, to send an embassy to the various countries of Europe and America, in order to bring to the notice of foreign governments China's right, as an independent Power, to manage her internal affairs without undue interference from outside. The mission, which included two Chinese officials, was placed under the leadership of Mr Burlingame, American Minister at Peking, who, in one of his speeches, took occasion to say that China was simply longing to cement friendly relations with foreign powers, and that within some few short years there would be "a shining cross on every hill in the Middle Kingdom."

Burlingame died early in 1870, before his mission was completed, and only four months before the Tientsin Massacre threw a shadow of doubt over his optimistic pronouncements. The native population at Tientsin had been for some time irritated by the height to which, contrary to their own custom, the towers of the Roman Catholic Cathedral had been carried; and rumors had also been circulated that behind the lofty walls and dark mysterious portals of the Catholic foundling hospital, children's eyes and hearts were extracted from still warm corpses to furnish medicines for the barbarian pharmacopoeia. On June 21, the cathedral and the establishment of sisters of mercy, the French Consulate, and other buildings, were pillaged and burnt by a mob composed partly of the rowdies of the place and partly of soldiers who happened to be temporarily quartered there. All the priests and sisters were brutally murdered, as also the French Consul and other foreigners. For this outrage eighteen men were executed, a large indemnity was exacted, and the superintendent of trade, the same Manchu official whose subsequent failure at St Petersburg has been already noticed, was sent to France with a letter of apology from the Emperor.

In 1872 T`ung Chih was married, and in the following year took over the reins of government. Thereupon, the foreign Ministers pressed for personal interviews; and after much obstruction on the part of the Manchu court, the first audience was granted. This same year saw the collapse of the Panthays, a tribe of Mahometans in Yünnan who, so far back as 1855, had begun to free themselves from Chinese rule. They chose as their leader an able co-religionist named Tu Wên-hsiu, who was styled Sultan Suleiman, and he sent agents to Burma to buy arms and munitions of war; after which, secure in the natural fortress of Ta-li, he was soon master of all western Yünnan. In 1863 he repulsed with heavy loss two armies sent against him from the provincial capital; but the end of the T`ai-p`ing rebellion set free the whole resources of the empire against him, and he remained inactive while the Imperialists advanced leisurely westwards. In 1871 he tried vainly to obtain aid from England, sending over his son, Prince Hassan, for that purpose. The following year saw the enemy at the gates of Ta-li, and by and by there was a treacherous surrender of an important position. Then a promise of an amnesty was obtained at the price of Tu's head, and an enormous indemnity. On January 15, 1873, his family having all committed suicide, the Sultan passed for the last time through the crowded streets of Ta-li on his way to the camp of his victorious adversary. He arrived there senseless, having taken poison before setting forth. His corpse was beheaded and his head was forwarded to the provincial capital, and thence in a jar of honey to Peking.

His conqueror, whose name is not worth recording, was one of those comparatively rare Chinese monsters who served their Manchu masters only too well. Eleven days after the Sultan's death, he invited the chief men of the town to a feast, and after putting them all to death, gave the signal for a general massacre, in which thirty thousand persons are said to have been butchered.

In 1874 the Japanese appear on the scene, adding fresh troubles to those with which the Manchus were already encompassed. Some sailors from the Loo-choo Islands, over which Japanese sovereignty had been successfully maintained, were murdered by the savages on the east coast of Formosa; and failing to obtain redress, Japan sent a punitive expedition to the island, and began operations on her own account, but withdrew on promises of amendment and payment of all expenses incurred.

CHAPTER 10 – KUANG HSÜ

In 1875 the Emperor T`ung Chih died of smallpox, and with his death the malign influence of his mother comes more freely into play. The young Empress was about to become a mother; and had she borne a son, her position as mother of the baby Emperor would have been of paramount importance, while the grandmother, the older Empress Dowager, would have been relegated to a subordinate status. Consequently,—it may now be said, having regard to subsequent happenings,—the death of the Empress followed that of her husband at an indecently short interval, for no particular reason of health; and the old Empress Dowager became supreme. In order to ensure her supremacy, she had previously, on the very day of the Emperor's death, caused the succession to be allotted, in utter violation of established custom, to a first cousin, making him heir to the Emperor Hsien Fêng, instead of naming one of a lower generation who, as heir to T`ung Chih, would have been qualified to sacrifice to the spirit of his adopted father. Thus, the late Emperor was left without a son, and his spirit without a ministrant at ancestral worship, the only consolation being that when a son should be born to the new Emperor (aged four), that child was to become son by adoption to his late Majesty, T`ung Chih. Remonstrances, even from Manchus, were soon heard on all sides; but to these the Empress Dowager paid no attention until four years afterwards (1879), on the occasion of the deferred funeral of the late Emperor, when a censor, named Wu K`o-tu, committed suicide at the mausoleum, leaving behind him a memorial in which he strongly condemned the action of the two Empresses Dowager, still regarded officially as joint regents, and called for a re-arrangement of the succession, under which the late Emperor would be duly provided with an heir. Nothing, however, came of this sacrifice, except promises, until 1900. A son of Prince Tuan, within a few months to espouse the Boxer cause, was then made heir to his late Majesty, as required; but at the beginning of 1901, this appointment was cancelled and the spirit of the Emperor T`ung Chih was left once more unprovided for in the ancestral temple. The first cousin in question, who reigned as Kuang Hsü (= brilliant succession), was not even

the next heir in his own generation; but he was a child of four, and that suited the plans of the Empress Dowager, who, having appointed herself Regent, now entered openly upon the career for which she will be remembered in history. What she would have done if the Empress had escaped and given birth to a son, can only be a matter of conjecture.
In 1876 the first resident Envoy ever sent by China to Great Britain, or to any other nation, was accredited to the Court of St James's. Kuo Sung-tao, who was chosen for the post, was a fine scholar; he made several attempts on the score of health to avoid what then seemed to all Chinese officials—no Manchu would have been sent—to be a dangerous and unpleasant duty, but was ultimately obliged to succeed. It was he who, on his departure in 1879, said to Lord Salisbury that he liked everything about the English very much, except their shocking immorality.

The question of railways for China had long been simmering in the minds of enterprising foreigners; but it was out of the question to think that the Government would allow land to be sold for such a purpose; therefore there would be no sellers. In 1876 a private company succeeded in obtaining the necessary land by buying up connecting strips between Shanghai and Woosung at the mouth of the river, about eight miles in all. The company then proceeded to lay down a miniature railway, which was an object of much interest to the native, whose amusement soon took the form of a trip there and back. Political influence was then brought to bear, and the whole thing was purchased by the Government; the rails were torn up and sent to Formosa, where they were left to rot upon the sea-beach.

The suppression of rebellion in Turkestan and Yünnan has already been mentioned; also the retrocession of Kuldja, which brings us down to the year 1881, when the Eastern Empress died. Death must have been more or less a relief to this colorless personage, who had been entirely superseded on a stage on which by rights she should have played the leading part, and who had been terrorized during her last years by her more masterful colleague.

In 1882 there were difficulties with France over Tongking; these, however, were adjusted, and in 1884 a convention was signed by Captain Fournier and Li Hung-chang. A further dispute then arose as to a breach of the convention by the Chinese, and an *état de représailles* followed, during which the French destroyed the Chinese fleet. After the peace which was arranged in 1885, a few years of comparative tranquility ensued; the Emperor was married (1889), and relieved his aunt of her duties as Regent.

Japan, in earlier centuries contemptuously styled the Dwarf-nation, and always despised as a mere imitator and brain-picker of Chinese wisdom, now swims definitively into the ken of the Manchu court. The Formosan imbroglio had been forgotten as soon as it was over, and the recent rapid progress of Japan on Western lines towards national strength had been ignored by all Manchu statesmen, each of whom lived in hope that the deluge would not come in his own time. So far back as 1885, in consequence of serious troubles involving much bloodshed, the two countries had agreed that neither should send troops to Korea without due notification to the other. Now, in 1894, China violated this contract by dispatching troops, at the request of the king of Korea, whose throne was threatened by a serious rebellion, without sufficient warning to Japan, and further, by keeping a body of these troops at the Korean capital even when the rebellion was at an end. A disastrous war ensued. The Japanese were victorious on land and sea; the Chinese fleet was destroyed; Port Arthur was taken; and finally, after surrendering Wei-hai-wei (1895), to which he had retired with the remnant of his fleet, Admiral Ting, well known as "a gallant sailor and true gentleman," committed suicide together with four of his captains. Li Hung-chang was then sent to Japan to sue for peace, and while there he was shot in the cheek by a fanatical member of the Soshi class. This act brought him much sympathy—he was then seventy-two years old; and in the treaty of Shimonoseki, which he negotiated, better terms perhaps were obtained than would otherwise have been the case. The terms granted included the independence of Korea, for centuries a tribute-paying vassal of China, and the cession of the island of Formosa. Japan had occupied the peninsula on which stands the impregnable fortress of Port Arthur, and had captured the latter in a few hours; but she was not to be allowed to keep them. A coalition of European powers, Russia, Germany, and France—England refused to join—decided that it would never do to let Japan possess Port Arthur, and forced her to accept a money payment instead. So it was restored to China—for the moment; and at the same time a republic was declared in Formosa; but of this the Japanese made short work.

The following year was marked by an unusual display of initiative on the part of the Emperor, who now ordered the introduction of railways; but in 1897 complications with foreign powers rather gave a check to these aspirations. Two German Catholic priests were murdered, and as a punitive measure Germany seized Kiaochow in Shantung; while in 1898 Russia "leased" Port Arthur, and as a counterblast, England thought it advisable to "lease" Wei-hai-wai. So soon as the Manchu court had recovered from the shock of these events, and had resumed its normal state of torpor, it was rudely shaken from within by a series of edicts which peremptorily commanded certain reforms of a most far-reaching description. For instance, the great public examinations, which had been conducted on much the same system for seven or eight centuries past, were to be modified by the introduction of subjects suggested by recent intercourse with Western nations. There was to be a university in Peking, and the temples, which cover the empire in all directions, were to be closed to religious services and opened for educational purposes. The Manchus, indeed, have never shown any signs of a religious temperament. There had not been, under the dynasty in question, any such wave of devotional fervor as was experienced under more than one previous dynasty. Neither the dreams of Buddhism, nor the promises of immortality held out by the Taoists, seem to have influenced in a religious, as opposed to a superstitious sense, the rather Boeotian mind of the Manchu. The learned emperors of the seventeenth and eighteenth centuries accepted Confucianism as sufficient for every-day humanity, and did all in their power to preserve it as a quasi-State religion. Thus, Buddhism was not favored at the expense of Taoism, nor *vice versa*; Mahometanism was tolerated so long as there was no suspicion of disloyalty; Christianity, on the other hand, was bitterly opposed, being genuinely regarded for a long time as a cloak for territorial aggression.

To return to the reforms. Young Manchus of noble family were to be sent abroad for an education on wider lines than it was possible to obtain at home. This last was in every way a desirable measure. No Manchu had ever visited the West; all the officials previously sent to foreign countries had been Chinese. But other proposed changes were not of equal value.

At the back of this reform movement was a small band of earnest men who suffered from too much zeal, which led to premature action. A plot was conceived, under which the Empress Dowager was to be arrested and imprisoned; but this was betrayed by Yüan Shih-k`ai, and she turned the tables by suddenly arresting and imprisoning the Emperor, and promptly decapitating all the conspirators, with the exception of K`ang Yu-wei, who succeeded in escaping. He had been the moving spirit of the abortive revolution; he was a fine scholar, and had completely gained the ear of the Emperor. The latter became henceforth to the end of his life a person of no importance, while China, for the third time in history, passed under the dominion of a woman. There was no secret about it; the Empress Dowager, popularly known as the Old Buddha, had succeeded in terrorizing everyone who came in contact with her, and her word was law. It was said of one of the Imperial princes that he was "horribly afraid of her Majesty, and that when she spoke to him he was on tenter-hooks, as though thorns pricked him, and the sweat ran down his face."

All promise of reform now disappeared from the Imperial programme, and the recent edicts, which had raised premature hope in this direction, were annulled; the old régime was to prevail once more. The weakness of this policy was emphasized in the following year (1899), when England removed from Japan the stigma of extra-territorial jurisdiction, by which act British defendants, in civil and criminal cases alike, now became amenable to Japanese tribunals. Japan had set herself to work to frame a code, and had trained lawyers for the administration of justice; China had done nothing, content that on her own territory foreigners and their lawsuits, as above, should be tried by foreign Consuls. One curious edict of this date had for its object the conferment of duly graded civil rank, the right to salutes at official visits, and similar ceremonial privileges, upon Roman Catholic archbishops, bishops, and priests of the missionary body in China. The Catholic view was that the missionaries would gain in the eyes of the people if treated with more deference than the majority of Chinese officials cared to display towards what was to them an objectionable class; in practice, however, the system was found to be unworkable, and was ultimately given up.

The autumn of this year witnessed the beginning of the so-called Boxer troubles. There was great unrest, especially in Shantung, due, it was said, to ill-feeling between the people at large and converts to Christianity, and at any rate aggravated by recent foreign acquisitions of Chinese territory. It was thus that what was originally one of the periodical anti-dynastic risings, with the usual scion of the Ming dynasty as figure-head, lost sight of its objective and became a bloodthirsty anti-foreign outbreak. The story of the siege of the Legations has been written from many points of view; and most people know all they want to know of the two summer months in 1900, the merciless bombardment of a thousand foreigners, with their women and children, cooped up in a narrow space, and also of the awful butchery of missionaries, men, women, and children alike, which took place at the capital of Shansi. Whatever may have been the origin of the movement, there can be little doubt that it was taken over by the Manchus, with the complicity of the Empress Dowager, as a means of getting rid of all the foreigners in China. Considering the extraordinary position the Empress Dowager had created for herself, it is impossible to believe that she would not have been able to put an end to the siege by a word, or even by a mere gesture. She did not do so; and on the relief of the Legations, for a second time in her life—she had accompanied Hsien Fêng to Jehol in 1860—she sought safety in an ignominious flight. Meanwhile, in response to a memorial from the Governor of Shansi, she had sent him a secret decree, saying, "Slay all foreigners wheresoever you find them; even though they be prepared to leave your province, yet they must be slain." A second and more urgent decree said, "I command that all foreigners, men, women, and children, be summarily executed. Let not one escape, so that my empire may be purged of this noisome source of corruption, and that peace may be restored to my loyal subjects." The first of these decrees had been circulated to all the high provincial officials, and the result might well have been an indiscriminate slaughter of foreigners all over China, but for the action of two Chinese officials, who had already incurred the displeasure of the Empress Dowager by memorializing against the Boxer policy. These men secretly changed the word "slay" into "protect," and this is the sense in which the decree was acted upon by provincial officials generally, with the exception of the Governor of Shansi, who sent a second memorial, eliciting the second decree as above. It is impossible to say how many foreigners owe their lives to this alteration of a word, and the Empress Dowager herself would scarcely have escaped so easily as she did, had her cruel order been more fully executed. The trick was soon discovered, and the two heroes, Yüan Ch`ang and Hsü Ching-ch`êng, were both summarily beheaded, even though it was to the former that the Empress Dowager was indebted for information which enabled her to frustrate the plot against her life in 1898.

Now, at the very moment of departure, she perpetrated a most brutal crime. A favorite concubine of the Emperor's, who had previously given cause for offence, urged that his Majesty should not take part in the flight, but should remain in Peking. For this suggestion the Empress Dowager caused the miserable girl to be thrown down a well, in spite of the supplications of the Emperor on her behalf. Then she fled, ultimately to Hsi-an Fu, the capital of Shensi, and for a year and a half Peking was rid of her presence. In 1902, she came back with the Emperor, whose prerogative she still managed to usurp. She declared at once for reform, and took up the cause with much show of enthusiasm; but those who knew the Manchu best, decided to "wait and see." She began by suggesting intermarriage between Manchus and Chinese, which had so far been prohibited, and advised Chinese women to give up the practice of footbinding, a custom which the ruling race had never adopted. It was henceforth to be lawful for Manchus, even of the Imperial family, to send their sons abroad to be educated,—a step which no Manchu would be likely to take unless forcibly coerced into doing so. Any spirit of enterprise which might have been possessed by the founders of the dynasty had long since evaporated, and all that Manchu nobles asked was to be allowed to batten in peace upon the Chinese people.

The direct issue of the emperors of the present dynasty and of their descendants in the male line, dating from 1616, are popularly known as Yellow Girdles, from a sash of that color which they habitually wear. Each generation becomes a degree lower in rank, until they are mere members of the family with no rank whatever, although they still wear the girdle and receive a trifling allowance from the government. Thus, beggars and even thieves are occasionally seen with this badge of relationship to the throne. Members of the collateral branches of the Imperial family wear a red girdle, and are known as Gioros, Gioro being part of the surname—Aisin Gioro = Golden Race—of an early progenitor of the Manchu emperors.

As a next step in reform, the examination system was to be remodeled, but not in the one sense in which it would have appealed most to the Chinese people. Examinations for Manchus have always been held separately, and the standard attained has always been very far below that reached by Chinese candidates, so that the scholarship of the Manchu became long ago a by-word and a joke. Now, in 1904, it was settled that entry to an official career should be obtainable only through the modern educational colleges; but this again applied only to Chinese and not to Manchus. The Manchus have always had wisdom enough to employ the best abilities they could discover by process of examination among the Chinese, many of whom have risen from the lowest estate to the highest positions in the empire, and have proved themselves valuable servants and staunch upholders of the dynasty. Still, in addition to numerous other posts, it may be said that all the fat sinecures have always been the portion of Manchus. For instance, the office of Hoppo, or superintendent of customs at Canton (abolished 1904), was a position which was allowed to generate into a mere opportunity for piling a large fortune in the shortest possible time, no particular ability being required from the holder of the post, who was always a Manchu.

Then followed a mission to Europe, at the head of which we now find a Manchu of high rank, an Imperial Duke, sent to study the mysteries of constitutional government, which was henceforth promised to the people, so soon as its introduction might be practicable. In the midst of these attractive promises (1904-5) came the Russo-Japanese war, with all its surprises. Among other causes to which the Manchu court ascribed the success of the Japanese, freedom from the opium vice took high rank, and this led to really serious enactments against the growth and consumption of opium in China. Continuous and strenuous efforts of philanthropists during the preceding half century had not produced any results at all; but now it seemed as though this weakness had been all along the chief reason for China's failures in her struggles with the barbarian, and it was to be incontinently stamped out. Ten years' grace was allowed, at the end of which period there was to be no more opium-smoking in the empire. One awkward feature was that the Empress Dowager herself was an opium-smoker; the difficulty, however, was got over by excluding from the application of the edict of 1906 persons over sixty years of age. Whatever may be thought of the wisdom of this policy, which so far has chiefly resulted in the substitution of morphia, cocaine, and alcohol, the thoroughness and rapidity with which it has been carried out, can only command the admiration of all; of those most who know China best.

CHAPTER 11 – HSÜAN T`UNG

The health of the Emperor, never very good, now began to fail, and by 1908 he was seriously ill; in this same year, too, there were signs that the Empress Dowager was breaking up. Her last political act of any importance, except the nomination of the heir to the throne, was to issue a decree confirming the previous promise of constitutional government, which was to come into full force within nine years. Not many weeks later the Emperor died (November 14), the Empress Dowager having already, while he lay dying, appointed one of his nephews, a child barely three years old, to succeed him, in the vain hope that she would thus enjoy a further spell of power until the child should be of age. But on the following day the Empress Dowager also died; a singular coincidence which has been attributed to the determination of the eunuchs and others that the Emperor should not outlive his aunt, for some time past seen to be "drawing near the wood," lest his reforming spirit should again jeopardize their nefarious interests.
The Regency devolved upon the Emperor's father, but was not of very long duration. There was a show of introducing constitutional reform under the guise of provincial and national assemblies intended to control the government of the empire; but after all, the final power to accept or reject their measures was vested in the Emperor, which really left things very much as they had been. The new charter was not found to be of much value, and there is little doubt that the Manchus regarded it in the light of what is known in China as a "dummy document," a measure to be extolled in theory, but not intended to appear in practice. Suddenly, in September 1911, the great revolution broke out, and the end came more rapidly than was expected.

It must not be imagined that this revolution was an inspiration of the moment; on the contrary, it had been secretly brewing for quite a long time beforehand. During that period a few persons familiar with China may have felt that something was coming, but nobody knew exactly what. Those who accept without reservation the common statement that there is no concealment possible in a country where everybody is supposed to have his price, and that due notice of anything important is sure to leak out, must have been rather astonished when, without any warning, they found China in the throes of a well-planned revolution, which was over, with its object gained, almost as soon as the real gravity of the situation was realized. It is true that under the Manchus access to official papers of the most private description was always to be obtained at a moderate outlay; it was thus, for instance, that we were able to appreciate the inmost feelings of that grim old Manchu, Wo-jen, who, in 1861, presented a secret memorial to the throne, and stated therein that his loathing of all foreigners was so great that he longed to eat their flesh and sleep on their skins.

The guiding spirit of the movement, Sun Yat-sen, is a native of Kuangtung, where he was born, not very far from Canton, in 1866. After some early education in Honolulu, he became a student at the College of Medicine, Kongkong, where he took his diploma in 1892. But his chief aim in life soon became a political one, and he determined to get rid of the Manchus. He organized a Young China party in Canton, and in 1895 made an attempt to seize the city. The plot failed, and fifteen out of the sixteen conspirators were arrested and executed; Sun Yat-sen alone escaped. A year later, he was in London, preparing himself for further efforts by the study of Western forms of government, a very large reward being offered by the Chinese Government for his body, dead or alive. During his stay there he was decoyed into the Chinese Legation, and imprisoned in an upper room, from which he would have been hurried away to China, probably as a lunatic, to share the fate of his fifteen fellow-conspirators, but for the assistance of a woman who had been told off to wait upon him. To her he confided a note addressed to Dr Cantlie, a personal friend of long standing, under whom he had studied medicine in Hong Kong; and she handed this to her husband, employed as waiter in the Legation, by whom it was safely delivered. He thus managed to communicate with the outer world; Lord Salisbury intervened, and he was released after a fortnight's detention.

"Well might Sun Yat-sen now say—
"They little thought that day of pain
That one day I should come again."

More a revolutionary than ever, he soon set to work to collect funds which flowed in freely from Chinese sources in all quarters of the world. At last, in September 1911, the train was fired, beginning with the province of Ss{u}ch`uan, and within an incredibly short space of time, half China was ablaze. By the middle of October the Manchus were beginning to feel that a great crisis was at hand, and the Regent was driven to recall Yüan Shih-k`ai, whom he had summarily dismissed from office two years before, on the conventional plea that Yüan was suffering from a bad leg, but really out of revenge for his treachery to the late Emperor, which had brought about the latter's arrest and practical deposition by the old Empress Dowager in 1898.

To this summons Yüan slily replied that he could not possibly leave home just then, as his leg was not yet well enough for him to be able to travel, meaning, of course, to gain time, and be in a position to dictate his own terms. On the 30th October, when it was already too late, the baby Emperor, reigning under the year-title Hsüan T`ung (wide control), published the following edict:—

"I have reigned for three years, and have always acted conscientiously in the interests of the people, but I have not employed men properly, not having political skill. I have employed too many nobles in political positions, which contravenes constitutionalism. On railway matters someone whom I trusted fooled me, and thus public opinion was opposed. When I urged reform, the officials and gentry seized the opportunity to embezzle. When old laws are abolished, high officials serve their own ends. Much of the people's money has been taken, but nothing to benefit the people has been achieved. On several occasions edicts have promulgated laws, but none of them have been obeyed. People are grumbling, yet I do not know; disasters loom ahead, but I do not see.

"The Ss{u}ch`uan trouble first occurred; the Wu-ch`ang rebellion followed; now alarming reports come from Shansi and Hunan. In Canton and Kiangsi riots appear. The whole empire is seething. The minds of the people are perturbed. The spirits of our nine late emperors are unable properly to enjoy sacrifices, while it is feared the people will suffer grievously.

"All these are my own fault, and hereby I announce to the world that I swear to reform, and, with our soldiers and people, to carry out the constitution faithfully, modifying legislation, developing the interests of the people, and abolishing their hardships—all in accordance with the wishes and interests of the people. Old laws that are unsuitable will be abolished."

Nowhere else in the world is the belief that Fortune has a wheel which in the long run never fails to "turn and lower the proud," so prevalent or so deeply-rooted as in China. "To prosperity," says the adage, "must succeed decay,"—a favorite theme around which the novelist delights to weave his romance. This may perhaps account for the tame resistance of the Manchus to what they recognized as inevitable. They had enjoyed a good span of power, quite as lengthy as that of any dynasty of modern times, and now they felt that their hour had struck. To borrow another phrase, "they had come in with the roar of a tiger, to disappear like the tail of a snake."

On November 3, certain regulations were issued by the National Assembly as the necessary basis upon which a constitution could be raised. The absolute veto of the Emperor was now withdrawn, and it was expressly stated that Imperial decrees were not to over-ride the law, though even here we find the addition of "except in the event of immediate necessity." The first clause of this document was confined to the following prophetic statement: "The Ta Ch`ing dynasty shall reign forever."

On November 8, Yüan Shih-k`ai was appointed Prime Minister, and on December 3, the new Empress Dowager issued an edict, in which she said:

"The Regent has verbally memorialized the Empress Dowager, saying that he has held the Regency for three years, and his administration has been unpopular, and that constitutional government has not been consummated. Thus complications arose, and people's hearts were broken, and the country thrown into a state of turmoil. Hence one man's mismanagement has caused the nation to suffer miserably. He regrets his repentance is already too late, and feels that if he continues in power his commands will soon be disregarded. He wept and prayed to resign the regency, expressing the earnest intention of abstaining in the future from politics. I, the Empress Dowager, living within the palace, am ignorant of the state of affairs but I know that rebellion exists and fighting is continuing, causing disasters everywhere, while the commerce of friendly nations suffers. I must enquire into the circumstances and find a remedy. The Regent is honest, though ambitious and unskilled in politics. Being misled, he has harmed the people, and therefore his resignation is accepted. The Regents seal is cancelled. Let the Regent receive fifty thousand *taels* annually from the Imperial household allowances, and hereafter the Premier and the Cabinet will control appointments and administration. Edicts are to be sealed with the Emperor's seal. I will lead the Emperor to conduct audiences. The guardianship of the holy person of the Emperor, who is of tender age, is a special responsibility. As the time is critical, the princes and nobles must observe the Ministers, who have undertaken a great responsibility, and be loyal and help the country and people, who now must realize that the Court does not object to the surrender of the power vested in the throne. Let the people preserve order and continue business, and thus prevent the country's disruption and restore prosperity."

CHAPTER 12 – SUN YAT-SEN

On January 1, 1912, Sun Yat-sen entered the republican capital, Nanking, and received a salute of twenty-one guns. He assumed the presidency of the provisional government, swearing allegiance, and taking an oath to dethrone the Manchus, restore peace, and establish a government based upon the people's will. These objects accomplished, he was prepared to resign his office, thus enabling the people to elect a president of a united China. The first act of the provisional government was to proclaim a new calendar forthwith, January 1 becoming the New Year's Day of the republic.

On January 5 was issued the following republican manifesto: –

"To all friendly nations, – Greeting. Hitherto irremediable suppression of the individual qualities and the national aspirations of the people having arrested the intellectual, moral, and material development of China, the aid of revolution was invoked to extirpate the primary cause. We now proclaim the consequent overthrow of the despotic sway of the Manchu dynasty, and the establishment of a republic. The substitution of a republic for a monarchy is not the fruit of transient passion, but the natural outcome of a long-cherished desire for freedom, contentment, and advancement. We Chinese people, peaceful and law-abiding, have not waged war except in self-defense. We have borne our grievance for two hundred and sixty-seven years with patience and forbearance. We have endeavored by peaceful means to redress our wrongs, secure liberty, and ensure progress; but we failed. Oppressed beyond human endurance, we deemed it our inalienable right, as well as a sacred duty, to appeal to arms to deliver ourselves and our posterity from the yoke to which we have for so long been subjected. For the first time in history an inglorious bondage is transformed into inspiring freedom. The policy of the Manchus has been one of unequivocal seclusion and unyielding tyranny. Beneath it we have bitterly suffered. Now we submit to the free peoples of the world the reasons justifying the revolution and the inauguration of the present government. Prior to the usurpation of the throne by the Manchus the land was open to foreign intercourse, and religious tolerance existed, as is shown by the writings of Marco Polo and the inscription on the Nestorian tablet at Hsi-an Fu. Dominated by ignorance and selfishness, the Manchus closed the land to the outer world, and plunged the Chinese into a state of benighted mentality calculated to operate inversely to their natural talents, thus committing a crime against humanity and the civilized nations which it is almost impossible to extirpate. Actuated by a desire for the perpetual subjugation of the Chinese, and a vicious craving for aggrandizement and wealth, the Manchus have governed the country to the lasting injury and detriment of the people, creating privileges and monopolies, erecting about themselves barriers of exclusion, national custom, and personal conduct, which have been rigorously maintained for centuries. They have levied irregular and hurtful taxes without the consent of the people, and have restricted foreign trade to treaty ports. They have placed the *likin* embargo on merchandise, obstructed internal commerce, retarded the creation of industrial enterprises, rendered impossible the development of natural resources, denied a regular system of impartial administration of justice, and inflicted cruel punishment on persons charged with offences, whether innocent or guilty. They have connived at official corruption, sold offices to the highest bidder, subordinated merit to influence, rejected the most reasonable demands for better government, and reluctantly conceded so-called reforms under the most urgent pressure, promising without any intention of fulfilling. They have failed to appreciate the anguish-causing lessons taught them by foreign Powers, and in process of years have brought themselves and our people beneath the contempt of the world. A remedy of these evils will render possible the entrance of China into the family of nations. We have fought and have formed a government. Lest our good intentions should be misunderstood, we publicly and unreservedly declare the following to be our promises:—

"The treaties entered into by the Manchus before the date of the revolution, will be continually effective to the time of their termination. Any and all treaties entered into after the commencement of the revolution will be repudiated. Foreign loans and indemnities incurred by the Manchus before the revolution will be acknowledged. Payments made by loans incurred by the Manchus after its commencement will be repudiated. Concessions granted to nations and their nationals before the revolution will be respected. Any and all granted after it will be repudiated. The persons and property of foreign nationals within the jurisdiction of the republic will be respected and protected. It will be our constant aim and firm endeavor to build on a stable and enduring foundation a national structure compatible with the potentialities of our long-neglected country. We shall strive to elevate the people to secure peace and to legislate for prosperity. Manchus who abide peacefully in the limits of our jurisdiction will be accorded equality, and given protection.

"We will remodel the laws, revise the civil, criminal, commercial, and mining codes, reform the finances, abolish restrictions on trade and commerce, and ensure religious toleration and the cultivation of better relations with foreign peoples and governments than have ever been maintained before. It is our earnest hope that those foreign nationals who have been steadfast in their sympathy will bind more firmly the bonds of friendship between us, and will bear in patience with us the period of trial confronting us and our reconstruction work, and will aid the consummation of the far-reaching plans, which we are about to undertake, and which they have long vainly been urging upon our people and our country.

"With this message of peace and good-will the republic cherishes the hope of being admitted into the family of nations, not merely to share its rights and privileges, but to co-operate in the great and noble task of building up the civilization of the world.

The next step was to displace the three-cornered Dragon flag, itself of quite modern origin, in favor of a new republican emblem. For this purpose was designed a flag of five stripes,—yellow, red, blue, white, black,—arranged at right angles to the flagstaff in the above order, and intended to represent the five races—Chinese, Manchus, Mongols, Tibetan, Mussulmans—gathered together under one rule.

On February 12, three important edicts were issued. In the first, the baby-emperor renounces the throne, and approves the establishment of a provisional republican government, under the direction of Yüan Shih-k`ai, in conjunction with the existing provisional government at Nanking. In the second, approval is given to the terms under which the emperor retires, the chief item of which was an annual grant of four million *taels*. Other more sentimental privileges included the retention of a bodyguard, and the continuance of sacrifices to the spirits of the departed Manchu emperors. In the third, the people are exhorted to preserve order and abide by the Imperial will regarding the new form of government.

Simultaneously with the publication of these edicts, the last scene of the drama was enacted near Nanking, at the mausoleum of the first sovereign of the Ming dynasty (A.D. 1368-1644). Sun Yat-sen, as provisional first president, accompanied by his Cabinet and a numerous escort, proceeded thither, and after offering sacrifice as usual, addressed, though a secretary, the following oration to the tablet representing the names of that great hero: –

"Of old the Sung dynasty became effete, and the Kitan Tartars and Yüan dynasty Mongols seized the occasion to throw this domain of China into confusion, to the fierce indignation of gods and men. It was then that your Majesty, our founder, arose in your wrath from obscurity, and destroyed those monsters of iniquity, so that the ancient glory was won again. In twelve years you consolidated the Imperial sway, and the dominions of the Great Yü were purged of pollution and cleansed from the noisome Tartar. Often in history has our noble Chinese race been enslaved by petty frontier barbarians from the north. Never have such glorious triumphs been won over them as your Majesty achieved. But your descendants were degenerate, and failed to carry on your glorious heritage; they entrusted the reins of government to bad men, and pursued a short-sighted policy. In this way they encouraged the ambitions of the eastern Tartar savages (Manchus), and fostered the growth of their power. They were thus able to take advantage of the presence of rebels to invade and possess themselves of your sacred capital. From a bad eminence of glory basely won, they lorded it over this most holy soil, and our beloved China's rivers and hills were defiled by their corrupting touch, while the people fell victims to the headman's axe or the avenging sword. Although worthy patriots and faithful subjects of your dynasty crossed the mountain ranges into Canton and the far south, in the hope of redeeming the glorious Ming tradition from utter ruin, and of prolonging a thread of the old dynasty's life, although men gladly perished one after the other in the forlorn attempt, heaven's wrath remained unappeased, and mortal designs failed to achieve success. A brief and melancholy page was added to the history of your dynasty, and that was all.

"As time went on, the law became ever harsher, and the meshes of its inexorable net grew closer. Alas for our Chinese people, who crouched in corners and listened with startled ears, deprived of power of utterance, and with tongues glued to their mouths, for their lives were past saving. Those others usurped titles to fictitious clemency and justice, while prostituting the sacred doctrines of the sages: whom they affected to honor. They stifled public opinion in the empire in order to force acquiescence in their tyranny. The Manchu despotism became so thorough and so embracing that they were enabled to prolong their dynasty's existence by cunning wiles. In Yung Chêng's reign the Hunanese Chang Hsi and Tsêng Ching preached sedition against the dynasty in their native province, while in Chia Ch`ing's reign the palace conspiracy of Lin Ching dismayed that monarch in his capital. These events were followed by rebellions in Ss{u}-ch`uan and Shensi; under Tao Kuang and his successor the T`ai-p`ings started their campaign from a remote Kuangsi village. Although these worthy causes were destined to ultimate defeat, the gradual trend of the national will became manifest. At last our own era dawned, the sun of freedom had risen, and a sense of the rights of the race animated men's minds. In addition the Manchu bandits could not even protect themselves. Powerful foes encroached upon the territory of China, and the dynasty parted with our sacred soil to enrich neighboring nations. The Chinese race of to-day may be degenerate, but it is descended from mighty men of old. How should it endure that the spirits of the great dead should be insulted by the everlasting visitation of this scourge?

"Then did patriots arise like a whirlwind, or like a cloud which is suddenly manifested in the firmament. They began with the Canton insurrection; then Peking was alarmed by Wu Yüeh's bomb (1905). A year later Hsü Hsi-lin fired his bullet into the vitals of the Manchu robber-chief, En Ming, Governor of Anhui. Hsiung Chêng-chi raised the standard of liberty on the Yang-tsze's banks; rising followed rising all over the empire, until the secret plot against the Regent was discovered, and the abortive insurrection in Canton startled the capital. One failure followed another, but other brave men took the place of the heroes who died, and the empire was born again to life. The bandit Manchu court was shaken with pallid terror, until the cicada threw off its shell in a glorious regeneration, and the present crowning triumph was achieved. The patriotic crusade started in Wu-ch`ang; the four corners of the empire responded to the call. Coast regions nobly followed in their wake, and the Yang-tsze was won back by our armies. The region south of the Yellow River was lost to the Manchus, and the north manifested its sympathy with our cause. An earthquake shook the barbarian court of Peking, and it was smitten with a paralysis. To-day it has at last restored the government to the Chinese people, and the five races of China may dwell together in peace and mutual trust. Let us joyfully give thanks. How could we have attained this measure of victory had not your Majesty's soul in heaven bestowed upon us your protecting influence? I have heard say that the triumphs of Tartar savages over our China were destined never to last longer than a hundred years. But the reign of these Manchus endured unto double, ay, unto treble, that period. Yet Providence knows the appointed hour, and the moment comes at last. We are initiating the example to Eastern Asia of a republican form of government; success comes early or late to those who strive, but the good are surely rewarded in the end. Why then should we repine to-day that victory has tarried long?

"I have heard that in the past many would-be deliverers of their country have ascended this lofty mound wherein is your sepulchre. It has served to them as a holy inspiration. As they looked down upon the surrounding rivers and upward to the hills, under an alien sway, they wept in the bitterness of their hearts, but to-day their sorrow is turned into joy. The spiritual influences of your grave at Nanking have come once more into their own. The dragon crouches in majesty as of old, and the tiger surveys his domain and his ancient capital. Everywhere a beautiful repose doth reign. Your legions line the approaches to the sepulchre; a noble host stands expectant. Your people have come here to-day to inform your Majesty of the final victory. May this lofty shrine wherein you rest gain fresh luster from to-day's event, and may your example inspire your descendants in the times which are to come. Spirit! Accept this offering!"

We are told by an eye-witness, Dr Lim Boon-keng, that when this ceremony was over, Sun Yat-sen turned to address the assembly. "He was speechless with emotion for a minute; then he briefly declared how, after two hundred and sixty years, the nation had again recovered her freedom; and now that the curse of Manchu domination was removed, the free peoples of a united republic could pursue their rightful aspirations. Three cheers for the president were now called for, and the appeal was responded to vigorously. The cheering was taken up by the crowds below, and then carried miles away by the thousands of troops, to mingle with the booming of distant guns."

The End

Of

China and the Manchus

Leaves from My Chinese Scrapbook

By

Frederic H. Balfour

CHAPTER 1. THE FIRST EMPEROR

AN eminent writer of the present century has hazarded the conjecture that in the unwritten history of the globe might be found the names of many great and distinguished men of whom the world knows nothing; that in bygone ages and in distant lands there have been Ciceros and Caesars, Hannibals and Homers, may we suggest, in all seriousness, Beaconsfields and Bismarcks? whose fame has never reached the shores of Europe, and whose memories have perished with their lives. Strange to say, we have heard this striking notion characterized as shallow. The criticism seems ungracious: profound it may not be, but there can be no question of its truth, nor of the fact that it is very little realized or thought of. That there are great countries in the world, with long and eventful histories, of which not one man in ten thousand knows the smallest trifle, is a statement which no one acquainted with China will dispute. The educated European is versed only in the ancient and modern history of the continent to which he belongs, and in that of Western Asia. The rise and fall of the Greek and Roman powers; the development of their intellectual life; the varying fortunes of their component states; the prowess of their commanders; the writings of their dramatists and poets, and the speculations of their philosophers: all these are familiar enough, in a general way, to the well-read gentleman of Europe. But does it ever enter his consciousness that Greece may not be the only land which ever produced a Plato or a Sophocles; that other worlds than that he is so well acquainted with may lie beyond the Ural Mountains and the Caucasus, the literatures of which present a treasure-house of instruction and delight, to which he may have access if he will; that Europe has not monopolized the statesmen and the warriors, the poets and reformers, the men of mark and women of command who have hitherto appeared among the nations of the earth; that deeds of heroism and daring, scenes of voluptuousness and revelry, triumphs of intellect and skill, brilliant campaigns and hard-won victories, revolutions, restorations, and reforms all the phenomena, in a word, of national and social life have signalized the history of a giant land whose past is shrouded in obscurity, and whose present is substantially ignored? Hardly; or, if such a speculation were to cross his mind, he would dismiss it as treating of persons and events as far removed from his sphere of being as if they belonged to another planet than our own. It is this apathy and this ignorance which future years we hope, dispel.

"We have decided to take the reign of the great Emperor Ch^ng as the subject of the present sketch, because it marks, in many ways, a new departure in the national life of China. For at least four hundred years prior to this time the country had been in a condition so unsettled as almost to border upon anarchy. It was split up into independent states continually at war with one another and among themselves. No fewer than nine sovereigns reigned over the territory bounded by the modern Chih-li on the north, and Ssii-ch'uan on the south; of these the most powerful was the King of Ts'in, whose domains comprised a fifth part of the whole of China, and whose subjects amounted to a tenth of the entire population; while the next in power and importance to Ts'in was his overlord, the King of Chou, who represented the dynasty from which this period of Chinese history takes its name. Now, at the time of which we are writing, there had been war between the states of Chao and Ts'in, at the conclusion of which a treaty had been made and hostages exchanged, according to the fashion of the day, as a guarantee of mutual good faith. Into the details of the dispute itself it is unnecessary to enter; the only point we need remark about it being that the end of the struggle left the state of Chao enfeebled, while the state of Ts'in had proportionately gained in strength. The convention concluded between the two was, however, not entirely one-sided; the King of Ts'in entered into recognizances on his part to abstain from further aggressions, and was forced to include, among the hostages offered to the King of Chao, his own grandson I-jen, then a child of very tender age. This lad spent several years in the principality of Chao, and seems to have become a great favorite with all who were brought into contact with him. He grew up a bright, clever, high-spirited youth, with frank and engaging manners, and much semblance, at any rate, of amiability; we hear nothing of any leaning to ambition or intrigue, and probably, had he been left to himself, he might have enjoyed a better if not more brilliant future than was actually in store for him. But, by one of those strange and most unlikely contretemps which so often turn the course of the world's affairs when seemingly most full of promise, he became the tool of an adventurer whose daring was only equaled by the success which crowned his schemes.

The man whose influence affected so remarkably the fortunes of the young Prince, and, through him, of China generally, was a travelling jeweler. How the two strangely assorted companions were first brought together is not very clear; but it appears that the Prince, who was very fond of gems, ornaments, and other articles of virtue, was attracted to the merchant by the tempting quality of his wares. The fact that Lii Pu-wei was a compatriot of his own, too, may have had some influence in cementing the regard felt towards him by the exiled Prince; but, however it may have been, Lii was not the man to lose whatever advantage might be reaped from intimacy with a scion of the royal house. He accordingly attached him-self more closely to the person of the Prince, and let no opportunity pass of insinuating himself into his confidence. Unlike most adventurers, however, he did not rise from humble aspirations step by step to more audacious projects. The curious thing about this man was that he conceived, from the very first, the grand design which he afterwards kept steadily in view; a design so impudent, and so apparently impossible of accomplishment, that we can hardly help admiring the coolness and fixity of purpose which eventually carried it through. What this plan was, may be stated in two words. It amounted to no less than the acquisition of the throne of Ts'in for his own son.

The difficulties in the way of this project were even greater than might be at first supposed. The Prince, through whom it was to be brought about, was not only a younger son of the heir-apparent his father, but was the offspring of a concubine. The first step, therefore, was to procure his recognition as the legitimate son and successor of the future King; and to this end was the ingenuity of the merchant now directed. Conversing with the Prince one day on affairs of family and state, he took the opportunity of pointing out to him the unsatisfactory nature of his position. He reminded I-jen that, as simply one of a numerous family of children, his present prospects of ever coming to the throne were absolutely nil. The old King could not live much longer; the heir-apparent, then a man in the prime of life, would immediately succeed him, and his choice of a successor would probably fall on one or other of his elder sons. Now the future Queen herself was childless, a matter of great grief to both her husband and herself; and as there seemed no chance of her ever becoming a mother, the only thing that she could do would be to adopt one of her husband's children by a concubine. The great point, therefore, urged the merchant, was that the Princess's choice should fall upon I-jen; to further which, he offered to repair to the court of Ts'in with rich presents of jewellery from the Prince himself, and do all he could to interest that lady on his behalf.

The Prince entered warmly into the scheme, and begged the merchant to set off at once. That worthy lost no time in commencing his journey, and soon presented himself at the court of Ts'in, where, as the accredited friend of the absent Prince, he met with a cordial welcome. The old King asked him a thousand questions about his grand-son; what sort of a youth he was, how he lived, and what the country itself was like. Nor, as may be supposed, were the Prince and Princess less anxious for information; and so skillfully did the envoy play his cards that he succeeded eventually in securing the adoption of his protege by the latter with her husband's full consent, and the rank of preceptor to His Highness for himself.

So far, therefore, the fortune that had attended his efforts was brilliant in the extreme. He was already the acknowledged guardian of the heir-presumptive; a few more years might see him the confidential adviser of the King. But he aspired to be, not the adviser only, but the father, of a king; and now commenced the most difficult part of his intrigues. The first thing to be done was to secure himself a son; for up till now he seems to have been childless. He accordingly repaired to a professed pander, or dealer in female slaves, and gave him an order for the handsomest and most attractive girl that he could find. She was required, also, to be above the average in mental accomplishments, and no difficulty was to be made about price so long as she came up to all the stipulated requirements. The dealer was not long in producing a suitable person; the bargain was soon struck, and the merchant conveyed his purchase in triumph to his house.

As the Prince had insisted upon Lli Pu-wei occupying a palace near his own, in order that their intercourse might be as free and unrestricted as possible, no very consider-able time elapsed before his eye fell upon the lovely mistress of his tutor. This girl, instructed by Lii Pu-wei, simulated an excessive coyness, which, added to the many personal graces with which she was endowed, inflamed still more the growing passion of the Prince. The prospect of becoming Queen, and mother of a King, was sufficiently dazzling to one who was even then no more than the property of her employer, and she fell readily into his schemes. At last the fish was hooked; I-jen avowed his passion to his friend, and begged him to let him have the girl. Lii Pu-wei hung back, and affected some resentment. The Prince, however, returned so frequently to the charge, that Lli Pu-wei found no difficulty in pretending to be won over by degrees, and eventually gave his consent. "I give you my most cherished possession," he said, as he yielded to his victim's importunities; "and I only ask that you will see in this act of self-sacrifice a proof of my complete devotion to your person."

It is probable that the merchant so arranged the matter as to make his concubine over to the Prince as soon as ever she declared herself enceinte. Some writers have hesitated to believe that the child she afterwards bore was really the son of Lii Pu-wei, on the ground that she had been already living with the latter for a considerable time, and the child was not born for a full year afterwards. It has been urged, too, that as the name of Ch^ng is held in execration by the literati of China generally, as the incendiary of books, they have framed this story by way of throwing dishonor on his birth. But it is as difficult to believe that so clever a scamp as Li Pu-wei would have made so clumsy a blunder in his calculations, as that the future Emperor was born after an abnormal pregnancy of twelve months. The fact appears to be that only eight months elapsed between the surrender of the slave-girl to the Prince, and the birth of the child; and in this case the probabilities are certainly in favor of the popular version of its paternity.

No suspicion, however, seems to have suggested itself to the mind of the confiding Prince. He was so much in love with his new bride, and so delighted with the son she presented to him, that he declared his resolution to raise the former to the rank of legal wife, and the latter to the position of his acknowledged heir. As regards the second part of his intention, there need have been no difficulty; for though married for a considerable time, he had no other children. But his wish to make the mother of the child a Princess was firmly resisted by that lady herself, who, acting under the instructions of her accomplice, declined the proposed honor, on the score of her humble origin. She continued to busy herself with household affairs; she nursed her infant herself, and treated her less fortunate companions in the harem with so much meekness and docility as to disarm all jealousy, and even to win their love. She played a waiting game, and lost nothing by her un-aspiring policy.

And now we must glance for a moment at what had been going on in the state of Ts'in. It seems to have been a necessity on the part of the old King, Chao Hsiang Wang, to be perpetually at war with somebody; and having no pretext for attacking the states of Han, Wei, and Chou, he persuaded himself that the treaty he had formerly concluded with the King of Chao was not sufficiently favorable to his own interests to be allowed to stand. He therefore recommenced operations against this state by attempting to gain possession of Yen-yii, a town situated at some distance from Hantan, the capital of his rival's kingdom. This place, although in an outlying district, was deemed worthy of preservation by the King of Chao, and a general named Chao Chih was forthwith dispatched with a large army to its relief. On his arrival, however, at the scene of action, he found that it had already been invested by the enemy; and the invading general, on hearing of his approach, immediately decided to [give battle. A short but decisive engagement took place, which, owing to good generalship on the part of the Chao commander, ended in the forces of Ts'in being entirely routed. The siege was raised, and the army of Chao Hsiang Wang ignominiously put to flight. But this defeat, though unexpected, did but little to weaken the growing power of Ts'in; and the King of Wei, who had been subdued but a short time previously, thought it prudent to avail himself of its temporary repulse to form a defensive alliance with the King of Tsi. Tor this purpose he deputed a man named Hsu Chia as his ambassador, accompanied by the philosopher Fan Tsii. The envoys received an honorable welcome at the court of Tsi, the King being so struck with the wisdom and prudent conversation of Fan Tsii that he presented him with a quantity of gold on his departure. This so excited the jealousy of Hsu Chia, who had received no such mark of favor, that on his return to the court of Wei he denounced his col-league as a traitor, representing the present he had received in the light of a shameless bribe. The evidence against Fan Tsli appeared so crushing that the Premier, before whom the accusation was made, caused him to be beaten within an inch of his life, and left him lying on the highway for dead. The unlucky philosopher, however, managed to crawl away under cover of the night, and immediately repaired to the Ts'inese Embassy, where he offered his services to the ambassador then residing at the court of the King of Wei. The ambassador took in the situation at a glance, accepted the philosopher's proposals, and accompanied him without loss of time to the court of Chao Hsiang Wang.

The entrance of the philosopher at his first audience seems to have been characterized by extreme rudeness. The old King, on the other hand, no sooner saw that his visitor was clad in a sage's robes than he caused the audience-chamber to be cleared, descended from his throne, and received him on his knees. A dialogue then ensued, in which Fan Tsii rebuked the King for certain disorders in his government, and urged such reforms as he thought necessary. The King took his scolding in good part, and promised that the changes should be made; indeed, such was the effect made upon his mind by the uncompromising counsels of the philosopher that he took him from henceforth into his full confidence, and did nothing without first asking his advice. It is but fair to say, however, that the counsels of Fan Tsii were of a nature in them-selves to please the King, as they had for their object the aggrandizement of his territories. "I am the only one in your Majesty's dominions," he said on one occasion, "who fears that your descendants will not remain masters of your present holdings."This remark struck the King with force, and caused him to place himself unreservedly in the hands of his new Minister.

And now, by a singular freak of fortune, who should come to the court of Ts'in, as ambassador from the King of Wei, but the philosopher's old enemy, Hsu Chia. It must have been a disagreeable surprise to him to meet the rival he fancied he had killed, and still more galling to be compelled in a measure to pay his court to him. Nor did Fan Tsii feel disposed to make things easier for him. He received him with a stern and haughty air, bidding him return to his master and say that it was useless for him to talk of peace until he chose to send the head of Wu Chih, the Premier who had committed so barbarous an outrage upon his person; threatening that, if this were not soon done, he, Fan Tsli, would lead his armies to the very heart of Wei, and lay the capital in ruins. The required head not being forthcoming, two towns of Wei were taken by the troops of Ts'in; but by way of indemnifying himself for his clemency in not razing the capital itself, he set on foot a bloody campaign against the King of Han. The success which attended these cruel measures served only to make the King of Ts'in more anxious for fresh conquests; and irritated by the recent defeat of his soldiers by the forces of Chao, at the attempted capture of Yen-yii, he decided to march straight upon the capital, where his grandson was still living as a hostage.

On receiving a private communication from his grand-father warning him of the impending danger, I -Jen escaped from the court of Chao, and soon arrived at his ancestral state. His wife and child he left in the care of Lii Pu-wei; but no sooner was his flight known than Lii himself became the object of suspicion. His connection with the Prince had been long no secret, and he now found himself for the first time under arrest. The stake for which he had been playing was too high, however, to be relinquished without an effort; and, great as were the difficulties surrounding him, he succeeded in corrupting his guards and making his escape. He soon arrived at the court of Ts'in, bringing with him the Princess for such she may now be styled and her son, now a growing lad; where, we need scarcely say, he was enthusiastically received by the King and the heir-apparent, and loaded with gifts and honors.

Then commenced a series of triumphs on the part of the King of Ts'in, followed in each case by massacres of the most wholesale and horrible description. Forty thou-sand prisoners of war were beheaded in Han and ninety thousand in Chao. Like a swarm of hungry locusts, the troops of Ts'in found lands as the garden of Eden before them which they left a desolate wilderness; nothing escaped their devastations, and the terror of them spread over the whole country. In despair, the King, or Emperor as he has been called, of Chou, ordered a blind attack to be made upon the advancing army by the other princes in a body, but it was too late; and, convinced of the infatuation of his design, he went of his own accord and tendered his submission to his conquering vassal. That monarch received his suzerain with condescension, accepted his humble apologies for the past, and took possession of thirty-six of his towns and thirty thousand soldiers. From this moment the dynasty of Chou may be said to have become extinct. Although the empire was not actually brought under the sway of a single scepter, the power of the state of Ts'in was growing so rapidly that it was clear the old order of things was irrevocably doomed; reverses were yet in store for the conquerors, but the day was fast approaching when the great object they had held in view should be once and for all attained.

During this campaign against the states of Han and Chao the King of Ts'in died. But, as if the fates had ordained that nothing should intervene to delay the consummation of his hopes, or retard the accession of the Coming Man, who was to complete the work he had left unfinished, his two successors were speedily cut off. The heir-apparent died a few days Rafter the decease of his father, and I-jen took possession of the throne. He continued the wars which his grandfather had bequeathed to him, and gained great victories over the states of Chao, Han, and Chou; but, in an evil moment, he allowed his energies to be diverted to the state of Wei, and here he received a check. Five princes joined together to resist the rapacious invader, and a bloody engagement took place, in which the ever-victorious army was routed and put to flight. But this disaster was the almost immediate cause of the final triumph of Ts'in. The King took it so much to heart that he sickened and soon died, after a turbulent reign of only five years, thus making way for the son of the adventurer and the courtesan, who was then just thirteen years of age.

To write a sketch, however slight, of the reign of Shih Huang Ti, or the "First Emperor," without giving a de-tailed account of the steps by which he succeeded in bringing the empire under a single sway, will probably seem to most readers as absurd and vain a task as to write a history of Queen Anne without dwelling upon the great military achievements of the Duke of Marlborough and Prince Eugene. We have elected, nevertheless, to pursue this course in a certain measure. To our mind, there is nothing drearier or more sickening than the minute chronicles of petty wars; wars involving no great principle, directed to no righteous end, but simply undertaken to glut the greed of the aggressor or satisfy his taste for blood; wars prompted by the meanest and most unworthy motives, and aided by the foulest perjury and intrigue. That the unification of the empire was an eventual benefit to China we do not dispute; that it called into play the powers of an almost master mind, whose boldness and originality, courage and perseverance, are more or less entitled to our admiration, will be as readily acknowledged. "What must be done," asked the King of Liang in conversation with Mencius two hundred years before, "for the empire to be tranquillized? " "It must be united under one sway," replied the philosopher. So far Shih Huang Ti seems to have been at one with Mencius. But the means he took to accomplish this great end would have been utterly condemned by that high authority. "Who can so unite it?" pursued the King. "One," replied his interlocutor, "who has no pleasure in killing men." It was by a liberal, just, and unselfish policy towards the people that the empire should have been consolidated; a wise, firm, but merciful system of government, which, as Confucius said, would have imparted joy to contiguous states and attracted distant ones. But the times of which we are writing were not calculated to produce the beneficent and prudent ruler here described;

and it is no more than justice to Shih Huang Ti to say that he was the natural offspring of the period in which he lived. We shall therefore hurry over the unpleasing details of his wars and devastations, believing that the laconic style of the Spring and Autumn Classic is the one most suitable for imitation in dealing with a subject so distasteful.

Aided by Lii Pu-wei, who now found himself a Prince of the Realm and confidential adviser to his own son, and the eminent statesman Li Ssu, of whom more anon, the new King commenced his operations by sowing dissensions between the states of Chao and Yen. When their mutual animosity had culminated in the outbreak of hostilities, the King of Ts'in affected to espouse the cause of the latter state on the ground of its having come off second best; and, under pretext of rendering assistance to Yen, captured nine cities from Chao, which he added to his own possessions. He then availed himself of a struggle that was going on between Chou and Wei to play a precisely similar game; and, making common cause with the former state, succeeded in reducing the latter to submission. This accomplished, he turned his arms once more against the state of Chao; but on this occasion he suffered a reverse, owing to the bravery and good general-ship of Li Mu, the leader of his adversary's forces. Smarting under this check, the baffled conqueror had resort to artifice. By dint of bribes and promises he succeeded in suborning a certain minion of the King of Chao named Ku Kai; and this degraded being, who be-longed to a class unhappily never rare at Chinese courts, undertook to ruin the General Li Mu by representing him as a traitor to his master. This infamous design was facilitated by the loss of three most important fastnesses belonging to the state of Chao, which fell into the hands of the enemy, and the unhappy general was forthwith put to death. The state of Chao being thus enfeebled and disorganized, the next victim was the King of Han. This unfortunate Prince, foreseeing the inevitable calamities in store for him, tendered his submission of his own accord; but the ruthless conqueror, not content with what his neighbor voluntarily relinquished to him, marched upon the capital, made prisoners of the King, his family, and his nobles, and butchered them to a man.

And now occurred an event which shows how utterly heartless and devoid of all human feelings the King of Ts'in had become. It appears that while he and his father, then Prince I-jen, were living as hostages at the court of Chao, he had formed a close friendship with Prince Tan of Yen, a child of his own age or thereabouts, who was stationed there in the same capacity as himself. This Prince, weary of the listless life he was leading in his father's palace, came to the court of Ts'in, never doubting that he would meet with an affectionate welcome at the hands of his former friend; but he little knew how different a person was the conquering King of Ts'in from the playmate of his childhood, and so insultingly cold was the reception he met with, and so mortifying the treatment he continued to receive, that he returned to his father's in disgust. There the affair might have ended; a short time afterwards, however, before his rage had had time to cool, his protection was demanded by a general of Cheng's army, who had somehow incurred the displeasure of his sovereign. Prince Tan received him warmly; but so deep was his resentment towards the King of Ts'in that he thought more of vengeance than of hospitality towards the refugee. His object now was the assassination of Cheng, and he found a ready instrument for his purpose in a certain man named Ching K'o, a native of Wei, who had private reasons for hating the powerful despot. The great difficulty was to obtain an audience of the King; and Ching K'o suggested that the best means would be to take him, as a present, the head of the offend-ing general. The King of Yen, however, peremptorily for-bade so gross a breach of hospitality as the murder of his guest; and the plan would in all probability have fallen through had it not been that a strange but most original idea suggested itself to the intending assassin. He appealed to the general himself, representing that the injuries he had suffered at the hands of the King of Ts'in could only be mortally avenged through the sacrifice of his own life." By giving me your head," urged Ching K'o, " you place it in my power to kill your own enemy, and to rid the world of its common oppressor; the whole empire will thus owe its enfranchisement to you." " I have but one desire left," replied the general, " and that is, revenge; " with which word he cut his throat, and fell dead upon the spot. Ching K'o then took off the head and repaired with it to the court of Ts'in, obtained an audience of the King, and presented him with his horrible offering. While Cheng was bending forward to examine it, the assassin struck at him with a dagger; but, owing to a quick motion of the King's body, he missed his aim. Recovering himself, he threw the dagger at the King; but it only grazed his robes, and the wretched man was overpowered after a brief struggle, in which he lost a leg. He then made a full confession of the whole conspiracy, and was accordingly put to death.

No better pretext than this could have been forthcoming for Cheng to turn his arms against the state of Yen.

Here he was again victorious, though in consideration of the fact that the King of that state repudiated all know-ledge of the plot, and decapitated his son, the Prince of Tan, for being its prime instigator, he left him in tempo-rary possession of his throne. He then, after a brief campaign, succeeded in annihilating the state of Wei; and flushed by his continued triumphs, set on foot a final attack upon the state of Chou. He first dispatched an army of two hundred thousand men, under the leadership of Li Hsin; but this force proving terribly insufficient, he entrusted the famous general Wang Ts'ien with another army three times as numerous, and sent him to the relief of his vanquished colleague. In less than a year the entire principality was subdued, and, owing to the moderation of Wang Ts'ien, with comparatively little carnage. This achieved, the King of Ts'in gave the coup-de-grace to the King of Yen, and assumed possession of his state. Seeing the desperate condition of affairs, the King of Tsi came with all his family, in very humble guise, and offered his submission too; upon which the King of Ts'in, now master of the whole of China, allowed him, with unusual clemency, to escape into a barren wilderness, where he died of hunger and destitution. The conqueror then assumed the title of Shih Huang Ti, or the First Emperor, and ordained that all his successors should call themselves Second Emperor, Third Emperor, and so on, from that time forward and forever.

The events above recapitulated have brought us to the year 221 B.C., being the twenty-sixth year of his reign and the thirty-ninth of his age. We are now at liberty to return to the time of his accession, and trace the course of the more interesting events which marked his domestic history. During the first decade of his reign, affairs of state were placed under the direction of the Emperor's guardian, Lii Pu-wei, whom he created Marquis of Wen Hsin. Now, it will he remembered that the Queen Dow-ager, widow of the Prince I-jen, had begun her career as the concubine of this man, then a travelling vendor of curiosities; and no sooner was the Prince her husband dead than the relations formerly existing between the two became renewed. For some time the secret of their intercourse seems to have been pretty successfully preserved; but it could not remain so always, and the other Ministers of State began to suspect some scandal. The new Marquis then hit upon a very strange and crooked expedient for averting the danger that might come upon himself. Among his retainers there was a young and very handsome lad named Lao Ai, who, from his soft and beardless face, might very well pass for a eunuch. He suggested, then, to the Queen Dowager that Lao Ai should be admitted into the number of her attendants, in order that, should any further scandal arise about his own familiarities with Her Majesty, suspicion might be diverted towards this boy. The one-sidedness of this scheme seems curious enough, and we are at first disposed to wonder that the selfishness of her paramour did not turn the Queen's affection into disgust. But this insatiable woman, who was but thirty years of age, no sooner saw the beautiful page provided for her than she consented at once to the arrangement, and forthwith abandoned herself to the unrestrained indulgence of her new passion.

This intrigue resulted in the birth of two sons, the influence of the soi-disant eunuch growing rapidly greater as the months went by. Soon he was created a Marquis, with the title of Chang Hsin; the territory of T'ai-yuen in the modern province of Shansi was conferred upon him as his fief; the government of the country passed almost entirely into his hands, and strangers from distant parts came and sought employment in his service.

Among the courtiers of the King, however, were certain persons who had on several occasions come into collision with the Queen's paramour, and who consequently bore a hearty grudge against him. Nothing was easier than to effect his ruin, both on account of his gross violation of power, and also on that of his criminal intimacy with the Queen Dowager. These nobles accordingly discovered the state of affairs to the young King, and denounced Lao Ai as an impostor of the worst description. The King immediately dispatched some high officials to investigate the affair; whereupon Lao Ai, taking the alarm, stole the royal seal, put himself at the head of an army, and attacked the palace as an avowed rebel. Two eminent commanders, named Chang P'ing and Chang Wen respectively, who held the rank of Princes of the State, then marched against him, and a battle took place at Hsien Yang, in which, says the historian, many hundred heads were struck off. The insurgents were routed, and their leader put to flight; but he was soon captured, and then the true horrors of the whole affair began. The carnage and the cruelty were awful. Every member of the families of his father, his mother, and his wife was put to death. Lao Ai and all his creatures were then tied severally to carts by their four limbs, and torn to piece, even the relations of those in his employ were ruthlessly butchered. Those who had but little to do with his crimes were banished to the modern province of Ssii-chuan, to the number of four thousand families; the Dowager was exiled to a place called Yung in Shansi; and her two innocent children were barbarously dashed to pieces in sacks. The King then issued a decree warn-ing all against daring to expostulate with him respecting his treatment of the Queen Mother, threatening that all who did so should be put to death, their limbs cut off, and heaped together in front of the palace gate.

This brutal threat, however, was powerless to restrain the righteous indignation of the people. No fewer than twenty-seven noble-minded men braved the royal monster, and a hideous stack of bloody arms and legs was soon to be seen in the courtyard of the palace. But soon after, a certain man named Mao Chiao, a native of the state of Tsi, undauntedly demanded audience; avowing in the most intrepid manner that his object was the same as that for which his twenty-seven predecessors had been so barbarously murdered. When the King heard of the application, he was lost in astonishment and rage; but being almost incredulous that any one should be so infatuated, and, possibly, satiated for the moment with his recent slaughters, he dispatched an attendant to investigate the matter more closely.

"One would think you had never seen the heap of arms and legs in front of the palace gate," was the grim remark of His Majesty, delivered by the messenger to Mao Chiao.

"I have heard," returned Mao Chiao coolly, " that, in the sky, there are just twenty-eight constellations. Up till the present time, only twenty-seven persons have been killed; I come, because I wish to complete the number. I have no fear of death."

So the messenger returned and reported Mao Chiao's answer to the King. In the meantime all the members of Mao Chiao's family, who lived in the same neighborhood as he, got wind of the affair, and made off with all speed, carrying their clothes and provisions with them on their backs. The King flew into a terrible rage when he heard what Mao Chiao had said. "This man has come with the deliberate intention of insulting me," he exclaimed." Let a cauldron be immediately prepared, that he may be boiled to death; the punishment inflicted on the others would be far too merciful for him." Then, grasping a two-edged sword, the ogre seated himself, his mouth in a froth with fury, and ordered the attendants to bring in the delinquent. Mao Chiao advanced quietly to the foot of the throne, prostrated himself twice, then rising, said:

"There are those living who do not fear death; there are states which do not dread being overthrown. Those who fear death lose their lives; those who dread the overthrow of their states are unable to preserve them. Now wise monarchs are all most eager to hear about life and death, extinction and preservation; does your Majesty desire to do so? "

"What do you mean? " inquired the King.

"Your Majesty's conduct is cruel and outrageous," was the undaunted rejoinder; " don't you know it yourself? You have torn your sham-father to pieces with carts; you tied your two brothers up in sacks and then dashed them to death; you have sent your mother into exile, and barbarously slaughtered all the worthy men who expostulated with you. The vilest tyrants never went to such lengths as this. When the world hears of it, all hearts will be estranged from you, and not a man will come near the state of Ts'in. Your servant presumes to tremble for your Majesty. This is all I have to say."

So saying he stripped off his clothes, and placed himself in readiness to be taken up with the pincers and put into the cauldron to be boiled. But the King, descending from his dais, stretched forth his hand and stopped him." Eise, Master," said he, " and put on your robes again. I am willing to receive instruction at your hands." Then he raised him to an honorable place among his counselors, and set off himself in his royal chariot to fetch the Dowager from her place of banishment, leaving the seat on his left vacant, in order that she might occupy it on the return journey. The lion's mouth was stopped for that time, and the King, rendered uneasy, probably, by the warnings of Mao Chiao, promised that he would not be more truculent than he could help in future.

This incident occurred in the ninth year of his reign, and seventeen years before his assumption of the Imperial title. The year afterwards Lu Pu-wei was banished to the state of Chao, where he led a miserable and discontented life, eventually putting an end to his own existence by poison just twelve years after the accession of his son to the throne. His fate, compared with that of the other actors in the tragedy, was merciful in the extreme.

Ten years after this the Queen Dowager also died. She appears from all accounts to have been a commonplace character, who would have been harmless enough had she not been made the tool of an audacious and unscrupulous adventurer. Her ruling passion seems to have been sensuality; in other respects she was simply an ignorant woman, characterized by the vulgar ambition to shine so often found among her class. Her part in the events we have detailed was a passive rather than an active one.

In the twenty-eighth year of his reign the Emperor made a grand progress through his dominions. He visited all the famous mountains and rivers in the kingdom, arriving at length on the shore of the Eastern Sea. There, with great pomp and ceremony, he offered solemn .sacrifices to the Lords of Heaven and Earth, the canonized spirit of Ch'ih Yu, the Lords of the Yin and Yang, the Sun, the Moon, and the Four Seasons. After these religious exercises he turned south and ascended the mountain of Lan Ya, the prospect from the summit of which so delighted him that he stayed there three months, and built a terrace, on which he erected a monolith in commemoration of his visit. On this he inscribed a lengthy catalogue of his virtues and achievements, for doing which he incurred a severe remonstrance at the hands of the local worthies; but the Emperor, to his credit be it spoken, instead of boiling them alive for their impertinence, contented himself with recommending his disinterested advisers to confine themselves in future to their own concerns.

The event we are now about to relate is so mixed up with legend, and so differently described by different authors, that it is by no means easy to arrive at the actual truth. According to Ssii-ma Kuang, there was, at this time, a certain mystic in the state of Yen, who had acquired considerable fame by his ability to go through all the Taoist pranks and capers which conduce to the exorcism of demons and the sublimation of the body. Numbers of people in both Yen and Tsi, who had a taste for the marvelous, were in the habit of resorting to him for instruction; while three Princes had, successively, given in their full adherence to his pretensions, and, in deference to his assurances, sent expeditions across the ocean in search of the Three Isles of Fairyland P'eng Lai, Fang Chang, and Ying Chou. These islands were said to be situated in the "North Sea," as it was then called, and were, of course, no other than Japan. It was currently believed that those who had made the voyage had actually arrived, had seen the Immortals who in-habited the mystic realm, and had drunk of the Elixir of Immortality. When, therefore, the Emperor arrived in the state of Yen, all the old mystics of the place, among whom was a man named Hsu Fu, overwhelmed him with memorials upon the subject, representing the islands as easy of access, and the acquisition of the wonderful elixir as a certainty. The Emperor, who was neither more nor less superstitious than his contemporaries, turned a ready ear to the story, and forthwith commissioned Hsu Fu to make a new attempt. A ship was then fitted out, and Hsu Fu, accompanied by a thousand virgin boys and girls, set sail for the fair realm. Just as they got within sight of the islands, however, a contrary wind arose and they were driven back to China; nor did they, as far as we are informed, attempt another voyage, it being a condition that, if they were destined to arrive, the wind would certainly be in their favor, so that it was useless to try and counteract the atmospheric influences by skilful navigation. So for the Chinese historian. We know for a fact, however, through Japanese histories, that Hsu Fu actually did arrive; indeed, his tomb is still shown to travelers.

"In the seventy-second year of Kore Tenno," says the Kolc Shi Riak, " a man named Hsu Fu arrived in Japan from the state of Ts'in, accompanied by a thousand persons, consisting of men, women, and children. He also brought with him a certain book, and the object of his visit was to find the Elixir of Immortality. In this he was unsuccessful, and he therefore never went lack. He took up his abode at Fusiyama, and his memorial temple is still to be seen at Kumanosan." It would appear from this, then, that a second expedition was fitted out and dispatched at a later period; unless we are to conclude that the version given by Ssii-ma Kuang is altogether erroneous. The Chinese themselves say that Hsu Fu was the first mortal who ever set foot in Japan, and that it is from him that the entire nation of the Japanese are descended. This theory is to be traced, we believe, to Ou-yang Hsiu, the well-known historian and statesman of the Sung dynasty. The story of his voyage to Japan forms the basis of a curious legend which, though largely mixed with fable, is worth repeating here." In the reign of Ts'in Shih Huang Ti," we read, " a number of murders were committed in Khokand, and the roads were strewn with corpses. But birds came, holding a certain sort of grass in their beaks which they spread over the faces of the dead men, where-upon the corpses immediately revived. The local authorities having reported the circumstance to the Emperor, he dispatched messengers in search of this wonderful grass, commanding them to make inquiries upon the subject of Wang Hsu, the recluse of the Demon Valley, who told them that in the Eastern Sea there was an island called Tsu Chou, where the Herb of Immortality was to be found. ' It grows,' he said, ' in the Coral Fields, and is known as the plant which nourishes the spirit. Its leaves resemble the water-grass called M; it grows separately, and a single blade of it is sufficient to revive a thousand corpses.' Then the Emperor ordered an expedition to go and procure some of it, and sent Hsu Fu with three thousand boys and the same number of girls over the sea in search of the island Tsu Chou. They did not return, and nobody knew what became of them. But some time afterwards, a man named Shen Hsi having attained to immortality, the Yellow Emperor and Lao-tzu sent Hsu Fu in a chariot drawn by white tigers, Tu-shih Chiin in a chariot drawn by dragons, and Po-yen Chih in a chariot drawn by white stags, to receive Shen Hsi; after doing which they all returned together. There-fore it became known that Hsu Fu had attained to immortality. Later, in the reign of Hsiian Tsung, of the T'ang dynasty, there was a scholar who was afflicted with a very strange disease, half of his body being dried up and black. As the imperial physicians could make nothing of the case, the patient called his friends together and said, ' My body being in this condition, how can I live any longer? Now I hear that in the Eastern Sea there is an abode of Immortals, and it seems to me that I might go and beg them for a prescription to cure me/ His family were one and all against the project; he insisted, however, and, taking a servant and a supply of provisions with him, he soon arrived at Teng-chou [near Chefoo] on the sea-coast. There he found an empty boat in which he put all the things he had brought with him, hoisted sail, and went whither the wind carried him. In ten days' time he came in sight of a solitary island, on which there were several hundreds of people, all engaged apparently in some act of worship. On the beach there was a woman washing herbs, of whom he inquired what they were all about. ' The personage in the middle, with white hair and beard,' replied the woman, pointing, 'is the Prince Hsu.' ' And who is the Prince Hsu? ' inquired the stranger. Don't you know about Hsu Fu, who lived in the reign of Ts'in Shih Huang Ti? ' asked the woman. ' Certainly I do,' he answered. ' Well, that is he,' said the woman. Then the assembly dispersed, and the traveler disembarked and went to pay his respects to Hsii Fu, telling him the object of his visit and begging for relief. ' Your malady will be cured now that you have seen me,' replied Hsii Fu. Then he set some fine rice before him, inviting him to eat; but in such tiny bowls that the stranger was rather offended, and complained of the niggardliness of his entertainment. ' As soon as you have eaten what I have set before you,' said the Immortal, ' I will give you more; but I fear you will be unable to finish what you already have.' Then the guest began to eat, and found that one of these little basins contained more than a great many large ones, so that he was more than satisfied. So with the wine; for though it was all in a little cup not bigger than a thimble, there proved to be so much of it that he made himself quite drunk. Next day, the Immortal gave him some black pills; and when he had taken them he evacuated several pints of black fluid, and found that his malady had disappeared. Then the patient besought Hsii Fu to permit him to remain in the capacity of his attendant; but the Immortal would not hear of it. ' You have still duties to perform and a position to keep up in the world,' he replied; ' you may stay no longer here. But do not fear the length of the journey; I will cause an east wind to blow which will escort you safely home/ Then he gave him a bag of yellow drugs, saying, ' This medicine is a universal panacea. When, on your arrival in China, you meet any sick person, dilute a little with water and give it him to drink.' Then the traveler set sail, and on his arrival showed the elixir to Hsiian Tsung, telling him the story of his adventures; and many were the afflicted persons whom His Majesty caused to be healed by its use."

To return, however, from fable to history. "While occupied with his travels through the empire, the Emperor incurred a very narrow risk of assassination. It appears that in the state of Han there was a family named Chang, of high respectability and worth, five generations of whom had served successive kings in the capacity of ministers. At the time of the conquest of Han by the King of Ts'in, this family seems to have been represented by a youth named Liang, who, indignant at the misfortunes of his country, made a secret vow to be revenged upon the usurper. He therefore bided his time, sacrificing lands, time, and all the money he possessed, to the one great object of his life. Eventually, he was in a position to offer a large reward to any man who would undertake to rid the world of such a monster as the King of Ts'in, and ere long a certain bold adventurer presented himself as a candidate for the prize. Chang Liang soon came to terms with him, and the assassin, armed with an enormous hatchet, a hundred and twenty pounds in weight, concealed himself by the side of the road along which the Emperor was expected to pass. The royal cortege at length came in sight, headed by the chariot of the sovereign; and the assassin, rushing out of his ambush, dealt a blow at it which, had His Majesty been inside, would most effectually have quieted him forever. It is conjectured that the Emperor had got wind of the conspiracy, and consequently rode in the second chariot instead of in the first; but, however this may be, the fact remains that the vehicle attacked was empty, the intended victim being in another part of the procession. Suspicion seems to have been immediately directed towards Chang Liang, and search was made for him far and near; but he evaded all pursuit, and lived to see the complete overthrow of the usurper's dynasty. His name has since been handed down to posterity as the reputed author of the celebrated Su Shu, and the man who contributed most to founding and consolidating the glorious dynasty of Han.

The lamentable poverty of all the native histories we have consulted precludes us from giving a proper account of the next great occurrence in the reign of Shih Huang Ti. We refer to the building of the Great Wall; an undertaking which is dismissed, with a bare mention of the fact, in about a couple of lines of large type." In the thirty-second year of his reign " B.C. 2 1 5 " the general Meng T'ien drove out the invading Huns at the head of 300,000 soldiers, and took possession of the modern province of Honan, dividing it into forty-four departments. He then built the Great Wall, extending it over hill and dale, from the western extremity of Shansi as far as Kuantung in Manchuria; thus covering a stretch of country ten thou-sand li in length." The event is not considered of sufficient importance to be more particularly described; the genius of the Chinese people, probably, not being such as to render them curious respecting the number of men employed, the cost of the materials and labor, the time occupied in the work, and such like trivial details. The bare fact is all we have: that, in the thirty-third year of Cheng's reign, Meng T'ien built the Wall. And if this is sufficient for the Chinese, it does not behove a European to be hypercritical.

Nor are we much better off when we approach the great achievement, par excellence, of this extraordinary person. That a man of letters should deem a vulgar piece of brick-laying beneath the dignity of his pen, we can well conceive; but that he should pass over the Burning of the Books with almost equal laconism is wonderful indeed. All we are told is, that, in the thirty-fourth year of his reign, the Minister Li Ssii presented the following memorial to the Emperor." In former times," he wrote, " when the empire was divided, and all the feudal princes were fighting among themselves, the peripatetic Sages were in great request. But now that the empire is settled and brought under a single sway, the services of these men are no longer required. The energies of the people should be directed simply to tilling the ground for their livelihood; the educated classes should devote themselves to studying law and the decrees of Government. But instead of this, they guide themselves, not by the present, but by the past, condemning the present order of things as wrong; they put erroneous notions into the heads of the common people, and thereby promote much disorder. If they hear of any decree having been promulgated by your Majesty, each man takes upon himself to discuss its merits and criticize it by the standard of his own erudition; in private, their hearts are disloyal, while in public they make the laws of the realm the subject of their talk in all the streets of the city. They acquire reputation by ostentatiously extolling your Majesty, and render themselves conspicuous by an affectation of eccentricity, misleading the people by all sorts of unfounded statements. If this is not put a stop to your Majesty's power will be imperiled, and sedition will become rife; while if measures are taken in time, it will be for the good of the empire. I therefore beg that your Majesty will cause all books to be burnt, excepting those on medicine, divination, agriculture, and astronomy, and such as have been written during the present reign; but let all others, particularly poems, histories, and philosophical works, that may be privately possessed, be burnt in a heap at the city gates. If any man dare so much as to mention the two words poetry and history, let him be immolated in the market-place. If any still dare to regard ancient times as preferable to the present, let them and all their families be destroyed. If any officers hear of such offences being committed and fail to report them, let them be regarded as guilty of the same crime them-selves. And let all those who have not burnt their books within thirty days after the promulgation of the Decree, be sent into penal servitude. If any persons are desirous of studying law and the Imperial decrees, let them take officers of state for their preceptors."

What a situation have we here for the historian! In what vivid colors might he not depict the consternation and alarm which such a project must have caused through-out the empire, the consultations which no doubt took place among the literati, the means devised for evading the cruel decree, and, above all, the scenes which ensued when volume upon volume of precious lore was flung into the bonfire before the very eyes of the indignant owners!

Or, looked at from the more dispassionate standpoint of statesmanship, what an opportunity for weighing the immediate and subsequent results of the decree, for pointing the moral deducible from the eventual failure of the object held in view, and gauging in some measure the real motives which influenced the memorialist in recommending so barbarous and futile a policy to the tyrant! But all this is far beneath the dignity of Chinese history, the highest ideal of which appears to consist in as close an approximation as possible to an almanac. Three words, and three words only, follow the text of the memorial as given by Ssii-maTsien: "The Emperor agreed." The subject is then dismissed, and another event portrayed in as brief and laconic a style as the preceding. Ssu-ma Kuang, however, does add a little incident, for which it behoves us to be duly grateful. It appears that at this time there was a certain descendant of Confucius, named K'ung Fu, who stood foremost among the literary men of the day. To him remarked Ch'en-yii, a native of the state of Wei, " His Majesty intends to destroy all the books of the former kings. Now you, Sir, as the descendant of the Holy Man, may be considered the representative and chief of the literary world; so you are in great danger." " The know-ledge I possess," replied K'ung Fu, " is of no use in the present state of affairs; it is only my friends, such as you, who know me. Now the Emperor, not being my friend, knows nothing of me; in what danger, then, do I stand? I shall just retire into concealment, and wait until he sends after me; and when he does that, there will be no more to fear." One would think that the historian might have deemed it worthwhile, by the addition of four or even three more characters, to have chronicled the fact that many books were preserved through the instrumentality of this prudent man; but the narrative finishes abruptly, as above, and we are left utterly in the dark as to whether the misguided .monarch ever recovered his senses sufficiently to " send after " K'ung Fu or not. The truth is, we believe, that the descendant of Confucius never had any opportunity of admonishing the Emperor, but continued in retirement for the remainder of his life.

From other sources, however, we may obtain an insight into the circumstances under which the Decree was pro-posed and carried out. Like Nebuchadnezzar of Babylon, the vain-glorious Emperor of China made a great feast, to which he invited all the princes, no-bles, and officers who called him lord. The great plain where this monster entertainment took place was covered with splendid tents, in the midst of which rose the imperial pavilion; tables were set, spread with the richest viands and the most sparkling wines; a thousand flags floated lazily in the breeze, and strains of ceremonial music added due solemnity to the occasion. Instead, however, of erecting an image of gold, like the Western sovereign, to which it was incumbent upon all to offer homage, the Emperor of China was content with a more economical and satisfactory arrangement, by virtue of which he was himself the object of his people's worship. At the conclusion of the grand banquet, the Emperor ascended his throne, and, in the hearing of the assembled thousands, invited any who might wish to do so, to offer their opinion upon the general policy of his government; declaring, in the frankest way, that he should be happy to receive any criticisms or suggestions which might be offered for his consideration.

The first speaker, of course, led off in a laudatory strain. He was a person named Chou Tsing-chen, who held some office under government at Pu-yeh; and who doubtless owed his rise in life to the successful policy of his master." If," said this man, " the whole country is now placed under a single sway, accorded the blessings of internal peace, and defended from the incursions of the Tartars, it is simply the result of your Majesty's bravery, foresight, wisdom, and good government. What more do we want, or what more can anyone give us? All the virtues and achievements of all the ancient kings ' together do not reach the sum of those of your Majesty; for you surpass every monarch who ever went before you, from the most ancient down to the present times."

This speech was greeted with immense applause, and the Emperor sat brimming over with self-complacency and delight. But his transports were soon moderated. A certain scholar of rank, named Shun Yu-yueh, indignant at this adulation of one whom he looked upon as a barbarous and uncultured tyrant, and exasperated at the reflection cast upon his beloved antiquity, rose from his seat and denounced the speaker as a sycophant and a flatterer." The person who has just had the impudence to praise your Majesty in such terms," he said, " does not deserve the title of a Grandee of the Empire, with which he is honored. He is nothing but a base courtier, a vile flatterer, who, meanly attached to the good fortune to which he has no claim, has no other object than to give you pleasure at the expense of the public weal and your Majesty's own fame. I shall in no way imitate his ex-ample; " and then went on to give the Emperor perhaps the severest scolding he had ever received from any of the lettered class, drawing the most invidious comparisons between the state of things which then existed and that of the early ages. Here he made a mistake; for Shih Huang Ti plumed himself, above all, upon his character as an innovator and an original, and nothing seems to have exasperated him so much as being continually pestered about antiquity. On the present occasion, breathing the incense of flattery and surrounded by a myriad realizations of his triumphs, he found it impossible to put up with such remonstrances, and, placing a strong restraint upon his rage, he interrupted the would-be Nathan, and told him not to waste his breath."

These points," he said, " have long ago been discussed and settled; and you have no business to bring them up again. Still, since you have been so ill-advised as to do so, I am ready to go into them once more, and listen to all that can be said upon both sides." Then he called upon Li Ssu for his opinion; and Li Ssii replied, in a somewhat lengthy speech, which embodied the famous proposal for burning all antiquated books whatever. The effect of such a suggestion, made in the presence of the Emperor and all the nobles, princes, and men of letters, in the midst of an imposing ceremonial, must have been dramatic in the extreme, and would furnish a grand theme alike for painter or for poet. But, whatever may have been the immediate circumstances which led to the adoption of the proposal, and whether it was " inspired " in the first instance by the Emperor or not, we know that it was put in force, and that it was the embodiment and culminating-point of the one great policy of change which was the guiding principle of this mad monarch from the beginning to the end of his reign.

The next enterprise undertaken by the Emperor of China was one of the highest public utility. It was none other than the construction of a magnificent highway, reaching from the city of Chiu-yuen, not far from the modern capital, to Ylin-yang; a distance of eighteen hundred li, or six hundred English miles. This great work involved no little engineering skill, for there were valleys to be filled up, rivers to be crossed, mountains to be pierced, and marshes to be drained; and, what was worse, the literati began to express opinions of the Emperor and his undertakings unfavorable to his general policy. Of these two classes of obstacles, however, the physical and the moral he ignored the one and overcame the other; but not until many years had 'passed away, and an enormous number of men had spent their energies in accomplishing the task. Yet this was but the commencement of his constructive mania. He now addressed himself to the building of innumerable palaces, the plans, extent, and general description of which were extraordinary in the extreme. His original reason for this was that the capital was fast becoming too populous, and he longed for a quieter abode; so he first decided to build a new palace for himself in the Imperial Forest Park, where he could retire and live at ease. An idea of the magnitude of this suburban retreat may be formed from the fact that its main entrance or front gate was on the peak of a mountain, many tens of li to the south, from which stretched three great pathways leading to the palace; while the front hall of the residence itself was five hundred paces from east to west and fifty from north to south. These dimensions, however, are difficult to reconcile with the statement that the upper storey was spacious enough to accommodate more than ten thousand persons; nor are we much impressed by the fact that it was possible to erect a flagstaff five yards high downstairs. But the most remarkable feature of the whole was the plan on which it was arranged. The various edifices were so disposed as to correspond with and otherwise represent that part of the heavens which lies between the North Star, the Milky Way, and the constellation Aquila, the vacant spaces being denoted by courts, corridors, and winding paths. This, it is said, was intended partly as an acknowledgment of the benign celestial influences to which the Emperor ascribed the brilliant success that had always attended him, and partly as a monument of the vastness of his dominions, which could only be symbolized by an imitation of the starry vault on high. Seven hundred thousand workmen who had suffered the punishment of castration were engaged in this enormous undertaking; stone was brought from the mountains to the north, and wood from the modern provinces of Ssu-chuan and Hunan, as far as that of Shansi. Nor was this enough for his ambition. Three hundred palaces were built in the city of Hsien-yang itself, and four hundred more outside, a ponderous monolith being erected on the shores of the Eastern Sea to serve as one entrance to the gigantic labyrinth. Seventy thousand families were told off to live in the palaces when ready, farmers and bonzes being the most numerous, all of whom were instructed to prosecute the duties of their respective callings with assiduity. As the time had not yet arrived for the Emperor to receive the rewards of his achievements in Heaven itself, he anticipated that epoch by transforming that part of Earth honored by his more immediate presence into a terrestrial Heaven in miniature.

By this time, however, the whole body of his ancient foes, the literati, were up in arms, and their indignation at his extravagances took the form of a most cutting satire or lampoon, in which he was represented in sufficiently odious colors. The Emperor was furious, especially as one of the principal movers in the affair was an old favorite of his, a person named Lu Shn, who had won his patronage by having pandered to his royal master's love of the marvelous and supernatural. The defection of his most trusted sorcerer cut him to the heart, and he had no mind for leniency. The consequence was that over four hundred and sixty literati, proving contumacious, paid for their temerity by a barbarous death, which so excited the indignation of Fu Su, the heir-apparent, as to draw from him a powerful and solemn protest. For this he was sent into exile, being compelled to proceed forthwith to Chang-chun and join the army under General Meng-t'ien.

Many other instances of atrocity, each one more monstrous and detestable than the other, are recorded of the Emperor about this time, the most cruel massacres on the most trivial pretexts, and in obedience to the dictates of pure caprice and unwarranted malignity, occurring with fearful regularity. There were, however, other exercises of his power and restlessness which are less revolting to humanity. He instituted a system of investigations by which all the characteristics of every part of his wide domains were accurately ascertained and noted down; all the productions of the various provinces catalogued and valued; the state of agriculture and commerce carefully inquired into; and, in short, the whole empire parceled out and tabulated. The emblem of the Chou dynasty had been Fire; he, therefore, as the conqueror of the Chou, adopted as the symbol of his domination the element Water, before which Fire itself is extinguished, He also consecrated the number Six, which was assigned by the astrologers to Mercury, the watery planet; and in pursuance of this fancy instituted a species of senary arithmetic, which formed the basis of all astronomical, geometrical, geo-Romantical, commercial, and musical calculations, as well as of all standard weights and measures. The head-dress or crown he wore on state occasions was six inches high; his chariot, which was drawn by six horses, was six feet long; and the empire itself was divided by the square of six, being distributed into thirty-six provinces. He also selected black as the imperial color, in which somber tint he and all his officers were dressed on state occasions; the very flags, banners, furniture, and hangings of the palace being of the same gloomy though appropriate hue. But these and other harmless vagaries were insufficient to distract the attention of the people from his crimes, and the empire was by this time in a state of the profoundest dissatisfaction. Belief seemed hopeless. The imperial power, or, rather, the personal power of the Emperor, was beyond attack. Appeals to his compassion were worse than futile, for they served only to inflame the natural ferocity of his character. There was one weak point, however, and apparently only one, in the composition of this monster, which seemed open to assault; and this was his superstition. On this, then, it was determined to play; and a plot was speedily hatched, which culminated in the presentation to the Emperor of a bit of stone said to have fallen from the skies, and inscribed with an undeniably treasonable sentence. The shot missed; for the Emperor, shrewdly remarking that the inscription bore no signs of celestial workmanship, had the stone publicly burnt in the presence of a large concourse of persons, and concluded the solemnity by the massacre of all the spectators. It may seem surprising that, after so signal and unexpected a defeat, the malcontents should have resorted to a precisely similar ruse a second time; but such was the line they pursued. Brave as was the face that the Emperor put upon the menace he had already received, it was easy to see that he was seriously perturbed. He became gloomy and sullen, while his love of cruelty was fostered by the jealousy and suspicion which now made him their prey. In this condition, we may well imagine the effect upon his superstitious mind when a second stone was placed in his hands a block of jade, engraved with an imitation of the tortoiseshell. This, he was gravely assured, had been presented to a courier, on his way from a distant province, by a strange and mysterious being clad in flowing robes, with an injunction to lose no time in delivering it to his imperial master: " for," affirmed the apparition, " in less than a year the Dragon Ancestor will be no more." Whether the Emperor really believed the fabrication, or whether he was shrewd enough to recognize the terrible truth that the danger threatening him came from his own subjects, we need not stop to inquire. He turned pale as he took the cold stone up in his hands, and appeared greatly agitated. It was some time before he could recover himself sufficiently to speak; and when at last the words came, they amounted only to a feeble utterance that, the Dragon being immortal, the legend was absurd. Alas! the very fact that that acceptation of the term Dragon involved an absurdity should have taught him that its true meaning was to be found nearer home. Per-haps it did; for the astrologers having been consulted, they unanimously advised the Emperor to take a journey. The recommendation was put in force. The doomed monarch bent his steps to the beautiful province of Che-kiang, offering sacrifices as he went to the spirits of the holy Emperors Yao, Shun, and Yii. But, as if the mockery were too great, there his proud steps were stayed. The man who could lift up hands red with the blood of a million innocents in adoration of the three most saintly of the ancient kings, brought by this crowning outrage the doom upon his head. The last sacrifice had been completed, and preparations were being made for the worship of the Spirits of the Mountains, when the Emperor fell sick. Careless of his condition, he neglected the needful remedies till it was too late; and after suffering agonies for some days, he died.

The epoch whose events we have thus hastily and imperfectly sketched is perhaps the saddest in the whole of China's history. Sad, not because of the tyranny, the treachery, the bloodshed, and the crime which were its salient characteristics, but because of the fatal influence it has had upon the minds of the Chinese people ever since. A merely wicked sovereign does no harm to posterity. The memories of Chieh Kuei and Chou Hsin are execrated, but men are no worse for the wretches having lived. The mischief worked by Ts c in Shih Huang, how-ever, is well-nigh irreparable; for he has inspired in the Chinese mind a rooted and consummate horror of change. Apart from his depravity, Shih Huang Ti aspired to be, and was, a great reformer. He sought to build the world afresh; to substitute new and better things for old ones to wean men's minds from their slavish adherence to the past; to instill into them the great truth that intellect and energy must march with the times; and to remodel worn-out institutions on a new basis. Was not this admirable? Was it not, indeed, the very thing that China needs to-day, and that we foreigners are spasmodically attempting to bring about? And yet the entire scheme was frustrated and brought into lasting disrepute by the selfishness, tyranny, and barbarity of its projector. His motive, in the first place, was impure. He did not aim at the regeneration of China for its own sake, but to feed his personal ambition and self-love. His power was un-bounded; but he used it entirely with a view to his own glory and renown. His intellect was grand; but its grandeur was the very means of its abuse. The unpopularity of the reforms he made required the utmost conciliatoriness of policy to reconcile men's minds to them; instead of which we find remonstrances the most respectful being met with punishments of unequaled cruelty, and barbarous tortures being inflicted by way of example on those he knew were guiltless. Who can wonder, then, that the very word Reform should be hateful to the Chinese people, and that they should view any move in that direction with unfeigned suspicion and distrust?

CHAPTER 2. THE EMPRESS REGENT

IT is safe to predict that in the future history of China the name of Tz'ii Hsi Tuan Yu Kang I Chao Yii Chuang Ch'eng Huang T'ai Hou will be prominent as that of one of the most remarkable sovereigns who ever guided the destinies of the " black-haired people." And, in fact, there are many features of special interest in the personality and antecedents of the lady about whom we have lately heard so much in connection with the Franco-Chinese campaign, and whose indomitable force of will has been alone instrumental in securing for her the unrivalled position she now occupies. To begin with, it is a remarkable thing for a woman to hold the reins of empire for so long a period as that enjoyed by her present Majesty. The Salic law is rigorously enforced in China, and although a woman may be Regent, she can never become the acknowledged equal of an Emperor in his own right. She may be de facto Empress of China, governing as well as reigning; but there must always be an Emperor, in whose name and as whose representative she wields the supreme power. Under no circumstances is a female ever permitted to succeed to the Dragon Throne in her own person; and while this law was undoubtedly the result, in the first instance, of the same just conviction on the part of the Chinese as that which is now working in England to keep Miss Helen Taylor out of Parliament, the inflexibility of its observance is justified by the infamous examples of female imperial profligacy which in two cases have disgraced the annals of China. The first occurred in the dynasty of Han, an epoch which is regarded by every good Chinese as one of the most glorious in the history of his country. The Emperor Kao Tsu, or Lofty Ancestor, having abdicated in favor of his son, who died soon afterwards, the Empress Dowager, Lti T'ai Hou, usurped the throne, and reigned wickedly and unjustly for eight years. Jealousy of a more youthful and beautiful rival, the Lady Ch'i, had, even in the lifetime of the Emperor, developed all that was evil in the nature of this woman; and it is related that her vengeance at length prompted her to cut off her rival's hands and feet, put out her eyes, render her deaf and dumb, and then throw her alive upon a dunghill, bidding her young son go and inspect for him-self the " human sow." When, on the death of both the old and young Emperors the latter of whom died a drivelling imbecile, in horror at his mother's crimes she assumed full power in the state, her reign was a series of the most mischievous political intrigues, and her decease was hailed with deep and heartfelt satisfaction in all parts of her dominions. The other instance occurred in the time of the T'angs, the period when China was most brilliant, most luxurious, most cultured; the golden age of poets and courtiers, musicians and fair women; the time, in short, when China excelled in everything but domestic virtue and political strength. One of the inferior concubines of the reigning sovereign, the future Empress Wu, a woman of low birth, retired from court on the death of her protector and embraced a religious life. She is said to have been extraordinarily fascinating, though it must be confessed that the only portrait of her we have ever seen represents her as particularly plain. But eventually she was discovered in her convent by the successor of the monarch, and after years of the cleverest and most audacious intrigue, found herself in a position of power which for an entire generation proved absolutely unassailable. She was the female counterpart of the great, bad sovereign who burnt the books, boiled the sages, buried courtiers alive, and arrogated to himself the title of The First Emperor. From a purely artistic standpoint, it is a thousand pities that this woman was so vile; for the splendid audacity of her genius, and her wonderful originality and independence of character, would otherwise have combined to make her a true heroine of romance, and one of the most extraordinary and attractive characters in the history of the world. Stories of her strange extravagances are legion. Everybody has read how she claimed authority over nature, and pretended to make the peonies bloom at her command as she walked in the palace gardens; how she had one good, great counselor, to whom she remained steadfast throughout in spite of her evil propensities; how she strengthened her power by foreign alliances; how she altered the style of her reign no fewer than seventeen times; how she attempted to change the mode of writing Chinese characters; how she held the reins of government for over twenty years in the teeth of the universal execration with which she was regarded; and how, in spite of the actual existence of a real Emperor on one hand, and the Salic law on the other, she assumed and was accorded the title of " Most Holy Emperor " herself. The end of this woman was in violent antagonism to poetical justice. She was eventually de-posed; but she lived her life out in a splendid palace, and passed peacefully away at the last. Her memory and the memory of the Empress Lii are both infamous, and the Chinese point to the reigns of these two women as justifications of the national policy with respect to the exclusion of women. But now another precedent appears on the page of history. The late Eastern Empress, Tz'u An Tuan Yli Chien Ching Chao Ho Chuang Ch'ing Huang T'ai Hou, who died some years ago, is said to have been a virtuous and amiable woman, but devoid of commanding genius. The Chinese speak differently of the Western Empress, the lady who then became sole Regent. She, according to all accounts, is a person of great originality and force of will. Some years ago she was dangerously sick, and for months her condition caused the gravest anxiety at Court. The only food it was possible for her to take was milk, and no fewer than sixty wet-nurses were engaged to keep Her Majesty alive. Physicians were sent for from all parts of the empire, some of whom, in despair of their own nostrums, went secretly and begged medicine from Dr. Dudgeon of Peking, a well-known practitioner who reckons some of the highest mandarins in the metropolis among his patients. The applicants, however, were unsuccessful; the doctor told them plainly that if the Court chose to swallow its pride and call him in he would undertake the case of the illustrious patient with pleasure, but that he certainly objected to confiding his drugs to other people, and letting them reap all the credit in the event of Her Majesty getting well. Suddenly it was announced that the Empress was dead. But it was the wrong Empress, the Dowager or Eastern Empress, who was believed to be in perfect health! The event caused a profound sensation in the capital, and numberless were the rumors that passed from mouth to mouth. It was, however, shrouded in mystery, and we shall probably never know the truth about it. Suffice it to say that Tz'u An unexpectedly died, and Tz'ii Hsi unexpectedly recovered; and she has continued in excellent health ever since. It is she who now holds the reins of power, and is the undisputed mistress of China. When the present writer saw her a few years ago, she was about three and forty years of age. Her hair was dressed " butterfly-fashion " that is, twisted in thick coils along a sort of bar stretching across the top of the head, and protruding on either side and fastened with gold hairpins; her straight, well-formed features had an austere look, as she gazed stolidly straight in front of her; and she wore a plain robe of lavender or light mauve silk, as half-mourning for her son, the late Emperor T'ung Chih. That was before the death of her sister-Empress. Since then her personal influence has very materially increased, and she has dared on several occasions to set all precedent and etiquette aside whenever such restrictions interfered with her own caprices. Tired of her long confinement to the Winter Palace, and in defiance of popular opinion, Her Majesty now goes constantly to the beautiful gardens known as the Nan and Chung Hai, and there gives audiences and holds her court. So thoroughly is she said to throw off the restraints of royalty as to practice archery, and is even reported to have taken lessons in boxing, attired in a sort of Bloomer costume, from an old eunuch. The sight must be vastly entertaining. Her Majesty, who is no longer in the first bloom of youth, has a dignified presence and a set, stern expression of face. Her appearance, at the age of fifty, in short skirts, hitting out at her venerable preceptor, and, we presume, occasionally receiving punishment herself, must, to say the least of it, cause some scandal to the strait-laced Censors who recently remonstrated with her upon the undue smartness of her head-dress; for if it be indecorous for a lady, to say nothing of an Empress, to so far forget her age, her widowhood, and her dignity as to wear showy caps, what must they think when they see her actually pummeling and being pummeled? Many widow ladies are not insensible to the consolations of pretty cap-ribbons; but how many indulge in the relaxation of la loxe? We, however, who are only barbarians, can afford to take a more generous view; and it is pleasant, to our mind, to see the Manchu Empress of China credited, even by rumor, with setting so good an example of independence. According to precedent, it would have been more virtuous for Her Majesty, on being left a widow, to have dressed in sackcloth for the rest of her life, used thorns instead of hairpins, and perhaps even starved herself to death. The Empress Tz'ii Hsi has, happily for herself and for China, far more human nature about her; and her name will certainly descend to future generations, in the histories now being compiled, as that of the best

Empress that China has ever had, in spite of the archery, the boxing-matches, the smart caps, and the too great economy of skirt.

CHAPTER 3. THE FIFTH PRINCE

OF the three surviving brothers of the late Emperor Hsien Eng, the one best known to foreigners is of course His Imperial Highness Kung Ch'in-wang, usually referred to in Chinese as the Sixth Prince. His younger brother Ch'un, the Seventh Prince, and father of the reigning Emperor, is less familiar to us, and for many years was credited with being the uncompromising foe of foreigners. This may have been true in a political sense, though recent events tell a far more favorable tale; and we are able to recall at least one instance in which the Seventh Prince, who happened to be staying at the same temple as a foreign gentleman intent on botanical researches, treated him with the utmost courtesy and cordiality, even going so far as to appoint an hour to receive him for a friendly conversation and the inevitable cup of tea. The position of Prince Ch'un at Court is, of course, of an exceedingly difficult and delicate nature. It is probable that when the Emperor attains his majority the Seventh Prince may be raised to the otium cum dignitate of T'ai Shang Huang-ti (" Emperor above the Emperor "), in which he would hold precisely the same position as his son as an Empress-Dowager towards the reigning monarch. But, as matters stand at present, it is impossible for him to see his son except in private and in an informal manner. Were he to attend Court in public he would either have to Jc'o-t'ou to his own child which is a sufficiently horrifying idea to a Chinese or the Emperor would have to k'o-t'ou to one of his own subjects which would be an equal outrage on propriety. He, therefore, only sees his son unofficially, and devotes him-self to supervising the lad's education in the privacy of the inner apartments. But there is yet another member of the Imperial fraternity, the eldest of the three, who is known as the Fifth Prince. This gentleman lives in a rather tumbledown-looking palace with green tiles just inside the Ch'i-hua Men, and is said to be a very original character. He holds the sinecure post of President of the Tsung Jen Fu, or Court of the Imperial Clan a department which regulates all affairs relating to the Emperor's kindred, and preserves the Yli Tieh or Genea-logical Record. In this capacity he has the title of Tsung Ch'ing, or Prince regulator of the Affairs of the Imperial

Clan. The Prince is both popular and poor. Many are the stories told at the capital about the escapades of the Prince of Tun. On one occasion he went to the palace in a very seedy sedan chair. After he had been there some time the Prince of Kung arrived, and also went in for audience. While the latter was engaged inside, the Prince of Tun came out again, and espied the handsome palanquin of his younger brother." Whose is this chair? " he asked the attendants." It belongs to the Sixth Prince," was the reply. "Just the one I wanted," rejoined His Imperial Highness, and before the servants of Prince Kung could recover from their surprise the Fifth Prince stepped nimbly into his brother's chair, and was carried off in triumph. Whether the Sixth Prince saw the point of the joke when he came out and found the shabby equipage that had been left behind in the place of his own handsome turn-out, history does not record; but this much is vouched for, that, sooner than accept the exchange, His Imperial Highness trudged back to his palace on foot. Soon afterwards the brothers met, and the interview is described as having been like that of the two augurs who did not laugh. Not a word was said about the elder Prince's escapade, and the demeanor of the two was characterized by the most scrupulous solemnity and politeness. Sometimes, however, the Prince of Tun's vagaries take a more generous form. One day, so the story goes, a very poor carter, with a cart of the worst and most rickety description, and drawn by a donkey instead of the mule which is employed by all but the very poorest, was hailed by a shabby-looking person about half a mile from the palace of the Prince of Tun. The shabby man took the inside place, and began to chat with the carter, who was sitting, as usual, on the shaft. The conversation turned upon the Imperial family; and the fare, who was apparently a stranger in Peking, evinced a good deal of curiosity to hear all about the much-talked-of Prince of Tun. The carter, who, like the rest of his race, was a gossipy, simple sort of man, informed the stranger of everything he knew. The Prince of Kung, he said, was not very popular; he had the reputation of receiving too many presents, and enriching himself at the expense of the people. But the Prince of Tun, he thought, was not open to that sort of charge. " What kind of a person is the Fifth Prince? " inquired the shabby man. " A very good man indeed," replied the carter. "And does he never take bribes? " pursued the fare. " Not he," was the reply; " but people do say that he sometimes waylays the fine presents that are being carried to the Prince of Kung, and keeps them for himself just by way of a joke, you know; and of course the Prince of Kung does not dare object." This idea seemed to amuse the stranger vastly. Then the carter asked where he should set him down. " Drive me to the Liu-yeh Fu " (Prince Kung's palace), said the fare. When they were within a reasonable distance of the door the carter stopped. The stranger asked why he did not go on. The carter replied that it was not permitted to go farther in that direction. The shabby person, however, insisted on his proceeding, and the carter eventually did so, protesting that if he got into trouble his fare should bear the blame. In a few minutes the dirty cart, with the donkey, and the shabby man inside, drew up at the palace of the Sixth Prince. The front doors were immediately flung open, and a cry was raised by all the servants in attendance, " The Fifth Prince has arrived! " The carter looked round in trepidation for the approaching cortege, and heartily wished himself a mile underground; when his shabby fare, jumping out, indulged in a good-natured laugh at the poor man's terror, telling him he need not fear, for he was no other than the Prince of Tun himself. That was the last occasion, however, on which the carter drove that cart and donkey, for the next day the Fifth Prince sent him a present of a new and handsome vehicle, with a good stout mule, by means of which he has been earning a comfortable living ever since. Stories of this kind, be they strictly true in every particular or not, are constantly told about the Prince of Tun, and we may see in him a member of the Imperial family who, without any political position to compare with that of his more illustrious brothers, has achieved an amount of popularity amongst the common people that cannot be without its value to the reigning dynasty.

CHAPTER 4. A PHASE OF COURT ETIQUETTE

A VERY amusing chapter in the history of official etiquette in China might be written under the heading of " The Emperor is Thanked." Many years ago the present writer was acquainted with a certain pedagogue, part of whose system of education consisted in extorting the formula, " Thank you, Sir," from his pupils in reply to any question or remark of whatsoever nature that might be addressed to them. If he asked a pupil what the time was, " Half-past two, Sir, thank you," was the correct rejoinder; and the same expression of gratitude was enforced even in acknowledgment of a severe rebuke or the imposition of a task. We may be permitted to doubt whether this practice was conducive to any very high standard of sincerity in the schoolboy mind, and to ask how much real value was attached to the compulsory employment of a formula so servile. The schoolmaster, however, was sup-ported by a precedent of no small authority, had he only known it. The constitutional maxim that "the King can do no wrong " might be translated into the official language of China, " The Emperor can do nothing that is not benevolent." It is entertaining to study the circumstances under which thanks are offered to His Majesty, and the strange inversion of thought and language by which every relation between the Emperor and the subject is made to appear in the light of favors bestowed and received. Every edict is a benign mandate, which it is an honor, a privilege, an act of grace, to be permitted to obey. This theory extends even to the infliction of punishments. When, some years ago, the boy-Emperor T'ung Cliih, in a fit of passion, thought proper to degrade his uncle from the first to the second degree of Imperial rank, the Prince humbly thanked His Majesty for permitting him still to exercise his function as a Grand Councillor. When reinstated on the following day, His Imperial Highness thanked the Emperor in still more grateful terms; and two days after, on the receipt of a bowl of bird's-nest soup, his gratitude could only find expression in a flood of tears. It may be doubted, however, whether the weeping of Prince Kung upon this affecting occasion was of a less ceremonial nature than the performance of hired women who wail and howl at funerals. The Imperial wish for the retirement of an official who is unpopular at Court is generally anticipated by the mandarin himself, who, in a memorial teeming with un-pleasantly graphic details of some imaginary complaint, implores the Emperor to let him remain in private life, comparing his fidelity to that of a dog or a horse, and vowing that when his health is re-established he will be readier even than either of those useful animals to roll his head in the dust and die in his master's service. It is noteworthy that a refusal on the part of the Emperor to accede to similar requests is oftener the occasion of thanks than when His Majesty accedes. Only a short time ago the eminent statesman Pao-t'ing implored the Emperor in most moving terms to permit him to retire.

The Emperor refused, sharply reproving him for ingratitude, and the snubbed official meekly thanked His Majesty for not acceding to his request. The gift of a fur cloak, especially when the fur round the neck of the animal is retained and made up, is another and more comprehensible occasion for thanksgiving; and so is the permission to ride on horseback through certain portions of the Imperial enclosure, which are sacred ground as regards less favored servants of the Throne. One of the most amusing incidents in connection with this practice of perpetual thanksgiving occurred not very long ago. A Manchu officer of high rank, no less a personage indeed than Wulahsich'ungah, President of the Board of Ceremonies, returned thanks for the honor of having been invited to a sacrificial feast by the Emperor. Next day, however, a terrible snubbing Was administered to Wulah-sich'ungah. The Emperor had received his expression of. gratitude with astonishment, for, as it happened, he had never been invited to the feast at all! " His name," says the Decree, " does not appear in the list of guests approved of by Us, and in thus thanking Us he has been guilty of a great piece of carelessness." The unfortunate President is then and there to be committed to the Board of Punishments for the determination of a penalty; and he will probably be less eager to thank the Emperor for invitations not accorded to him in future. It is a remarkable fact that Wulahsich'ungah does not express his gratitude either for the snubbing or the omission of his name from the list of guests; but as a loyal subject he no doubt is duly conscious of the honor done to him in both instances. If, however, the Emperor exacts all this deference and professional gratitude from his subordinates, it must be admitted that he shows equal politeness, on his side, towards Heaven. Two most auspicious occurrences were some time ago reported to the Throne a fall of snow in the metropolitan district, nearly half a foot in depth, and the sudden setting of the wind from the north-east a phenomenon which presages longevity and plenteous harvests. Immediately the Decree went forth, returning thanks for the timely blessing, and announcing His Majesty's intention to proceed in person to the temple outside the back-gate of the palace to offer up his acknowledgments; the imperial princes and dukes had to go to other temples for the same purpose, and the usual rewards were distributed among the Taoist priests of the Ta-kao Tien for the valuable assistance they had rendered in coaxing Heaven to send these happy and long-expected prognostications.

CHAPTER 5. FILIAL PIETY

WHEN the early Jesuit missionaries to China compiled their valuable Memoir esconcernant les Chinois, they de-voted the half of one large volume to the literature which has grown up around the doctrine of filial piety. It is noteworthy, however, that there is a marked abstention from either praise or blame of this celebrated article of faith for so we may almost call it on the part of the editors of the series. But we have heard the filial piety of the Chinese commended in the highest terms by foreign critics, and even by foreign missionary critics. One writer, at any rate, has gone so far as to say that in the long-continued existence of the Chinese Empire we have a fulfillment of the Fifth Commandment "Honor thy father and thy mother, that thy days may be long in the land." It would be idle to speculate what connection there may be between respect to parents and a prolongation of land-tenure in any given society, and equally idle to attempt to prove, from what we know of Chinese history, that the doctrine of filial piety as practiced in China has directly or indirectly conduced to the preservation of that country in a national and political sense. Our object is less ambitious, and we will state our meaning in the fewest and most pointed words at our command. Briefly, then, the doctrine of filial piety, as practiced and interpreted in China, is in many ways a curse and a calamity to the people. It is a flagrant and flagitious example of a virtue exaggerated into a vice. The admiration of the Chinese is extorted for numerous instances of filial piety that have come down from antiquity, and they are taught to believe that upon this is based their loyalty to the Throne. No brighter pattern of this so-called virtue exists than that of the great Emperor Shun, who, cursed with an unnatural father and a malignant stepmother, who on one occasion burnt his house down over his ears, and on another threw him down a well, went about roaring and weeping to Compassionate Heaven in the channeled fields. And why? because of his parents' cruelty? No; but because of his own imagined vileness, vileness which can have been the only cause of their ill-treatment of him, so virtuous a person shrinking from imputing any blame to those who had given him life. Is not such a type degrading? Then there was another bright example, an old philosopher, who at the age of seventy used to dress himself up in a baby's frock and dance around and roll about the floor, shaking a rattle or beating a little drum, simply to amuse his doting parents, who are said to have cackled with delight as their venerable offspring jerked himself about and frolicked for their entertainment. Nearly all the instances of filial piety held up to the Chinese for imitation are equally grotesque and mischievous. But worse remains behind. No man, be he a viceroy or a general, or what he may, or whatever age he may have attained, is a free agent so long as his father is alive. In the eye of custom and the law he is a child and a minor. The highest and most cultured man in China may thus be legally at the disposal of an un-lettered and narrow-minded boor, if it happens that his father was born and has remained a peasant, and he himself has risen. The ethical works of China teem with admonitions to children how to perform their duty to their parents, but there is scarcely one that touches upon the duty that parents owe their children. It is not too much to say that a Chinese father has more absolute power over the members of his family than the Emperor has over his realm. Only last year the Peking Gazette recorded the horrible fact of a mother burying her own child alive, and the Emperor condoning, even if not actually approving, the loathsome crime. Had that son, even by accident or in a fit of lunacy, caused the death of the virago, he would have been slowly sliced to death and the flesh peeled off his bones. Sometime after this, an unhappy woman, in trying to save herself from outrage at the hands of her father-in-law, killed him; and instead of being commended for her virtue, was condemned to death by the slicing process. Such is the doctrine of filial piety in China, so much cried up by those who have never studied it. It was the vile and intolerant spirit that hated, persecuted, tortured, and did to death all who took the liberty of thinking for themselves. That spirit exists still, and everywhere, though in a different form. It is that which gives the license or affords an excuse for all cruelty and rank injustice, and we deliberately affirm that there is no cruelty or injustice ever perpetrated in China grosser than that which is based upon this pernicious doctrine of filial piety. To be filial a man must be a groveling slave, ready to repudiate his own knowledge and sacrifice his prospects in life at the dictum of a possibly prejudiced and ignorant father. To be filial a man must never dare to cherish a new or independent thought, for his ancestors had never had such thoughts, and would probably have condemned them if they had. Superstition and obstructiveness of the most fatal type are thus made to hinge upon the doctrine of filial piety which is by no means confined to a domestic application, but runs through the entire social policy of China just as they were made to hinge upon Church traditions in the Middle Ages. Fanaticism and its offspring cruelty the spirit that leads men to bind each other's souls and torture each other's bodies constitute, to our mind, a sin for which a new name ought to be discovered. It may almost be called sacrilege against the human race, and this is the unpardonable sin, or what should be considered such by all wishers for the mental and corporeal enfranchisement of their fellow-men. The worst feature of it all is, that the evil of which we complain, like evil in the abstract, is simply poisoned and distorted good. Reverence for parents is a natural and human feeling. It has been the mainspring of some of the most beautiful actions ever per-formed by men. No one will dispute the propriety of the Chinese in placing the relation of paternity and son-hood among the five primary relationships of mankind. But where it is pushed to such an extreme as it is in China, where the father is endowed with the authority of an absolute and irresponsible despot, and the son lowered to being the slave of another man simply because that other man was instrumental in bringing him into the world, it becomes an outrage, a mischief, and a folly. It strikes at the root of all sense of right and wrong. Such is the perversion of that sense among the Chinese at present that probably not one man who reads the Peking Gazette will think there is anything strange in the fact of the Emperor protecting the human tigress who murdered her own son in cold blood. The child is taught even by the proverbial philosophy of China to look upon his parent as a god, while the parent appears to wield autocratic power over the life he has been the accidental means of giving.

There is possibly only one element in this distorted doctrine which is at all healthy. The Emperor, as Son of Heaven, owes filial duty to his Celestial Progenitor, and if he does not pay it his commission is withdrawn. In plain language, if he is a bad sovereign, the disfavor of Heaven is shown by manifold disasters and portents; and when this is the case the people have a right to rebel against the man whom Heaven thus openly rejects. So far, the extreme phase of filial piety results beneficially for the people. But in all other respects it is liable to prove a blight and a hindrance to the country, at once representing and encouraging the old bad spirit of conservatism and cruelty which worked such desolation among men in the bygone ages of the world.

CHAPTER 6. CHINESE IDEAS OF PATHOLOGY

THERE are few things more amusing, and at the same time more exasperating, to a European than the utter confusion of thought which characterizes the Chinese as a race. The extreme difficulty of getting a direct reply to a simple question, in examinations before a magistrate, for instance, has become almost proverbial. There seems a looseness of reasoning, a want of consecutiveness, in the mental processes of the Chinese which argues an inherent defect in their constitutions; and it is a fact that can be proved by experience, that scarcely a Chinaman will be found free from this strange defect who has not been brought into long and intimate contact with Europeans.

The same phenomenon is, of course, observed in all their so-called scientific theories. Physiology and meta-physics appear to form but one science according to Chinese notions, no clear distinction being recognized between phases of matter and phases of mind. This is almost incomprehensible to a European intellect; but it is none the less a fact. Take, for instance, the idea of anger, in the view of a Chinese. In the native language it is cJi'i, which means, popularly speaking, breath or air. But this is not simply an instance of one word doing duty for two different ideas. Anger has been defined to us by Chinese as an actual rush of breath, or wind, from the heart to the head, which flushes the face and stiffens the muscles of the neck. No difference is allowed between the material and the immaterial, the cause and the effect. An angry man is said to sheng ch'i, produce breath or air, and this air is anger, the too great predominance or inrush of which into the human system is apt to bring about insanity or even death. It is a purely physical, not a mental, phenomenon in the eyes of native physicists; or, rather, the Chinese system does not recognize or admit of any element of the immaterial whatever. Another curious example is afforded by the use of the word hsin or heart, and the sense in which it is understood. In discussing metaphysical subjects with a cultured Chinese it is almost impossible to make him distinguish clearly between the physical organ and the word in its popular acceptation of mind. In the study of Taoist books the distinction is still more difficult to trace. But it is in what may be called the popular philosophy of the common people that the most glorious confusion arises. There we find the actual blood-pump made the seat or embodiment of the man's mental and moral characteristics; so much so, that every form of what we understand by the term heart-disease should logically be regarded as the sign of some special depravity or sin. Hence comes the curious Chinese doctrine of the effect of climate upon character. Now, the Chinese are sufficiently well acquainted with the functions of the heart, and the relation to that organ of the blood. They know that for perfect health of body it is necessary that the blood should be kept completely pure, and that everything that taints the blood 'has an injurious effect upon the heart, through which it passes.

It follows, therefore and we now quote the words of a certain curious old empiric of Peking, a strange compound of shrewdness and folly that the inhabitants of the northern capital are the most corrupt community in China. The reasoning is clear. The atmosphere of that city is intensely impregnated with two things foul smells and pulverized ordure. This impure air is inhaled by the lungs; from the lungs it passes into the blood, and the blood thus defiled pours into the heart, which is thus corrupted and contaminated in its turn. Consequently the people whose hearts are thus infected become treacherous and insincere; they lose all sense of morality, propriety, and good faith; and what is worse concluded our interlocutor, solemnly " foreigners them-selves are falling victims to this defiling process too." Of course to argue against this congeries of contradictions is generally a waste of time; for even if one's opponent is pushed into a corner and unable to reply, it by no means follows that he is convinced of the un-tenableness of his views. The earnest simplicity and seriousness with which an amiable and lettered man in China will sit and propound the most preposterous and fantastic theories that ever entered a human brain, and the profound unconsciousness he shows of the nonsense he is talking, affect one very curiously. Foreign science, such as that of medicine or anatomy, for example, impresses him with the notion of something strange and heterodox, which is too far removed from the traditions of the sages to be ever regarded as more than a bizarrerie to be wondered at, instead of a subject calling for grave investigation. He is firmly impressed with the belief that the heart is the seat of the intellect, and is situated in the centre of the body, although he can feel it beating on his left; that courage resides in the gall, the affections in the liver, the direction of bodily movement in the lungs, temper in the stomach, and mental force and wisdom in the kidneys. It is true that even we in the West appear to sanction this confusion of ideas by speaking of a coward as white-livered, and of a fastidious or haughty person as a man of delicate or proud stomach. But what are popular and figurative expressions with us are scientific axioms among the Chinese, and it will take a long term of educational courses before their eyes are opened to the untenable nature of their theories. At the same time, we must not forget that the action and re-action of the mind upon the body and the body on the mind is still a matter of much mystery even to Western thinkers, and the fact that deaths have actually occurred from the influence of imagination solely ought to make us lenient in dealing with the quaint confusions between mind and matter which exist in the Chinese intellect.

CHAPTER 7. CHINESE MEDICINES

THE medical remedies of the Chinese afford a promising field of inquiry to the student of curiosities. No one who is not fairly acquainted with the pseudo-philosophies of China, the strange affinities which are supposed to exist between the five points of the compass, the five colors, the five flavors, the five elements, and other fanciful phenomena, can rightly understand the principles on which certain substances are supposed to be antagonistic to certain humors and conditions of the body. For a rough list of the medicaments in common use in China one has only to study the ordinary Customs returns, which will be quite sufficient to show the very extraordinary character of the articles which go to make up the Chinese pharmacopoeia. Some of these medicines are, no doubt, useful enough. The Chinese are known to have a wide knowledge of herbs and simples, and their primitive ideas of surgery are in many instances founded upon true principles. A case in point is the practice of pinching and scraping the skin with a view to drawing out internal inflammation. A slight " touch of the sun " is unmistakably relieved by the hard tweaking of the skin between the eyes and on the breast with a couple of copper cash, until a livid red line or patch is raised upon the surface; and though the process is not agreeable, the result certainly goes far to justify the principle of counter-irritation on which the treatment is based. Many of the medicines in use, however, are exceedingly coarse and disgusting, and, we should hope, are never resorted to except in extreme cases. A very curious method of procedure is adopted by the doctor who is called in to see a patient. The sick man does not open the interview by detailing his symptoms, as with us. That would involve an insult to the perspicacity of his adviser. It is the doctor who, by feeling the patient's pulse, is expected to detail the various ailments of his patron, which can be correctly diagnosed by a clever practitioner from the slow or hurried beats. He then writes out his prescription, pockets his horse money or chair-money, as the fee is called, and takes his departure for the time. In most instances the medicine prescribed is of a very cheap and often very nasty description; there are, however, drugs highly prized among the faculty in China which are extremely precious. Diamond-dust is looked upon as a dangerous poison in India and the West; yet there are other precious stones, rare indeed in China, which are said to have a wonderful efficacy in curing certain disorders. A detailed description of one of these peculiar and certainly very expensive remedies lies before us. It consists of white and red coral, rubies or jacinth, pearls, emeralds, musk, and one or two earths in various quantities, crushed into powder, rolled into pills with gum and rose-water, and coated with gold-leaf. As a poison, one would think this composition must be quite invaluable; or as a tit-bit for an ostrich, did such birds exist in China; but as a medicine it is quite unique. It is said, however, to be an infallible cure for smallpox, measles, scarlet fever, and, in fact, all diseases which arise from blood-poisoning and break out in cutaneous eruptions. The strengthening qualities of the preparation are said, even on' European testimony, to be quite remarkable; and the old Jesuits who flourished here during the early part of the present dynasty deliberately affirm that they have seen men snatched from the last convulsions of death by its judicious use. Another famous remedy is called Tcu chiu, or bitter wine. This reminds one of the bitter cup sold by chemists in England some five-and-twenty years ago. The preparation seems to be a strong and invigorating tonic; it is said to have great efficacy in cases of bile, indigestion, colic, and intermittent fevers, and to be an excellent preservative of health if taken, much as Europeans take the nauseous waters of Carlsbad and Aix, the first thing in the morning on an empty stomach. Its ingredients are neither so indigestible nor so expensive as those of the other. It is composed of spirit, aloes, myrrh, frankincense, and saffron. These are to be mixed and exposed to the sun for one month; the bottle to be well shaken from time to time, and the fluid used when it is perfectly clear, and yet impregnated with the various contents. These two remedies are not of Chinese origin. They are said to have been brought from India, where they were originally discovered. Readers of the Hung Lou Meng, one of the most charmingly written novels in the whole world, will remember the burlesque prescription proposed by a Buddhist priest for the ailments of Mademoiselle Pao-chai. It consisted of the pistils of a white moutanflower or peony which had bloomed in the spring, of a white lotus that had bloomed in the summer, of a white poppy that had bloomed in the autumn, and of a white plum-blossom that had bloomed in the winter; of each of these twelve ounces. All these pistils were to be kept over till the vernal equinox of the succeeding year, dried in the sun, mixed into powder, and dissolved in twelve mace-weight of rain, and the same amount of pure dew, hoar-frost, and snowflakes, all of which must have fallen on that particular day. These ingredients were then to be mixed in equal pro-portions, made into pills the size of a dragon's-eye, and placed in an old porcelain jar, which must be buried under the root of a flower. When the patient felt her illness coming on, she was to dig up the jar and swallow one of the pills in a hot decoction of juniper-bark. It is, of course, evident that the due preparation of this medicine depends upon an impossible concatenation of coincidences; and it is just a bit of graceful humor at the expense of the medicos of China, whose abraca-dabra and affectation of mysticism are a fitting object of ridicule. The fact is, indeed, that the description is scarcely overdrawn, and anyone who has had the patience or the curiosity to dip into many of the books which deal with the pharmacopoeia in China will testify to the existence of so-called remedies almost, if not quite, as preposterous. In many instances, as in one for tooth-ache, the chances are that the patient would be either dead or cured weeks before the first ingredients of the marvelous panacea had been obtained.

CHAPTER 8. THE HORSE IN CHINA

THE China pony plays so important a part in the life of foreigners in the East that a short account of the antecedents of this famous animal in past ages may not be without its interest to our readers. In spite of the general inferiority it presents to its confreres of Arabia and the West, its culture has always been an object of considerable attention and solicitude among the Chinese; and though no one who sees the shaggy, unkempt brutes, with their tawdry garniture and jingling necklaces of bells, which are used by the gentry, soldiery, and mandarindom of the empire, is likely to form a very high idea of either the value set upon the animals or the care bestowed upon their welfare, the fact remains that they occupy a high place in the national esteem, and inherit all the prestige which four thousand years of national existence can confer upon them.

Now, apart from the assertion which we are in no way bound to believe that horses existed as early as the time of Fu Hsi, there is ample evidence in the Classics that they were both known and used in that golden age of China's history immediately preceding the establishment of the dynasty of Hsia. We read in the Shu Ching of the milk-white steeds which were harnessed to the chariot of Yao; and unless we belong to those who see in the name of this great sovereign no more than an impersonation of Heaven, we need not hesitate to accept the correlative inference that the animals referred to were the flesh-and-blood progenitors of the horses we drive today. Under the Emperor Yii and his successors the horse seems to have been regularly trained to the exercises of the battlefield, the labors of agriculture, and the excitement of the chase. In the dynasty of Chou it became the subject of special legislation. Horses were divided into six classes, viz., those for the Emperor and nobility, those to be used in war, those for draught and field labor, those for government posts, those for private riding or journeying, and those for carrying burdens. To the Emperor alone were assigned no fewer than forty thousand war-horses; to the princes and other nobles a smaller number, regulated according to their rank. The art of horsemanship was at this time greatly cultivated and admired. No man was permitted to become a cavalry soldier before the age of thirty-five, or to remain such after fifty. It was necessary for him to be tall, robust, and strong, active, and firm in his saddle. " The good rider," it was said, " is glued to his horse like bark to a tree, and characterized by the rapidity of lightning, the immobility of a rock, and the lightness of a feather." As long as this warlike spirit was kept up, and a simple hardy life recognized as that most honorable to the man of rank, the breed and mettle of horses were preserved at a high standard; but when a spirit of sloth and luxury began to prevail, and internal dissensions disturbed the general tranquility, the animals became the objects of a pampering and indulgent system which was attended by the most pernicious results. Not only were the horses themselves demoralized, but the people were actually impoverished by the enormous levies laid upon the land for the fodder necessary to their maintenance; insomuch that a certain scholar is said to have frankly told the Emperor that, for his part, he would far sooner be a viceroy's horse than a viceroy's secretary. Nor was this all: the unwholesome luxury in which the horses were reared, and the vast numbers of them which were appropriated to the imperial use, resulted first in the degeneracy of the breed, and then in an alarming mortality. So serious was the mischief which had taken place during the dynasty of Han, that when Kao Tsu, the first T'ang Emperor, ascended the throne, it was found that the entire cavalry of China consisted but of five thousand horses, all told. When he died he left his successor in a position to collect seven hundred thousand from the different provinces of his realm; and before long the stock of horses had so much increased that it was said they were actually more numerous than all the camels, sheep, and cattle in the land. Then the old abuses gradually crept back; corruption became rife in those departments of state to which was confided the care and maintenance of the Government studs; epidemics broke out among the animals; and when, at the close of the thirteenth century, the dynasty of Sung was overthrown by the Mongol hordes, the supply was found entirely inadequate to resist the charge of the invading cavalry. It was the horses of the Mongols which conquered China; but so badly did the humid atmosphere suit the animals themselves, and so widespread was the corruption practiced by the native cavalry inspectors, that, when the Yuens were ousted in their turn, they actually found themselves without sufficient horses on which to take to flight.

Such being the violent fluctuations which have characterized the fortunes of the horse in China, it may not be uninteresting to turn to the theories current among the Chinese with respect to the proper treatment of the animal. Horses, be it first observed, are said to be subject to the principle Yang, and under the influence of fire. It is therefore necessary that all their stables should face the south. It is also obvious that, for the same reason, no horse should ever be reared in the neighborhood of silkworms; for silkworms are subject to the opposing principle Yin, and under the influence of stars whose action is at direct variance with that of the stars which govern horses; and it is impossible to say what dire results might accrue to both were these hostile agencies ever allowed to clash. Indeed, a man has only to rub a horse's teeth with silkworms' droppings to prevent him from masticating his hay, while a few mulberry-leaves will, if placed in his mouth, deprive him of the power of eating for ever afterwards. The smallness of a horse's ears, say the Chinese naturalists, indicates a corresponding smallness of his liver; the size of his nostrils, that of his lungs, and consequent staying power in a race; the largeness of his eyes, that of his heart arguing courage and spirit; while a small stomach is a sure sign that he requires but little food. A horse has no gall; which, it is scarcely necessary to add, is the reason he is so constantly subject to sore eyes. He hates gal-loping with the wind behind him, but enjoys it when it blows in his teeth. He is believed also to have a strong objection to cinders, particularly fresh ones; and if he is kept long standing he will get ulcers in his legs. When he rolls in the dust and does not get up again, that is a sign that his bones ache; if on rising he does not shake off the dust, there is something the matter with his skin; if he shakes it off, but fails to snort through his nostrils, his chest is out of order. The maladies to which the horse is most subject are those of the heart, the liver, the stomach, the lungs, and the kidneys. When his heart is wrong the tongue becomes bright red; when his stomach is wrong his lips become discolored, and have an appearance of laughing; while the other diseases manifest their existence in a variety of ways, all equally relevant and unmistakable.

It is, therefore, highly desirable that in the treatment of horses no violence should be done to their natural constitution. That this excel-lent rule is, however, but seldom observed in its integrity is sufficiently proved by the fact that many horses die before the age of thirty-one, such being the average age of the quadruped as intended by nature. The longer the period of gestation, say the Chinese, the longer the life of the animal; and horses, who have a period of twelve months, live half the life of a man, and twice that of an ox. In order, therefore, to prolong the life of a horse to its full extent three things are necessary. The first is, that a horse should never be transported from the country where he is indigenous to any other. The Tartar horses, it is said, languish and die when carried into the warm, humid provinces of the South; the enervating climate and more generous food work great mischiefs in an animal accustomed to the bracing air and hardy life of the deserts of the West. This was specially found to be the case on one occasion in the T'ang dynasty, we believe when the vanquished Tartars were compelled to pay tribute to the Chinese in horses.

The animals not only sickened themselves, but introduced a terrible epidemic among the horses of the country a fact which was attributed to bad faith on the part of the Tartars, until experience and observation disclosed the true reason. The second is, that a stop should be put to the practices of gelding and of working mares in foal, one of which has a bad effect upon the present generation, and the other upon their descendants. The third and last is, that a horse should be always continued in the duties to which he was originally trained. The hack should not be turned into a beast of burden, nor the charger into a beast of draught. If this is done, say the Chinese veterinaries as in England, for instance, where many a fine racer ends his days between the shafts of a London cab the animal will most assuredly come to grief. It is related, as a case in point, that in the T'ang dynasty a certain man had trained his horse to dance and caper in time to the cadences of music an accomplishment which was considered very wonderful in those days, and brought in a fair amount of money. But one morning the owner died at a village near Han-kow, whither he was taking his horse to perform at a great fair then being held; and the animal had to be sold in order to procure a coffin for the deceased. He was purchased by a petty mandarin, who, being unaware of his terpsichorean talents, shut him up in a stable with a couple of mules and an ass. But the confinement was intolerable to the poor beast. He had done nothing but dance all his life, and as he was unable to follow out what was really his second nature without restraint, relieved his feelings as best he might by capering in his stall. The mules and the ass resented this extraordinary behavior, which naturally interfered with their own peace and comfort; and the owner, fancying that the animal must be mad, sold him to a neighboring butcher, who disposed of him, no doubt, for the good of his customers in general.

CHAPTER 9. HIPPOPHAGY AMONG THE TARTARS

THE use of animal food among the Chinese dates from the remotest times, and is said to have preceded the knowledge and use of fire. Before the advent of the mythical Emperor Fu Hsi the people ate raw flesh and drank blood warm from their flocks and herds; and when, he came he instructed them in the art of cookery, from which fact he derives his other title of The Butcher. From this time downwards the Chinese have been great meat-eaters, consuming, in addition to the various kinds used for food in civilized communities, the flesh of dogs, rats, and asses. These last, however, are only eaten by the poor. The solitary instance, we believe, of a universal food being rejected by a special class of persons is that of beef, which no rigid Confucianist will touch. An ox is euphemistically called the Ta Wu, or Great Beast, which, from its being offered in sacrifice to Heaven by the Emperor, acquires a sacred character; besides which, it renders services to agriculture too noble to permit of its being degraded into an article of food. We may add, however, that no prohibition of the kind is to be found in the Confucian books; it rests upon tradition solely.

It is for much the same reason, perhaps, that horse-flesh is hardly ever eaten in China. The only persons who are accused of doing so are the very poorest of the poor in Peking itself; and it is not likely that they are able to procure any carcasses but those of worn-out animals who have died a natural death. Among the Tartars, however, horse-flesh is not only a favorite but a staple dish; so much so, indeed, that they are said to have acquired, by long practice, a wonderful power of discriminating, while the animals are yet alive, those whose flesh will prove toothsome and nutritious, and those whom it would be dangerous and bad to eat. They have a way of preparing horse-flesh by first boiling, and then drying it in the cold breezes of the plain; after which they grind it into a sort of powder or meal, which may be preserved for almost any length of time. The Tartar nomad is thus always provided with a nutritious article of food, which can be put into an insignificant compass; since a very small quantity dissolved in boiling water furnishes him with a comfortable bowl of soup, in precisely the same way as a teaspoonful of Liebig's Extract will make a basin of beef -tea. Indeed, there is a very curious resemblance between the preserved horse-flesh powder of the Tartars and the meat-paste recently in-vented by M. Moride, and introduced by him to the French Academy under the name of " Nutricine." It is prepared by working raw meat into a pulp, and then mixing it with bread or farinaceous substances, which absorb the natural moisture of the meat and so form a paste. This paste is then dried, and the material ground into a powder which is said to last an indefinite time, and may be used in much the same way as its analogue in Tartar}^ Of course it is necessary that the Tartar horse-flesh should be kept as dry as possible, and also that it be used almost exclusively in cold climates. These two conditions being complied with, it forms the principal provision of armies when engaged on distant campaigns, or in forced marches through hostile or unproductive territories. It is then of inestimable value, for it renders the soldier entirely independent of harvests, and enables him to maintain his corporeal vigor upon the smallest possible cubic measurement of food.

The Tartar's meat, however, is the Chinaman's poison. All books upon the subject condemn the use of horse-flesh as unhealthy to the last degree, especially that portion of the back which is covered by the saddle. The liver is said to be so impure as to cause death in all who eat it; while the blood and the sweat are so impregnated with venom as to turn all wounds with which they may come in contact into bad gangrenes. But though not to be used as food, the tissues of a horse enter freely into the Chinese pharmacopoeia. Horse-broth is an excellent remedy for pleurisy and all sorts of malignant fevers, on account of its cooling properties; while well-cooked horse-nerves act as a general tonic to the system, and impart no small amount of strength to a man who has become weak through illness. Young mothers whose children are cutting their teeth will be glad to hear that by burning the tooth of a horse, grinding it to ashes, mixing it with the infant's saliva, and then rubbing it on the gums, the pain may be greatly moderated and the process of teething materially assisted. The milk of a white mare is useful in cases of phthisis and pulmonary complaints in general; while the hoof, if burnt to ashes, is an excellent preservative against pestilence. Many other parts and products of the animal are of great value in other cases of emergency; but the prophylactics found in Chinese medical works are, as may be imagined, not always suitable for transcription. In the majority of cases the remedy must be far worse than the disease, as any one may discover for himself by examining the ordinary Customs returns. Our readers may remember a story told of the late Earl of Derby which has no slight bearing upon this point. It appears that at one time his lordship was suffering from one of his severe attacks of gout. An obscure admirer whose name is of importance chiefly to himself sent the illustrious sufferer a case of sherry of some very particular brand, which, he said, was of priceless value as an antidote to that complaint. After a few days, however, the wine came back upon his hands, with a polite letter from Lord Derby thanking him most sincerely for his kind intentions, but saying that he had tasted the sherry, and very much preferred the gout.

CHAPTER 10. A PHILOSOPHER WHO NEVER LIVED

"Do you know," said a nephew of the Marquis Tseng to a friend of ours a few years ago, "that we have a book in China that bears a very close resemblance to your Bible? "

"I did not know it," replied our friend; " pray, which may it be? '

"It is called the Works of Lieh-tzu" answered the young Chinese.

Now, such a statement as this was quite sufficient to make us turn our attention to the volumes indicated with something more than usual anticipation; and if we find ourselves unable to endorse the description, we have nevertheless discovered much in the book to interest us, and much that deserves recording. Lieh-tzii is said to have flourished circa 400 B.C., and to have been one of the earliest and most illustrious disciples of Lao-tzu, the reputed founder of the Taoist philosophy. His book is a congeries of interpolations and additions of a considerably later date; still, it has been honored with special attention by more than one Emperor, and His Majesty Hsi-ian Tsung, of the T'ang dynasty (7 1 3-7 5 5), raised it to the dignity of a classic by the title of Ch l ung Hsu Ohing, or Sutra of Fullness and Emptiness. About the philosopher himself, however, scarcely anything is known: so little, indeed, as to lead the vanguard of modern sinologists to doubt, and even to deny, that such a person ever existed in the flesh. He is, in fact, now generally regarded as a sort of Isaac Bickerstaffe the literary creation of a sect or school, and so far holding a certain position in the Valhalla of Chinese letters, but not entitled to the honors due to a great historic character about whose personality there is no question. Such scruples are a marked feature of modern criticism; and not only has a blow been recently struck at the authorship and personality of Lao-tzu himself, but the destructive process is sanctioned and encouraged by no less eminent an authority than the Quarterly Review. " A book/' says the writer of an article on the ' Sacred Books of the East,' " to a modern mind suggests an author. It was not so then " in the days of old. " No one of them can be properly said to have had an author. And by this much more is meant than the mere suggestion that the books were at first anonymous, or that the names of their authors have not been handed down to us. In those early times a book was seldom or never composed originally in the shape in which it has come down to us. It was not made: it grew. Sayings, passages, legends, verses, were handed down in a school or were current among a body of disciples. These were gradually, and only gradually, blended together. They were added to; their connection or sequence was altered; they were collected by different hands and at different times into compilations of different tendencies. Finally one or other of these compilations became so much the favorite that all being handed down by memory alone, liable to 'have their root cut off and find no place of refuge ' if they were not popular it alone survived. It is the old story of the struggle for life, and of the survival of the fittest that is, of the fittest under certain circumstances, the fittest for the needs of the school in which it existed, the fittest for its peculiar environment; not, of course, the fittest absolutely, nor the fittest for the purposes of modern historical research. The books lived, or rather were kept alive, not for the sake of the author, but for the sake of their contents. Hence it is that, though certain of the wise sayings or verses it contains may have authors assigned to them, no really ancient book claims to have an author a human author. It is only later that the tendency is felt to satisfy the natural craving for a cause by assigning books to individual hands." Candor compels us to admit that these remarks apply with singular aptitude to the book which bears the name of Lieh-tzu. It presents all the features of a compilation, and a compilation made by different hands; it contains passage after passage, copied in some instances verbatim, in other instances with less exactitude, from at least two classical works of the Taoist school universally recognized as authentic; while nothing, or next to nothing, is known of the man to whom it is attributed, beyond references to him in the third person in the very book of which he is the alleged author. We consider, therefore, that we are justified in speaking of him as a philosopher who never lived, and in regarding the Lieh-tzii of the Ch'ung Hsu Ching as no more than a supposititious personage, projected from the minds of a Taoist literary clique.

But the book remains. That is a visible fact, and with it we now propose to deal. The criticism which finds in it a resemblance to the Christian Bible may be rejected at the outset as valueless, for the religious element in the work is extremely tenuous. Our readers, however, shall judge for themselves. The first chapter contains speculations respecting the nature and attributes of God, and the processes of Creation, which, as far as they go, are striking enough, and illustrative of that singular independence and originality of thought which forms so honorable a characteristic of the Taoist school. Here, for instance, is a piece of transcendentalism which occurs on the second page of the book. It would have shocked Confucius.

The Origin of Life and Motion.

There is a Life that is uncreated;

There is a Transformer who is changeless.

The Uncreated alone can produce life;

The Changeless alone can evolve change.

That Life cannot but produce;

That Transformer cannot but transform.

Wherefore creations and transformations are perpetual,

And these perpetual creations and transformations continue through all time.

They are seen in the Yin and Yang: They are displayed in the Four Seasons. The Uncreated stands, as it were, alone; The Changeless comes and goes; His duration can have no end, Peerless and One His ways are past finding out.

The philosopher, taking as his text a very obscure passage in the Tao Te Ching though he quotes the Book of the Yellow Emperor as his authority then proceeds to show how it is that the Creator is uncreated and the Transformer changeless; averring that the Supreme

Power is self-produced, self-transformed, self-shaped, self-manifested, self-intelligent, self-powerful, self-exhausting, self-reposing; though, he adds, to speak of these phenomena as actualities, in the common acceptation of the term, is inaccurate. Then he proceeds to describe the evolution of the visible universe:

The Four Stages

Now, seeing that that which has form was produced from formlessness, from what can the Universe have sprung . Thus it is that it is said there was first the period of the Great Calm, then of the Great Inception, then of the Great Beginning, and lastly of the Great Concretion. At the time of the Great Calm the primordial aura was yet invisible. The Great Inception was when the primordial aura first began to exist; the Great Beginning was when form first came into being; the Great Concretion was when simple matter first appeared. Then aura, form, and matter were in readiness, but had not yet been separated from one another; and for that reason the condition of things was called Chaos. Chaos means the indiscriminate mingling of everything together before their distribution.

"Invisible, though looked for; inaudible, though listened for; intangible, though clutched at " therefore was the primordium called the period of Calm, or Stillness; and there is no form to which that Calm was like.

Then the condition of Calm changed, and it became One 8C. t the primordial ether came into being. This One changed again, and became Seven j Seven changed, and became Nine; and the changes of the Nine were final. Then a reflex change took place back to the

One; and the One was the commencement of that change which resulted in the production of forms. The pure and light ascended, and became Heaven; the turbid and heavy descended, and became Earth; and the harmonious aurse, in combination, produced Man. Heaven and Earth containing in themselves the germinal essence of all things, the visible creation was evolved and came into existence.

The manner in which the various powers of nature supplement and assist each other is then shown with much perspicacity:

The energy of Heaven and Earth is not sufficient [of itself]; nor is the ability of the Sage, nor the usefulness of created things. For instance, the function of Heaven is to produce and to overshadow; the function of Earth, to shapen and to support; the function of the Sage, to instruct and to reform; and the function of things, to fulfill the purposes for which they were created. This being so, there are directions in which Heaven is deficient, but in which Earth excels; in which the Sage encounters obstruction, but in which things in general have free course. For it is clear that that which produces and overshadows cannot impart shape and support; that which shapens and supports cannot instruct and reform; and he who instructs and reforms cannot act in opposition to the natural purposes of things, which, being once fixed, can never depart from their proper stations in the universal economy. Therefore, the principle of Heaven and Earth, if not Yin, is Yang; the doctrine of the Sage, if not benevolent, is just; the natural property of a thing, if not soft, is hard; all these follow their inherent properties, and never leave the stations to which they belong. Thus, given Life, there are living creatures which produce other living creatures; given Form, there are forms which impart form to others , given Sound [in the abstract], we have tones which present sounds [in the concrete]; given Color, we have that which manifests chromatic phenomena; given Flavor, we have that by which we are enabled to perceive tastes. The actual beings produced from what has life themselves die; but the succession of births the production of living things from living things is endless. The forms imparted by that which has form are real enough; but that which imparted form in the first instance has no existence. The tones produced by sound [in the abstract] are audible; but the tone-producing sound has never gone forth. The hues manifested by color are varied; but that which imparts those hues color in the abstract has never been seen. The sensation produced by flavor is experienced by gestation; but the taste-producing flavor has not been discovered. All these phenomena are functions of the principle of Inaction. The ability to be inherent in the Yin and Yang, softness and hardness, shortness and length, circularity and squareness, life and death, heat and cold, floating and sinking, do and re, production and annihilation, blue and yellow, sweet and bitter, stench and fragrance, appears divorced from both consciousness and power; but really there is nothing beyond either the consciousness or the power [of this principle of Inaction].

Our philosopher has now fairly plunged into a swamp of metaphysical speculation, and soon gets beyond his depth. We will follow him a little farther in his researches, and then proceed to the stories and parables some comic, some very beautiful, but all quaint and interesting with which, this book abounds.

In the Book of the Yellow Emperor it is written: " When a form moves, it does not produce another form, but a shadow; when a sound is emitted, it does not produce another sound, but an echo. Immobility does not produce nothing; it produces a something. Forms must come to an end; the Cosmos is finite in point of time, just as I am myself; but where the end leads to nobody knows. ... It is the destiny of the living to be finite; the finite cannot but come to an end, just as that which is born cannot but give birth in its turn; so that the desire to prolong life, and to do away with one's end, is a misunderstanding of one's destiny."

The moral of all which is contentment with one's lot in life, and this forms the subject of the first story that we shall present to our readers. But first let us hear what Lieh-tzu and the Yellow Emperor have to say about death, as the illustrations which are given of their theory a little farther on are of incomparable beauty.

The spiritual or essential part of man's nature pertains to Heaven; his bony framework to the Earth. That which belongs to Heaven is pure and tenuous; that which belongs to the Earth is turbid and dense; and when the spiritual part of a man leaves the form in which it has resided, each reverts to where it first came from. Wherefore the disembodied spirit is called a kuei [or ghost], which is something that " reverts" \kuei\ ', for it reverts to its original dwelling-place.

The Yellow Emperor said, " The spiritual part enters the gate [it emerged from], the body returns to that from which it sprang; and then what becomes of Me? Between the birth of a man and his death there are four great transformations: from infancy to childhood, from youth to prime, from age to decrepitude, and from the last agonies to annihilation. . . . On reaching this last stage the man finds himself at rest, and thus returns to the point from which he started."

It is this idea of death as rest, as a cessation of all worry, fatigue, and strife, that is so touchingly brought out in the stories we are about to give. First, however, there is a charming little anecdote illustrative of a lesson previously given by our philosopher that we must not overlook. We will call it

The Secret of Contentment

As Confucius was on a journey to the Great Mountain, he fell in with a man named Jung Ch'i-ch'i, walking in a country place at Ch'eng. He was dressed in deerskin, with a girdle of cord; and he was playing a lute and singing.

"May I ask what makes you so happy, sir? ' said Confucius.

" There are many things that make me happy," replied the other. "Of all created beings, human beings are the noblest; it has fallen to my lot to be a human being, and that is one source of happiness. The difference between the male and the female consists in the former being honorable and the latter base; it has fallen to my lot to be born a male, and that is another source of happiness. Among the crowd of people who come into the world there are some who see neither months nor days who never live to get free from their swaddling-bands; I have already lived ninety years, and that is my third source of happiness. Poverty is the common lot of scholars, and death is the end of us all. What cause for sorrow is there, then, in quietly fulfilling one's destiny and awaiting the close of life? "

"Excellent! " exclaimed Confucius. " By this means can a man find tranquility and sereneness in himself."

Here death is regarded simply in the light of the inevitable. In the following stories it is represented in a far more beautiful and attractive guise:

The Blessedness of Death

Lin-lei, who had reached the age of a hundred years, and still wore fur clothes at the end of spring, went a-gleaning in the harvest-fields, singing as he walked. Confucius, journeying to the State of Wei, saw him in the field as he passed by, and, turning to his disciples, said

"That old gentleman is worth speaking to. Go up to him, one of you, and test him with a few questions."

Tzu. Kung offered to go, and, coming opposite to the old man just in front of a ridge of earth, " Sir," says he, with a sigh, " do you not repine at your lot, that you are singing as you glean? " But Lin-lei continued his course, singing as before; so Tzu Kung repeated his question again and again, until Lin -lei raised his eyes and answered him.

"What have I to repine at? " he said.

"Why, Sir," replied Tzu Kung, "not diligent in youth, neglectful of opportunities in middle life, wifeless and childless in your old age, and the time of death rapidly approaching, what possible happiness can be yours, that you are singing as you glean? "

"The sources of happiness that I possess," rejoined Lin-lei, smiling, "are equally possessed by all; the only difference is, that others turn them into sources of sorrow. It is just because I was not diligent in my youth, and did not seize on opportunities during the prime of life, that I have been able to reach my present age; it is because I am wifeless and child-less in my old age, and because the time of my dissolution is drawing nigh, that I am as joyful as you see me."

"Old age," remarked Tzu Kung, "is what all men desire; but death is what all men dread. How comes it, Sir, that you find joy in the thought of death? "

"Death," said the old man, "is to life, as going away is to coming. How can we know that to die here is not to be born elsewhere? I know that birth and death are outwardly un-like; but how can I tell whether, in their eager rush for life, men are not under a delusion, how can I tell whether, if I die to-day, my lot may not prove far preferable to what it was when I was originally born. "

Tzu Kung, being weary of instruction, said to Confucius, " I long for rest! "

"There is no rest to be had in life," replied Confucius.

"Then is there no possibility of rest for me?" exclaimed Tzu Kung.

"There is," rejoined the Sage. "Look upon the graves around you the mounds, the votive altars, the cenotaphs, the funeral urns; there can you know what rest is."

"How great, then, is death! " exclaimed Tzu Kung. " For the good man it is repose; for the bad man an engulfment."

"You now know the truth," observed Confucius. " Men all understand the joys of life, but they ignore its sorrows; they know the decrepitude of old age, but forget that it is the period of ease and leisure; they know the dreadfulness of death, but they do not know its rest."

"How excellent is it," exclaimed Yentzii, " that from all antiquity death has been the common lot of men! It is rest for the virtuous, and a hiding-away of the bad. Death is just a going home again. In ancient times it was said that the dead were those who had returned; if, then, the dead are those who have returned to their homes, it follows that the living are still travelers; and those who travel without a thought of returning have renounced their homes. Now, if a single person relinquishes his home, the whole world condemns him; but when the whole world relinquishes its [true] home [by avoiding death], there is no one who sees the error! "

We now come to a very curious subject of discussion, in which the disputants shall speak for themselves:

An Impending Cataclysm

In the State of Ch'i there lived a man who was so sadly afraid lest earth and sky should burst up and leave his body without a place of habitation, that he lost both his sleep and his appetite. A friend of his, feeling sorry for his anxiety, went to explain the matter to him. " The sky," he said, " is nothing but an accumulation of vapor, and there is no place where this vapor does not exist. Since, then, everybody sits down and stands up, breathes, moves, and rests all day long in the very midst of it, why should you dread its disruption . "

"But if the sky is nothing more than accumulated vapor," replied the nervous man, " does it not follow that the sun, the moon, and the stars will fall from their positions? "

"The heavenly bodies," said his counselor, " are themselves nothing but luminosities which exist in the midst of this accumulated air; so that even if they were to fall it would be impossible for them to hurt anybody."

"But supposing the earth were to burst up? " pursued the other.

"The earth," he replied, " is just an accumulation of clods, which pervade every empty space; there is no place where these clods or lumps of matter do not exist. Since, then, a man can hobble about or tramp along, walking and stopping alternately the whole day upon the surface of the earth, what reason have you to apprehend its destruction? ' '

Then the other, much relieved, experienced great joy; and the friend who had given him the explanation was satisfied, and experienced great joy too. But when Chang Lutzu heard about it, he laughed, and said, "Rainbows, clouds, mists, wind, rain, and the four seasons all are produced by accumulations of vapor in the sky. Mountains and hills, rivers and seas, metal and stone, fire and wood all these consist of accumulated forms upon the earth. Now, knowing what we do about these accumulations of vapor and accumulations of matter, how can it be said that their disruption is impossible [seeing that disruption did actually take place during the state of chaos]? Why, Heaven and Earth themselves are just one little particle in the midst of space; and yet, in the midst of Heaven and Earth there is that which is extremely great, difficult to exhaust, difficult to get to the end of, difficult to fathom, difficult to understand. This is a most certain fact. The man who is sorrowful lest all this should disrupt is really over-fearful; while the other, who says that disruption is impossible, is also far from right. Heaven and Earth cannot but disrupt; they will return to a condition when disruption must take place; but it will be quite soon enough to grieve about it when the time for their destruction comes."

When Lieh-tzu heard this, he smiled, and said, " Both those who say that Heaven and Earth will disrupt, and those who say they will not, make a great blunder. Whether disruption will or will not take place is a question about which I cannot know anything; yet each of the two theories has its advocate. Thus the living know nothing of death, the dead know nothing of life; the coming know nothing of their departure, the departing know nothing of their return. Whether there is to be disruption or not, why should I trouble myself about it either way? "

The following stories have a raciness that will commend them even to those who find it difficult to see a moral in them, though each is intended to illustrate some special doctrine peculiar to the philosophy of Taoism:

The Two Robbers

In the State of Ch'i there lived a very rich man named Kuo; in the State of Sung there lived a very poor man named Hsiang. One day Mr. Hsiang went from Sung to Ch'i to ask Mr. Ku5 what secret he possessed for acquiring wealth; and Mr. Kuo replied, " The fact is, that I am an extremely clever robber. When I had been robbing for a year, I had enough to eat; in two years I was in easy circum-stances; in three I enjoyed affluence; and from that time to this I have dispensed charity to all the people in my district."

Mr. Hsiang was delighted. He understood very well what robbery was, but he did not understand the principle of the robbery referred to. So he immediately took to climbing over walls and breaking into houses, and nothing that his hand could reach or his eye could see escaped his clutches; but alas! in a very short time the stolen goods led to the detection of his crimes, so that he lost even the property he originally possessed. Then Hsiang, beginning to think that he had been grossly misled by Mr. Kuo, went to him and reproached him bitterly. " In what way did you act the robber . " asked Mr. Kuo. So Hsiang described all that he had been doing. " What! " exclaimed Kuo, "have you really missed the true principle of robbery to such an extent as this? Let me now explain to you what that principle is. You know that Heaven has its seasons and Earth its pro-duce; well, what I steal are these two things. I employ the moistening and fertilizing influences of the clouds and rain, the productive and nurturing properties of the mountain and the marsh, to make my corn grow and to ripen my harvests, to build my houses and construct my walls. On dry land I plunder birds and beasts; in the water I plunder fishes and turtles. All this is robbery; for, seeing that corn and harvests, soil and trees, birds and beasts, fish and turtles, are all produced by Heaven, how can they belong to me? Yet in thus robbing Heaven I incur no retribution. But gold, jewels, precious stones, food, silken fabrics, wealth, and property are accumulated by men; Heaven does not bestow them. If, then, you plunder such things, and suffer for the crime, whom have you to reproach but yourself, pray? "

This puzzled Hsiang greatly, and he thought that Ku5 was just hoaxing him a second time; so he went and consulted a learned man named Tung Kuo about it. Tung Ku5, however, pointed out to him that even his body was, in a philosophical sense, stolen from the influences of Nature; that!Ku5 had simply plundered or used that which was the common property of all, and that, while his principle of robbery was just, and deserved no punishment, that of Hsiang was selfish, and led to his conviction as a criminal.

The Dream of the Yellow Emperor

During the first fifteen years of the reign of the Yellow Emperor he rejoiced in the love of the whole empire; so he fostered his life, and spent his time in the gratification of his senses; but his skin became shriveled, his complexion swarthy, his mind confused, and his passions out of gear. During the second fifteen years of his reign he had occasion to mourn over the disorder of his realm; whereupon he exerted all the powers of his mind and put forth all his strength and wisdom in caring for the people; but still his own health and appearance continued as bad as ever. Then the Yellow Emperor groaned, and exclaimed with a sigh, " My faults are indeed excessive! To think that all this misery should result first from my caring too much for myself, and now from endeavoring to benefit my subjects! " Whereupon he renounced the whole machinery of government, abandoned his imperial seraglio, dismissed his guards and eunuchs, removed the frame on which his bells hung, retrenched his table, and retired into a secluded chamber in the great court of his palace, where he purified himself and put on sad-colored robes, not meddling with State affairs for a period of three months. One day it so happened that he fell asleep and dreamed. He thought he wandered as far as the State of Hua-hsii, a place situated a very long way off. He had no idea how many thousand myriads of li he was from home; but certainly neither carts nor boats had ever succeeded in getting so far before. Of course it was only his spirit that was roaming. In this state there was neither general nor king everything happened of its own accord; the people had no passions, no predilections spontaneity reigned supreme. They knew nothing about the joys of life or the horrors of death, so that none died before their time; they knew nothing of loving themselves and avoiding those unconnected with them, so that there was neither affection nor hatred among them; they knew nothing of rebelliousness on one hand or obedience on the other, so that benefits and injuries were alike unheard of. There was nothing they loved and cherished, there was nothing they feared and shunned; if they fell into water they were not drowned, or into fire, they were not burned; if they were hacked or struck they suffered neither injury nor pain; if scratched by fingernails they felt no irritation. They rode through space as easily as treading solid ground, they reclined in vacancy as on a couch; clouds and mists did not obscure their vision, thunderclaps did not disturb their hearing, beauty and repulsiveness did not unsettle their minds, mountains and valleys did not impede their footsteps. Their spirits moved no more.

Then the Emperor awoke; and immediately the whole thing was plain to him. Beckoning to his three Ministers, he said, " We have now lived in retirement for three months, purifying Our heart and wearing a mourning garb, pondering how best to nourish Our own person and govern others; but all in vain We failed to discover the secret. At last, wearied out, We fell asleep; and, as We slept, We dreamed." The Emperor then detailed his dream. " Now We have attained to a comprehension of the perfect Way; and We can never more exercise Our mind in searching for it. We know it; We possess it; but We cannot impart it to you."

Twenty-eight more years passed, and the empire enjoyed perfect peace, almost like the State of Hua-hsii. At last the Emperor ascended to the Distant Land, and the people wept his loss for over two hundred years without ceasing.

The Power of Faith

A certain Mr. Fan had a son named Tzii-hua, who enjoyed a good reputation for his chivalrous and generous disposition. He was, in fact, highly respected in his native state, and much beloved by the Prince of Ts'in. He held no office, but his rank was superior to that of the three Ministers of State. All on whom he looked with favor received honors from the Prince; all of whom he spoke disparagingly were forthwith ruined men; all who had the run of his mansion were received as equals at Court. Now, among the hangers-on of Fan Tzii-hua some were clever and some were stupid, and these were constantly intriguing against each other. Some were influential, and others powerless; and these vilified and sought to injure each other. But although they thus attempted to ruin and discredit one another in the eyes of Fan Tzu-hua, he him-self bore no grudge against any one of them; on the contrary, he amused himself day and night in watching them, as though it was all a game or comedy; and this view of the matter soon became general all over the state.

One day Huo Sheng and Tzu Po, the most honored of Mr. Fan's guests, went out and wandered far from the town through a wild country place. Passing a night under the roof of a rustic watchman named Shang Ch'iu-k'ai, the two beguiled the hours by conversing upon the fame and power of Tzii-hua, saying how he held men's lives and deaths in his hands, and how he could enrich the poor and impoverish the rich. Now, Shang Ch'iu-k'ai had, up till then, been poor to the very verge of starvation; and secreting himself outside the window of his two lodgers, he listened to their conversation. What he heard had such an effect upon him that he forthwith armed himself with a basket, and went off to ask the loan of some grain at Tzii-hua's door. Now, Tzu-hua's proteges were all persons of considerable rank, who dressed in silken robes, drove showy carriages, dawdled along in a lordly style, and stared superciliously at others; and when these gentlemen set eyes on Shang Ch'iu-kai, with his weight of years, his feeble appearance, his swarthy, withered face, and his disordered cap and clothes, they were filled with contempt and scorn. Very soon they began to insult him and treat him with impertinence, pushing, hustling, and shoving him about; there was nothing, in fact, they did not do to show their superiority. Shang Ch'iu-k'ai bore all their rudeness without the slightest appearance of anger, until the ingenuity of his assailants was exhausted and they themselves tired with their game. Then they drove him to the top of a high tower, and one of them cried with a loud voice, " A thousand ounces of gold to any man who will jump down." The rest all vied with one another in professing their willingness to do it; but Shang Ch'iu-k'ai, believing them to be in earnest, threw him-self over at once. His body looked like a flying bird, and he alighted on the ground without sustaining the slightest injury. Mr. Fan's people all thought it was an affair of pure chance, and made as though there was nothing surprising or extra-ordinary about it; so they pointed out a place in the bend of the river, where the water was exceptionally deep, and said, " There is a precious pearl at the bottom; dive in and fetch it." So Shang Ch'iu-k'ai complied again, and plunged in; and, sure enough, out he came again with a fine pearl in his hand. Then, for the first time, the others began to wonder what sort of a man this was; and Tzu-hua ordered a residence to be prepared for him, where he could eat and dress. One day a fire suddenly broke out in the family treasure room; and Tzu-hua said to Shang, " If you will venture into the flames and save the dresses that are in danger, I will reward you in proportion to the number of garments you bring out." So Shang went straightway, without the slightest expression of fear, plunged into the burning room, and returned, free from dust and perfectly unscorched. Then they all came to the conclusion that he was in possession of the True Doctrine, and with one consent began to excuse themselves, saying, " We did not know that you possessed the Doctrine when we insulted you; we did not know that you had supernatural powers when we used you with dishonor. Treat us as clods, as deaf and blind! And then we will venture to ask you to instruct us."

"I have no doctrine," replied Shang. " I am perfectly unconscious of possessing any special power. Nevertheless, there is one point which bears upon the matter, and I will try and explain it to you. Lately, two of your number passed a night in my cottage, and I overheard them expatiate upon the great fame and influence of Mr. Fan; saying how he held men's lives in his hand, and how he could enrich the poor and impoverish the rich. All this I believed implicitly; so, regard-less of the distance, I came hither; and, having come, I sup-posed that every word you all uttered was absolutely true. I was only afraid that my own sincerity might fall short of perfection, and that my performance might consequently fall short too; so I ignored all my personal surroundings, and thought nothing of incurring benefits or injuries. My mind was just fixed on one thing, and one thing only; no external object stood in my way. That is my only secret. To-day I am made aware for the first time how I have been abused by your gang. Formerly I kept my amazement and my doubts to myself, and paid close attention to all I heard and saw; now, when I recall my good luck in escaping from death by fire and by water, I tremble at the very recollection and feel hot inside; I quake from head to foot with imaginary terror. Could I dare, think you, to brave such horrors over again? "

From that time forward, whenever the proteges of Fan Tzu-hua happened to meet even a starving man or a horse doctor upon the road, they did not venture to treat him rudely; on the contrary, they made a point of descending from their chariots and bowing to him.

The above occurrence came to the ears of Tsai Wo, who went and told Confucius. " Don't you know," said the Sage, in reply, " that the man of perfect faith can influence even external objects can move heaven and earth, as well as all ghosts and spirits and can pass freely throughout space without encountering any obstruction? Is it, then, such a great thing that he should be able to brave dangers, even so far as to enter fire and water? If, when the trustfulness of Shang Ch'iu-k'ai was exercised on hypocrites, he even then found no difficulties in his path, how much more when both parties, the trusting and the trusted, are equally sincere! Lay this to heart, my children."

Men and Brutes

When the Director-General of State Music, in the days of the Emperor Yao, played on the musical stones, all the animals were attracted by the sound, and came and danced to it; and as the pandean pipes blended harmoniously at the close, phoenixes drew near and listened reverently; thus music was made a means of influencing beasts and birds. In what, then, do the hearts of the brute creation differ from those of human beings. The only differences between them lie in their voices and their outward forms, and the fact that they are unacquainted with the principle of social intercourse. Now, the Sage knows and understands everything, and therefore he is able to induce their obedience, and so make use of them. And there is a department of the intelligence of animals which is naturally identical with that of men. All animals, for instance, are endowed with the instinct of self-preservation, and this without being at all indebted to men for the idea. Males and females pair together, mothers and their offspring love each other; they avoid the open and unsheltered plain, and take refuge in precipitous places dangerous to man; they flee from cold and seek warmth; they live in flocks, and wander with those of their own kind; the young stay inside their lairs, while the full-grown ones go outside; they go to watering in company, and feed when the muster is called. In high antiquity brutes lived in harmony with men, and walked with them without fear. Later, they began to fear men; then they were scattered and cast into disorder. In after ages they concealed themselves, lurking in ambush, and skulking far away in order to escape injury. In one state there were men from time to time who were able to distinguish the language of the different sorts of animals; but this was a special accomplishment, and confined to a few. In high antiquity, however, the men of supernatural wisdom enjoyed a complete knowledge of all the properties, external and internal, of the lower animals, together with a full understanding of their differentiations and of the sounds they uttered; so that when they called them together they assembled, and when they taught them they received the instruction that was imparted, exactly like human beings. . . . The conclusion of all which is, that the mental powers of all things that have blood and breath are very much the same in all instances.

King Mu and the Magician

In the reign of Mu, King of Chao, there came from a far Western country a certain magician gifted with the most extraordinary powers. He was able to enter fire and water, pass through stone and metal, remove mountains and rivers, change the position of cities, ride through space without falling, and encounter solid substances without his progress being impeded. The changes and transformations he effected were innumerable and endless; indeed, not only could he alter the external shape of objects, but was actually able to turn the current of other people's thoughts. King Mu received him with the reverence due to a divinity, and served him as though he were a prince; he also prepared a pavilion for him to take his rest in, brought fish, flesh, and fowl to present to him, and told off certain music-girls to play before him for his delectation. The magician, however, looked upon the King's palace as a wretched and sordid hut, and declined to stay in it. The royal banquet, he said, was disgusting, and refused to touch it; while, as for the court ladies who attended him, he condemned them as both ugly and offensive, and would have nothing whatever to do with them!

Thereupon the King caused a new mansion to be built, and set the people at work to paint the walls red and white with the utmost carefulness and skill. All his treasuries were empty by the time the tower was finished, the height of it being ten thousand feet; and he called it the Tower of the Central Heavens. Then he chose the fairest virgins from the States of Cheng and Wei, bright-eyed, beautiful, and alluring; and to them he presented rich perfumes and fragrant ointments, enjoining them to paint their eyebrows tastefully and adorn their heads, don delicate silks with trailing sashes, powder their faces, darken their eyes, and decorate their arms with jeweled bracelets. He then caused aromatic grass to be spread throughout the tower; the bands played royal music in a gladsome strain; changes of splendid raiment were offered to the guest at stated intervals, and exquisite viands prepared for him every morning. At first the magician again declined to take up his abode there; eventually, however, he was constrained to go, although he did not stay in it more than a few days.

One day, while having an audience of the King, the magician invited His Majesty to accompany him on a journey. The King accordingly laid hold of the magician's sleeve, and then both of them rose high into the air, as far as the very zenith of the heavens, where they found themselves at the magician's palace. It was roofed in with gold and silver beams, incrusted with pearls and jade. It stood far, far above the region of clouds and rain, and nothing led one to suppose that, when seen from below, it would look like nothing but a thick cloud itself. All the phenomena which appealed to the senses were quite different from those which prevailed among mortals, and the King fancied that it must be the Pure City, the Purple Hidden Palace, where the music of the spheres is heard the home of God Himself. He gazed downward, and saw his own palace far below, with its terraces and arbors, like a mere heap of clods and billets; and then he thought how he would stay where he was for some tens of years, and give over troubling himself about his kingdom. But the magician proposed a further move; so away they soared again, till they came to a region where, if they looked up, there was no sun or moon to be seen, and, if they looked down, no seas or rivers were discernible. The reflection of light and shade dazzled the King's eyes, so that he could no longer see distinctly; strange sounds confused his ears, so that he could not hear distinctly. His whole frame became convulsed with dread, his mind was bewildered, and there was no more spirit left in him. He implored the magician to let him go back; whereupon the magician gave him a gentle push; he experienced a sensation of falling, falling, falling, and then suddenly awoke. He was sitting just where he had been before, with his attendants still around him; in front of him was his wine, not yet cooled, and his viands were not yet ready. The King asked what had happened. His courtiers replied, " Your Majesty has been sitting wrapped in silent contemplation."

Thereupon the King fell into a state of abstraction and self-oblivion, which lasted for three months, at the expiration of which he again interrogated the magician about what had occurred. The magician replied, " Your Majesty and I only journeyed in the spirit; how could our bodies have moved? What difference is there between the abodes we lately visited and your Majesty's own palace? between the places through which we roamed and your Majesty's own grounds? During your Majesty's retirement you have been constantly filled with misgivings that these places were, for the time being, non-existent. Do you think that in so short a time you are able to fathom all the depths of my enchantments? "

The King was greatly pleased at this reply. He lost all interest in the affairs of State, took no more pleasure in his harem, and gave free rein to his imagination. Then he commanded that the six noble steeds, Beauty, Jasper, Buce-phalus, Alabaster, Topaz, and Swift-flyer, should be harnessed to his chariot, and off he set with his charioteers and retainers, the horses flying like the wind. They galloped furiously a thousand li, when they came to the land of the Mighty Hunter. The Hunter presented the King with the blood of a wild goose to drink, and prepared a bath of the milk of cows and mares for the royal feet. When all were refreshed they started again, and passed the night in a cavern of the Kwen-lun Mountains, to the south of the Vermilion Waters. The next day they ascended the mountain to visit the Palace of the Yellow Emperor, who invested the King with hereditary honors; after which His Majesty was entertained by the Royal Mother of the West, who spread a banquet for him by the side of the Emerald Pool. Then the Queen sang to him, and the King joined his voice with hers. The King's song was of a plaintive character, and as he watched the sun rapidly sinking below the horizon, and travelling a thousand li in the course of a single night, he heaved a profound sigh. " Alas! " he said, " my virtue is far from perfect; for I am still susceptible to the influences of this sweet music. Succeeding generations will not fail to censure me for this fault."

What! King Mu endowed with supernatural powers, think you? He was nothing but a man, able to exhaust the pleasures of which his body was capable, and then after a hundred years to depart this life, while the world imagined that he had ascended bodily from view.

The Dreamer Awake

The philosopher Lieh-tzu said, " The divine men of old never thought when they were awake, and never dreamed when they were asleep."

In a corner of the world towards the extreme West there is a state, the frontiers of which border upon I don't know where. The inhabitants mostly sleep; they wake only once in fifty days, when they believe that the dreams they have been experiencing constitute their real life, and that the realities they see in their waking hours are non-existent.

There was a wealthy man of the Chou dynasty, named Yin Ta-chih, who kept his servants constantly at work, morning, noon, and night, without allowing them a moment's rest. Among them was one old fellow, who, having used up all his strength, was at last entirely worn out. But his master only made him work the harder; so that all day long he groaned and panted over his tasks, and when night came was so thoroughly exhausted that he slept as soundly as a log. Then his mental equilibrium became upset, and he used to dream every night that he was the king of a state, high exalted over the heads of the people, with all the affairs of his realm upon his hands; roaming and taking his pleasure amid palaces and temples, and giving free rein to all his passions and desires, so that his enjoyment was beyond compare. During his waking hours he was nothing but a hard -worked drudge, and people would pity him, and condole with him upon his arduous life. But the old fellow would reply, " A man's life is passed under two separate conditions day and night. By day I am a slave, and miserable enough; but by night I am a prince, and happy beyond all comparison. So, after all, what reason have I for grumbling at my lot? "

Now Mr. Yin, his master, was careful and troubled about many things, and the affairs of his wealthy establishment occasioned him constant anxiety; so that when night came round he also fell asleep, exhausted and knocked up. And night after night he dreamt that he was a slave an over-worked runner, always on his legs, doing everything that one can think of, being scolded and sworn at, and beaten with a stick in fact, there was no hardship that did not fall upon him. The wretched man would sob and whimper in his sleep all night, and it was not till morning dawned that he was silent. At last he fell sick, and took counsel of a friend. " Your position in life," said his friend, " is one of sufficient splendor, and you have greater riches than you want; you surpass your neighbors far and away. And yet you dream that you're a slave! Well, this is nothing more than compensation; it is a proper adjustment of the good and ill that must befall every man in life; it is no more than the common destiny. Do you want your waking and sleeping experiences to be both pleasant? No, no; that is more than you have any right to expect."

Then Mr. Yin thought over what his friend had said, and, in accordance with it, treated his servants with greater kindness, and eased their tasks; while he abstained from undue worry and anxiety about his own affairs, and soon found his malady much relieved.

Which was the Dream?

As a man of the State of Cheng was gathering fuel in the fields, he met with a startled deer. Throwing himself in its way, he struck at it, killing it on the spot; then, fearing lest it might be found, he made haste and concealed the carcass in a dry ditch, covering it with leaves and sticks. This done, he rejoiced exceedingly. But in a short time he forgot where he had buried it; and thinking that the whole occurrence must have been a dream after all, he turned his face homeward, humming the affair over to himself. It so happened, how-ever, that he was overheard by a passer-by; and this man, taking advantage of what the woodcutter was saying, went and found the deer, and took it. Then he went home and told his wife. " A woodman," he said, " once dreamt he got a deer, but could not remember the place where he had put it; but now I have actually found it myself, so that his dream must have been a true one." "I expect it was you who dreamt about the woodman getting the deer," replied his wife; " how can there be any woodman in the case? It is you who have actually got the deer, so it is you who have had a true dream." " If I've got the deer, what does it matter which of us has been dreaming? " retorted her husband.

Meanwhile the woodcutter went home, feeling considerably put out at the loss of his deer; and that night he had a true dream of the place where he had hidden the carcass, and of the person who had taken it. So he rose with the sun, and hastened, in accordance with his dream, to find him. The up-shot was, that the affair was taken into court and argued before a magistrate, who gave the following decision: " The plaintiff, in the first instance, really did get a deer, and then foolishly said that it was all a dream. He did really dream about the man who afterwards took possession of it, and then foolishly said that his dream was a reality. The defendant really took the deer, and now disputes its possession with the plaintiff. The defendant's wife, again, says her husband only dreamt of the man and the deer; so that, according to her, neither of them got it. However, here we have a deer before us, so I decide that it be equally divided between the contending parties."

When the affair came to the ears of the Prince of Cheng he exclaimed, "The magistrate must have dreamt the whole case himself! " Then he consulted his Prime Minister about it; but the Minister professed himself quite unable to distinguish the dreampart of the business from the actual occurrences. " There have been only the

Yellow Emperor and Confucius," he said, "who were able to distinguish dreams from the waking state; and, as both of them are dead, nobody can discover the truth of the matter. All your Majesty can do is to uphold the decision of the magistrate."

The Advantages of having no Memory

When Yang-li Huatzu, of the State of Sung, reached the prime of life he suddenly lost his memory. If he received anything in the morning, he forgot all about it by the even-ing; if he gave anything away overnight, he forgot all about it by next day. Out of doors he would forget to walk; in the house he would forget to sit down. To-day he would forget what had taken place the day before; and to-morrow he would forget what had happened to-day. His family got perfectly disgusted with him, and engaged the services of a soothsayer to divine when and how he might be cured; but the effort was unsuccessful. Then they resorted to a magician, who came and prayed for the afflicted man; but no result followed. Finally they sent for a doctor; but again the attempt proved useless.

Now in the State of Lu there lived a man of letters, who, taking the initiative himself, volunteered to effect a cure. The sick man's wife and son immediately offered him half their fortune if he would only favor them with a prescription. But the scholar replied, " This is not a malady that can be cured by sortilege and divination, or affected by prayer, or attacked successfully by drugs. I shall address myself to his mind. His mind must be changed, and his thoughts diverted into another channel; if this can be accomplished, his recovery will almost surely follow." So saying, he caused Huatzu to strip naked; whereupon Huatzu begged that he might have his clothes again. Then he starved him; and Huatzii begged for food. Then he shut him up in the dark; and Huatzu begged for light. Thereupon the scholar turned joyfully to the patient's son, exclaiming, " His disease is curable! But my prescription is a secret that has been handed down from generation to generation, and may not be disclosed to others." So he turned them all out of the room, and remained himself alone with Huatzu for the space of seven days; and there is no one who knows what he did all that time. But the result was, that an illness which had lasted for years was cured, so to speak, in a single day.

When Huatzu. came to his right senses he flew into a great rage, turned his wife out of doors, flogged his son, and drove away the scholar with a spear. This came to the ears of a certain gentleman of the same state, who asked Huatzu why he behaved so strangely. Huatzu replied, " Formerly, when I had no memory, I had no cares; I lived at large, unconscious of anything in the wide world; existence and non-existence were all one to me. But now, all of a sudden, I find myself remembering everything that has occurred for ten years past; births and deaths, gains and losses, joys and sorrows, loves and hates, are mixed up in my memory in the most inextricable confusion, and the future bids fair to be as intolerable as the present. Would that I could recover my former happy state of oblivion! But that is impossible; and there you have the reason why I drove the whole pack of them away."

The Crazy Genius

There was once a man of the State of Ts'in, named P'ang, who had a son. The boy, when quite little, was extremely clever, and showed signs of an understanding beyond his years; but when he grew up he became crazy. If he heard anybody sing, he thought he was crying; he took white objects for black; perfumes he thought were stenches; if he ate sweet things, he imagined they were bitter; bad conduct he approved as good; in fact, whatever he thought about in the whole world water, fire, heat, or cold his ideas were always the exact reverse of the truth.

One day a man named Yang said to the lad's father, " The Superior Man of Lu (Confucius) has a multitude of resources; he will surely be able to effect a cure. Why not ask his help? " So the father set out for the State of Lu; but on his way he had to pass through the State of Ch'en, and there he fell in with Lao-tzu, to whom he told his story. Lao-tzu re-plied, " How is it that you only know your son to be crazy, and appear quite unconscious that everybody else in the world, by confusing right and wrong, injury and advantage, is suffering from precisely the same disease? I assure you that there is not a single sane man among them. Now, the craziness of one person is not sufficient to impoverish a whole family; that of a single family is not sufficient to impoverish a whole village; nor that of a village to impoverish a state, nor that of a state to impoverish the whole empire. And if the whole world went completely crazy, who would there be left to suffer by it? while, supposing the whole world to be in the same mental condition as your son, it follows that it is you who are crazy, and not he."

Confucius on Sageship

The Premier Shang, during an interview with Confucius, asked him whether he was a sage.

"A sage! " replied Confucius; " how could I dare claim to be a sage? And yet my learning is wide, and my knowledge considerable."

"Well, were the Three Princes sages? " asked the Premier.

"The Three Princes," said Confucius, "were virtuous, tolerant, wise, and brave; but whether they were sages I don't know."

"How about the Five Rulers? " inquired the Premier.

"The Five Rulers," replied Confucius, "were virtuous, tolerant, benevolent, and just; but whether they were sages I don't know."

"The Three Emperors, then? " pursued the Premier.

"The Three Emperors," said Confucius, "were virtuous and tolerant, and always acted in accordance with the times; but whether they were sages I don't know."

Then the Premier, greatly astonished, exclaimed, "If so, then, where is a sage to be found? "

Confucius, with a change of countenance, replied, after a short pause, " In the West there is a sage. He governs not, yet there is no disorder; he speaks not, yet he is naturally trusted; he attempts no reforms, yet his influence has free course. Vast and far-reaching are his aims! The people can find no name for it. I suspect that he is a sage; yet I cannot be sure whether even he is or no."

The Premier relapsed into silence, and pondered in his heart whether Confucius were not chaffing him.

We will skip over the next few pages, contenting ourselves with a brief summary of some of their more interesting contents. There is a description of several fabulous countries, their beauties and marvelous productions, together with the strange legends pertaining to their origin. One of these imaginary realms is called the Country of Salamanders, where, to show their filial piety, the people leave the corpses of their relations to rot, and then throw the flesh away and bury their bones; while in another a man drives away his aunt when his uncle dies, on the ground that it is impossible for people to live with the wife of a ghost. A still more curious passage is devoted to a discussion between the Emperor T'ang and his Minister, Hsia Ko, about the extent and eternity of matter. The Emperor begins by asking his Minister whether matter existed from the beginning of all things, and the Minister replies by asking how, if it did not, it came to exist at present, and whether their descendants would be justified in denying that matter existed in His Majesty's own day. The Emperor naturally enough rejoins that, by this argument, matter must have existed from all eternity a remark that the Minister parries by saying that no records remain of the time before matter existed, and that all such knowledge is beyond the scope of humanity. To the question of the Emperor whether there is any lim-it to the expanse of the universe, the Minister replies by avowing his entire ignorance; and when the Emperor presses the matter home by saying that " where nothing exists, that is the Infinite, but where there is existence there must be finality," the Minister says plainly that nobody can know anything about the Infinite, as, by the nature of the case, human knowledge is confined to what is limited and finite. Heaven and earth are simply contained in the great whole of the infinite Universe. How, he asks, can we know that there is not a larger Cosmos, over and above the manifestation of Cosmos that we can see? Then the conversation tails off into a mass of mythology, more curious than important, into which we have no space to follow it.

Confucius at Fault

One day, as Confucius was travelling in an easterly direction, he came upon two small boys quarrelling, and asked what was the matter. The first replied, " I contend that when the sun rises it is near to us, and that at the zenith it is a long way off." "And I," said the other, " say that it is farthest when it rises, and nearest in the middle of the day." " It isn't," protested the first. " When the sun rises it looks as big as the tent of a cart, while in the middle of the day it is only the size of a saucer. Isn't it clear that when it is farthest it looks small, and when nearest it looks big? " Then the second replied, " But when the sun rises it is quite chilly and cold, while at mid-day it is broiling hot; and doesn't it stand to reason that it is hottest when it is near, and coldest when far off? " Confucius confessed himself unable to decide between them; whereupon both the urchins mocked him, saying, "Go to; who says that you are a learned man."

The Mischievous Physician

Duke Hu of Lu, and Ch'i Ying of Chao, being both sick, begged a celebrated physician named Pien Ch'iieh to cure them. The doctor did so; and when they were quite well again he said, " The malady you have been suffering from came from outside, and invaded your interiors, and that is why it proved amenable to drugs. But now you have both fallen sick again together, and your malady is growing with your bodies. What do you say? would you like me to tackle it for you?" " We should first like to hear your diagnosis," replied the two gentlemen. Then the doctor said to the Duke, " Your will is strong, but you have a weak constitution; so, while you are equal to consulting, you are inadequate when it comes to arriving at a decision. Ch'i Ying, on the other hand, has a weak will, but a strong constitution; so that he is defective in deliberation, and therefore suffers from the decisions that he forms. If you two could only effect an exchange of minds, your powers would be equalized to perfection. " Where-upon the doctor gave each of them a strong anaesthetic, which caused them to lie in a dead stupor for three days, during which time he cut open their bosoms, took out their hearts, and changed one for the other. Then he poured a wonderful elixir down their throats, and soon they woke up again as well as they had been before. So they took their leave of him and set out for their homes; but the Duke went to the house of Ch'i Ying, where Ch'i Ying's wife and children lived, and of course they did not know him. Meanwhile Ch'i Ying went to the Duke's, where precisely the same experience awaited him; and the next thing was, that Mrs. Ch'i Ying brought an action against Duke Hu, and the Duchess brought one against Ch'i Ying. The magistrate, after hearing the cross-actions, confessed his inability to arrange the difficulty, and decided that it should be referred to the doctor who had done the mischief. The doctor recounted the facts of the case, which was thereupon dismissed, each man returning to the bosom of his own family.

The Power of Music

When Kua Pa only thrummed his lute, the birds danced and the fishes capered around. Wen, the Director of Music in Cheng, having heard of this, left his family and attached himself to Shih Hsiang another famous lutanist following him whithersoever he went. For three years he was never without his lute in his hand, and yet at the end of that time he was unable to play a single air. Shih Hsiang thereupon said to him, " I think you had better go home again." The Director flung aside his instrument with a deep sigh. " It is not that I cannot thrum the strings," he exclaimed; " it is not that I cannot learn a tune. What I pay attention to has nothing to do with the strings; what I aim at is not mere sound. If a man's heart is not in it, he will never be able to interpret his feelings on any instrument. Therefore it is that I do not venture to put forth my hand and strike the strings. Let me take only a short leave; we will see how I get on when I come back."

In a few days he returned, and went to see his teacher, who said, " Well, and how are you progressing with the lute? "

"I have succeeded," replied the Director of Music.

"Well, let's hear what you can do," rejoined his teacher.

Now, it was the time of spring. The lute-player struck a chord, sounding the second note in the scale, harmonizing with the lower fifth, when suddenly the wind blew chill and the plants and trees bore fruit. It was autumn! Then he struck the third note, setting in motion the second lower accord; and gradually a warm wind fanned their faces, and trees and shrubs burst into exuberant foliage. It was summer! Again, he struck the fifth note of the scale, harmonizing with it the first upper accord; whereupon hoar-frost appeared and snow began to fall, and the streams and pools froze hard. It was winter! Once more, he struck the fourth note of the scale, setting in motion the fourth upper accord; whereupon the sun burst out in an excess of brilliancy and heat and the fast-bound ice thawed rapidly. Finally he played a grand chord, the dominant of which was the first note of the scale, and immediately a delicious breeze sprang up, auspicious clouds floated across the sky, a sweet dew fell, and a fountain of pure water bubbled up from the ground.

The teacher, Shih Hsiang, stroked his breast and fairly danced with delight. " Wonderful, wonderful," he cried, " is your playing! You surpass the most gifted of the ancients."

Singing and Weeping

Once upon a time a certain man named Han Ngo, while on a journey, found that he had taken an insufficient quantity of provisions with him, so on arriving at the next town he had to sing for his food. When he left, the sound of his voice still hovered among the rafters of the room he had occupied, and continued to be heard for three days without interruption, so that the neighbors on either side imagined he was still there. When he came to another place, called Ni Lii, the populace insulted him, whereupon he burst out weeping in stentorian tones. All the children and old folks in the district caught the infection, and they all roared and wept in concert, sitting opposite to each other for three days and eating nothing. When Han Ngo went away they hastened after him, whereupon he returned, and sang them a very long ballad in a very loud voice. Then the children and old people danced with joy and capered delightedly about, quite unable to restrain their feelings and forgetful of their former grief. At last they loaded him with gifts and sped him on his way; and thus the people of that place have been great adepts at singing and weeping ever since, imitating to the present day the sounds bequeathed to them by Han Ngo.

The King and the Marionette

As King Mu was on his way back from a journey he passed by a place where a very accomplished conjuror, named Yen Shih, was presented before him with a view to His Majesty's entertainment. The King received him graciously, and asked wherein lay his special proficiency. " Your servant," replied the conjuror, "will endeavor to execute whatever commands your Majesty may be pleased to lay upon me; but I have in readiness a certain piece of mechanism of my own, which I beg your Majesty to inspect first." "Bring it with you another day," said the King, " and then we will look at it together."

Next day the conjuror again sought an audience of the King, and was accordingly ushered into his presence. " But who is this person you have brought with you? " asked the King. "This is my handiwork/' replied the conjuror, "and he can sing and act." The King, astonished at this statement, bent his gaze upon the figure as it stepped backwards and forwards, cast its eyes up and down, for all the world like a real man. The extraordinary creature, moving its jaws, then sang a tune, and, raising its hands, danced in time to it, throwing its body into a thousand diverting contortions in a most appropriate manner, so that the King was convinced that it was really a living person. Then he sent for the ladies of his harem to see it with him, when, towards the end of the performance, the actor winked at the Royal concubines, making signs to them with its hands. The King flew into a great rage, and, springing to his feet, made as though he would kill the conjuror on the spot; whereupon the conjuror, in a panic of terror, seized the actor, and then and there took him to pieces! He showed the King that it was simply an arrangement or combination of carved wood, glue, and varnish, painted white, black, scarlet, and blue; and the King, examining it himself, found that inside it contained liver, gall, heart, lungs, spleen, kidneys, bowels, and stomach all complete, while the framework consisted of sinews, bones, limbs, joints, skin, teeth, and hair every one of them an imitation of the real thing. Nothing was wanting; and when the whole contrivance was put together again it looked exactly the same as before. Then the King, to test it, removed the heart, where-upon its mouth could not speak. He removed the liver, and it could no longer see. He removed the spleen, and its foot refused to walk.

Then was King Mu delighted beyond measure, and ex-claimed, with a sigh, " Verily the skillfulness of man is on a par with that of the Creator Himself! "

The Two Archers

There was once upon a time a very celebrated archer named Kan Ying, who no sooner drew his bow than every animal crouched and every bird fell. He had a disciple named Fei Wei, who, having learned archery under him, eventually be-came more skilful than his master; and Fei Wei, in his turn, had a pupil named Ch'i Chang. . . . Now, Ch'i Chang, having probed the method of his instructor to the uttermost, and gained his enthusiastic praise, reflected within himself that he had only one rival in the world namely, Fei Wei himself. Thereupon he cast about how he might slay Fei Wei, and meeting him one day in a solitary place, he picked a quarrel with him. The two then shot at one another, but such was the unerring accuracy of each man's aim that their arrows met half-way, and the two points striking together, they fell harmless to the ground without raising a speck of dust. The arrows of Fei Wei gave out first; Ch'i Chang had just one left, and he shot it. Fei Wei replied with a twig of thorn, and again the two met midway. At this juncture the two men burst into tears, threw away their bows, prostrated themselves before each other in the dust, and vowed that they would live as father and son for evermore. Then they swore an oath never to divulge the secret of their skill, and branded it upon their shoulders.

Fate and Free Will

Free Will once said to Fate, " How can your merit be compared with mine? "

"What power have you in the affairs of life," retorted Fate, " that you presume to compare yourself with me? "

"Why," replied Free Will, "I claim to be the arbiter of long life and early death; failure and success, ignominy and honor, poverty and wealth, all depend on me."

"The wisdom of Peng Tsu," said Fate, "was certainly not superior to that of the great Emperors Yao and Shun, yet he lived eight hundred years. The abilities of Yen Yuen were not inferior to those of the common herd, and he died at the early age of thirty-two. The virtue of Confucius was certainly not inferior to that of the Feudal Princes, and he was brought to the direst extremities. The conduct of Chou Hsin t was not superior to that of the Three Philanthropists, yet he attained to the imperial dignity. The virtuous Ch'i Ch'a had no rank whatever in the State of Wu, while the infamous T'ien Heng managed to usurp the throne of Tsi. The incorruptible brothers Po I and Shu Ch'i died of hunger, while the traitor Chi Shih waxed rich. Now, pray, if you, Mr. Free Will, are as powerful as you say you are, how is it that all the good men died early and all the bad ones nourished till they were old? that the Sage was reduced to misery, while a rebel gained his ends? that the wise were slighted and the foolish held in honor? that the virtuous were poor, while the wicked rolled in wealth? "

"You have proved your case," replied Free Will. " It is clear that I have no power whatever. All these things were of your ordaining; the fault is yours, not mine."

"What! " exclaimed Fate. " If, as you say, these things are the result of Fate, pray, where does the ' ordaining ' come in? All I do is to go blindly forward, or, if I am so impelled, from side to side. How can I tell who are to live long or to not?"

The Puzzle Solved

Pei-kung Tzu said to Hsi-men Tzu, " You and I are contemporaries, and you have succeeded in life. We belong to the same clan, and you are held in honor. We have both the same cast of features, and you are generally popular. We are both able to speak, and you, in this respect, have only ordinary abilities. We both take an active part in public affairs, and you are no more than commonly honest. We are both in office, and your post is an honorable one. We both cultivate our fields, and you have grown rich. We both engage in commerce, and you make large profits. As for me, I dress in coarse rustic clothes, and my food is of the poorest and commonest; my dwelling is a thatched hut; and when I go out I walk on foot. But you! Your clothes are of embroidered silk; you dine on dainty viands; you live in pillared halls . At home you lead a proud and merry life, and treat me with contempt; at Court your manners are abrupt, and your bearing towards me is haughty; while, if we have occasion to go out, you will never walk in my company. Now, this has gone on for years; pray, do you consider yourself a more meritorious person than I? "

"Really," replied Hsi-men Tzii, " I cannot go into such details as these. All I know is, that whatever you turn your hand to fails; whatever I do succeeds; and here you have the experimental proof of it. And yet you say that we are equals in every respect. Such audacity is simply unheard-of!"

Pei-kung Tzu was silenced; and, greatly confused at the snubbing he had received, went home. On the road he met the teacher Tung Ku5, who said, " Where have you been, that you are walking all alone and looking so mortified? " So Pei-kung Tzii told him all that had happened; to which Tung Ku5 rejoined, " Never mind; I will cure you of your soreness.

“Let us go back to the man's house together, and see if we can't put him to the question."

When they arrived the teacher went up to Hsi-men Tzu and said to him, without any preface

"How is it that you have been speaking so insultingly to Pei-kung Tzii? Be good enough to inform me."

"It is simply this," replied Hsi-men Tzu. " Pei-kung Tzu maintained that all the conditions of our two lives were similar, while our fortunes were quite different. I told him that I couldn't account for it excepting on the ground that he was not so richly endowed with natural gifts as I was. How, I asked him, could he have the audacity to say that we stood upon an equal footing? "

"According to you," rejoined the teacher, "wealth and poverty of natural endowments amount simply to differences in ability and virtue. Now, my definition is quite another thing. The truth is, that Pei-kung Tzu is rich in merit but poor in destiny. You are rich in destiny but poor in merit. Your success in life is not a prize due to your wisdom. Pei-kung Tzu's failure is not a loss resulting from his stupidity. It is all a matter of fate; it does not rest with the individual. Again, you pride yourself at his expense because of your lucky star; he, on the other hand, suffers shame in spite of his wealth of worth. In short, you neither of you understand the doctrine of Predestination."

"Pray, Sir, forbear," said Hsi-men Tzu. " I do not dare to answer you."

Then Pei-kung Tzii, departing, found the common clothes he wore as warm as fur of fox or badger, his pulse of beans as toothsome as the finest rice, and his thatched house as protective as a lordly mansion; he mounted his old cabbage-cart as though it were a chariot of state, and spent the whole of his after-life in the happiest frame of mind, caring not a jot whether glory or shame fell to the lot of himself or anybody else.

The Patriot Friends

Kuan Chung and Pao Shu were bosom friends, living together in the State of Ts'i. The former was in the service of the young Prince Chiu; the latter served his brother, the young Prince Hsiao Po. Now, the reigning Duke, their father, had a large family, on whom he doted fondly, the Duchess and the ladies of his harem being all considered of equal rank. The people of Ts'i feared lest grave disorders might arise from this weakness of the Duke's; so Kuan Chung, accompanied by one Shao Wu, attended Prince Chiu to the State of Lu, while Pao Shu escorted Prince Hsiao Po to Chii. Their escape having been effected, the smoldering rebellion broke out; the Duke was killed, and the state left without a sovereign. Then both the young Princes contended for the throne; and Kuan Chung, on behalf of his master, Prince Chiu, gave battle to Prince Hsiao Po in the State of Chii, .in the course of which engagement he shot an arrow that struck the Prince in the clasp of his belt. Hsiao P5, however, was eventually successful j and afterwards, when he ascended the throne, he brought pressure to bear upon the State of Lu with a view to the execution, by being minced, of his brother and Shao Wu. The former was put to death, and the latter committed suicide, while Kuan Chung was thrown into prison. Then Pao Shu said to his royal master, " Kuan Chung has abilities which fit him to administer a state." " But he's my enemy," replied the young Duke, " and I should like to kill him." " I have heard," rejoined Pao Shu, "that virtuous sovereigns never bear private grudges. Besides, a man who is able to serve one master is also able to serve another, if he chooses. If your Highness wishes to become Chief of the Feudal Princes, it is absolutely necessary for you to secure the aid of Kuan Chung; so you really must set him at liberty." Thereupon the Duke commanded Kuan Chung to be brought before him, and he was accordingly given up by the authorities of Lu. Pao Shu went to meet him on the road, and brought him to the Duke, who received him with great honor, and gave him a post higher than that occupied by the two hereditary nobles of the state. Pao Shu contented himself with a subordinate position, and the entire administration of affairs was vested in Kuan Chung, who was soon called Father Chung. When, subsequently, the Duke aimed at the Chief-dom of the Feudatories, Kuan Chung heaved a sigh, and thus soliloquized:

"When I was young and poor I often traded with Pao Shu. On the profits being divided, I always took the larger share; yet Pao Shu never reproached me with covetousness, for he knew that I was poor. I often advised him about his affairs; yet when he came to grief through following my counsel he never reproached me with stupidity, knowing that times were sometimes favorable and sometimes the reverse. I held office thrice, and thrice was dismissed by my sovereign; yet Pao Shu never reproached me with degeneracy, knowing that I was simply unfortunate. Thrice did I wage war, and ' thrice was I defeated; yet Pao Shu never reproached me with cowardice, knowing that I had an aged mother. And then, when my royal master was defeated and my colleague killed himself, while I escaped with mere imprisonment, Pao Shu never reproached me with shamelessness; for he knew I felt no shame at trifles, but was only ashamed at my reputation not being coextensive with the world. It was my parents who gave me birth, but it is only Pao Shu who knows me."

Thus it is that Kuan Chung and Pao Shu have become a synonym for faithful friendship.

A Cynical Courtier

Once upon a time Duke Ching went on a journey to the Ox Mountain. As he approached the capital of his state, on his return from the north, he burst into a flood of tears, and exclaimed, " How beautiful is my kingdom, embedded in all the exuberant luxuriance of foliage! Why, then, should I weep? Because I must die, and leave it. Supposing that death had never entered the world in the olden times, and we were all immortal, whither should I bend my steps if once I left this spot?" Then two of his courtiers lifted up their voices and wept in company. " We depend on your Highness's generosity," they said, " for the coarse food and bad flesh we are able to obtain, and for the ill-tempered horses we harness to our carriages; yet even we do not wish to die, how much less, indeed, should your Highness?"

Yentzu, however, laughed at this scene as he stood apart. Thereupon the Duke, wiping away his tears, turned to him and said, "

My excursion to-day is a very sad one. My other courtiers join me in weeping; how is it that you alone begin to laugh? "

"If," replied the philosopher, " virtuous monarchs enjoyed perpetual tenure of the throne, Dukes T'ai and Huan would be in possession of it to this day; or if that were the case with brave monarchs, then Dukes Chuang and Ling would similarly be reigning still. If, in short, all these princes were perpetually in power, your Highness would to-day be wearing a straw hat and living among the ditches of some farm, where your occupation would be such as to leave you but little time for thinking about death. If your predecessors had been immortal, how would your Highness have been able to obtain the throne at all? It has now descended to you in the usual manner from those who previously occupied and vacated it, and yet you alone make it a cause of weeping! This is pure selfishness; and it was the sight of a selfish prince and a couple of sycophantic courtiers that led me to laugh on the sly."

The Duke was much abashed, and drank a glass of wine by way of punishing himself. He also exacted the same penalty from his two courtiers.

And now conies a chapter devoted to Yang Chu, a very celebrated philosopher indeed. He lived about the fourth or fifth century B.C., and may be called the Epicurus of China, being, curiously enough, a contemporary of the Western philosopher, whose doctrines his own resembled so closely. " With him," says Mr. Mayers, " he agrees in preaching a sublime indifference to life and death, and a regard for self in preference to the case of others. Thus Mencius " his unsparing enemy " rightly characterizes his philosophy as that of Selfishness." The following illustrations of his theory are exceedingly curious and interesting:

A Chinese Ecclesiastes

Yang Chu said, " A man who lives to be a hundred has a great allowance of years. There is not one in a thousand who attains to it. ... Yet what, after all, is a man's life worth to him? What true joy does it afford? Well, he may get elegance and comfort enjoy beautiful sounds and sights. Yet comfort and elegance cannot suffice him forever beautiful sounds and sights cannot be enjoyed indefinitely. Over and above this, there are punishments to deter and rewards to stimulate; and there are various methods of acquiring fame to guide one's policy of action. Thus men get into a constant fluster of work, bustling about in their little hour to acquire empty praise, that they may secure posthumous glory; ... so that, of course, they lose all the real pleasure there may be in life. For not one hour can they be at ease; for, hemmed up in a sort of prisoner's cage, bound and manacled hand and foot, how can it be otherwise with them? The sages of old knew that birth was just a Coming for a little while, and that death was just a Going; wherefore they followed the promptings of their own natures, and did no violence to their natural bent; never rejecting whatever delights there were to be had in life, never acting with a view to fame, but just following their own spontaneous inclinations," &c.

Now, this is not only a caricature of pure Taoism, but a gross libel on the sages of antiquity; for we shall soon see, in such a story, for instance, as The Virtuous Profligates, what Yang Chu meant by " doing no violence to their natural inclinations." Even the irreproachable Kuan Chung is subsequently pressed into the service and made to utter the most atrocious doctrines.

Live While You Can

Yang Chu said, " It is only the living who differ among themselves; the dead are all alike. When a man is alive, he may be wise or he may be foolish, he may be noble or he may be mean; thus do the living differ. But the dead all stink, they are all corrupt, they all decay till there is nothing left of them] and thus they are all alike. Both these facts are beyond the power of man; neither are they the result of any-thing that people themselves may do. Some die when they are ten, and some when they are a hundred; the wisest and best die, just as the vilest and worst; a man may live as a Yao or a Shun [the typical saintly Emperors], or as a Chieh or a Shou [say a Nero or a Philip the Second], but when he dies he is nothing but rotten bones in either case. In fact, there is no difference between the rotten bones of a dead saint and those of a dead rascal. Wherefore, in life let us attend to the things of life; why should we trouble our heads about what is to take place after death? "

How to Live Long.

Yen P'ing-chung asked Kuan Chung, saying, " What is the best way to take care of one's health? "

"To do precisely what you please, without hindrance or restraint," replied Kuan Chung; " nothing more."

"Pray descend to particulars," urged his interlocutor.

"The thing is very simple," said Kuan Chung. " What-ever your eye delights to look at, that look at to your heart's content; whatever your ear loves to hear, your nose to smell, your mouth to speak; whatever your body finds pleasure in; whatever your heart prompts you to do, enjoy it all! If there is any sound you love, and you can't hear it, that is restraint of one sense; if there is any beauty you delight to gaze on, and can't, that is restraint of another sense; and so on through all the desires of which your soul is capable. Now, all these different forms of restraint are the head and front of everything that is deleterious and cruel; so that if these are swept away, and a man quietly waits for death every day of his life in unrestrained enjoyment, you have what I call the true method of preserving one's health. But to be subjected to such restraints does not conduce to the preservation of men's health no, not if a man lives a hundred years, or a thousand, or ten thousand."

The Virtuous Profligates

Tzu Ch'an, Prime Minister of the State of Cheng, wielded complete power for three years, during which time the virtuous all submitted to his reforms, while the vicious feared his prohibitions; so that the State of Cheng, from its good government, commanded the respectful dread of all the feudal princes. Now, the Minister had two brothers, of whom Chao, the elder, was a drunkard, and Mu, the younger, was a lecher. Chao's house contained a thousand chung (about 750 tun) of wine; accumulations of yeast stood up like a barricade, and the odor of wine-dregs offended everybody's nose to a distance of a hundred paces from 'his door. The man was simply reckless in his self-indulgence, and neither knew nor cared what was going on in the world whether things were prosperous or in danger, whether public affairs were being wisely administered or not, whether his relations lived or died, or whether even his own life were or were not threatened. Mu, on his side, filled his inner rooms, to the number of thirty or forty, with concubines. The place just overflowed with the choicest, most delicate, voluptuous, and seductive girls imaginable. The man was simply a slave to lust, and broke off all intercourse with his relatives and former comrades, skulking away in his harem, where, not satiated with night pleasures, he prolonged them throughout the day. He only went out once every three months, and even then he would have preferred remaining inside. If ever he heard that there was a virgin of unusual beauty in some country place, he would send and tempt her with money, or employ a procuress to abduct her; and if he failed, he turned his pursuit elsewhere.

Now, all this caused daily and nightly distress to their good brother, the Prime Minister; and at last he went privately to a friend of his, one Teng Hsi, to consult him about the matter. "I have heard it said," remarked the Minister, in conversation with his friend, " that if a man can govern himself he can govern his family; and that if he can govern his family he may also govern a state. This saying reasons from the near to the far. But look at my case. I have governed the state successfully, but my family is in utter disorder; so the theory is contrary to fact. What method can I possibly adopt for rescuing these two lads? I pray you, point one out to me."

"For a longtime," replied Teng Hsi, "I have wondered greatly at all this; but I did not venture to mention the matter to you first. How is it, then, that you have taken no measures to set them straight? Your best way is to explain to them the dignity and value of life, and allure them, by gentle means, to a knowledge of the nobleness of decorum and rectitude."

So Tzu Ch'an acted upon his friend's advice, and took an early opportunity to seek an interview with his two brothers. " The superiority of man over the birds and beasts," he said to them, "consists in intelligence and the power of thought. Now, what intelligence and thought are calculated to promote is uprightness and decorum; and when these are perfected the man's good name is established. But if every desire and passion is gratified, and licentiousness indulged in without restraint, one's very life is put in jeopardy. Be advised by me; if you will only repent by dawn, you may enjoy emoluments from the State ere night."

"We have known all that for a long time," replied Chao and Mu, " and we made our choice ages ago. Do you really suppose we have had to wait for you to tell us? Life is not to be had for the asking, while death comes only too easily; and which, pray, is the more earnestly desired? What? To struggle after rectitude and decorum in order to make a show before others; to feign virtues we don't possess in order to acquire fame, why, we would very much sooner die at once. No; what we want is to exhaust all the pleasure we can in the course of our lives, and to get all possible delights out of the present time; all we are afraid of is, that our stomach may overflow, and our mouth be unable to enjoy un-restrained indulgence in wine, or that our strength may give out and leave us impotent to go to extremes in the sweets of lechery. We have no time to grieve over the foulness of our reputation or the danger to which we expose our health. Whereas you employ your administrative ability to sound your own trumpet; you desire to upset our minds by your glibness in talking, and try to please us with promises of glory and pelf. Is not this vile and pitiable on your part? No; we would rather not resemble you,"

The two profligates continue to rate the Minister in the same strain, until the poor man retires, speechless and abashed, only to be snubbed in the most heartless fashion by the treacherous Teng Hsi, who upholds the words of Chao and Mu as embodying the true philosophy of life.

Sage or Reprobate?

In the State of Wei there lived a man named Tuan-mu Shu, who inherited a fortune from his ancestors, which, by accumulation, had reached an enormous sum. He took no part in public affairs, but threw himself headlong into a whirlpool of pleasure. Everything that a man could think of he indulged in. He had towers and palaces, parks and pleasurance pools of ornamental water, banquets, chariots, music, and concubines, just like a sovereign prince. There was not a sense left un-gratified: what he could not obtain in his own state he sent for from another; in fact, there were no hills or streams, as far as the human foot could go, that were not ransacked for him. Every day he entertained a hundred guests in his pavilions; the fires in his kitchen never went out, and music resounded without ceasing in his halls and piazzas. What he had over, he distributed among his family; what they had over, they distributed among the people in the neighborhood; and what they were unable to use, they distributed broadcast over the state. But when Tuan-mu had lived sixty years he began to break up. His strength failed rapidly; his means of living were exhausted. In the course of a single year his treasuries became empty, his jewels disappeared, his chariots and his concubines were no more. Not a penny was left for his heirs; during his illness there was no money to buy medicine, and when he died there was no money to bury him. But all the people in the state who had enjoyed his benefits brought the money they had saved, and restored it to the sons and grand-sons of the dead man.

When Ch'in Kuli heard of this he said, " Tuan-mu Shu was a profligate, who brought disgrace upon his ancestors." Tuan-kan Sheng, on the other hand, said, " Tuan-mu Shu was a most intelligent person, whose ancestors were far inferior to him in virtue."

There is one more striking passage attributed to Yang Chu, scurrilously comparing the sad lives of the good and virtuous in Chinese history with the joyful careers of those whose names are execrated, and who are still happily unconscious of the curses heaped on them by posterity; and there are also a few more anecdotes in which he occupies a prominent position. But we have seen quite as much of the apostle of selfishness as is necessary to our purpose, and will proceed at once to a selection from the more pleasing stories with which the book concludes. We may remark, however, in taking our leave of Yang Chu, that Lieh-tzu, so far from endorsing his praise of cynicism and vice, says roundly that men who care nothing for integrity and everything for eating are no better than fowls and dogs, and need never hope for the respect of their fellow-men, for they will never get it.

The Leaf-maker

There was a man of Sung who made artificial leaves of jade for the King. The work took three years to finish; the artificer carving and paring the stalks and veins, and reproducing the very down and gloss, so that the result had all the appearance of a luxuriant cluster of bright leaves, in natural disorder, and impossible to distinguish from real ones. The man followed his art as a handicraft, receiving a regular stipend from the State. When Lieh-tzti heard of it he said, " Well! if when God created the world He was three years making a bunch of leaves, there would be very few leaves in the world today."

Therefore it is that the Sage sets store on good principles and social reformation, not on dexterity and skill.

Luck and No Luck

There was a certain Mr. Shih, of the State of Lu, who had two sons. One was devoted to study, the other to the profession of arms. The student went to seek his fortune at the Court of , the Marquis of Ch'i, who received him cordially, and appointed him tutor to his two young sons; while the soldier repaired to the State of Ch'u, where the Prince made him generalissimo of his forces, conferred large revenues upon his family, and ennobled all his relations.

Now, old Mr. Shih had a neighbor of the name of Meng, who also had two sons, whose respective professions were the same as those followed by the brothers Shih; but, alas! they were hampered in their life by poverty. Incited by the brilliant fortunes of the young men Shih, old Mr. Meng asked their father how they had managed to get on so well; and he told him exactly what had taken place. Whereupon he deter-mined that his own two sons should follow their example, and accordingly sent the studious one to the Court of the Prince of Ch'in. But the Prince said, " At present we feudatory princes are all engaged in internecine warfare, and all our thoughts are concentrated upon military equipments, commissariats, and such things; to talk, as you do, of governing my state on an ethical basis would be its ruin." So he castrated him and sent him away. The other son, who had studied military matters, meanwhile went to the State of Wei, in order to gain the interest of the reigning Marquis. But the Marquis said, " Mine is a weak state, hemmed in between two great ones. My policy is to conciliate the states that are larger than mine by being of service to them, and states that are smaller than mine by dealing kindly with them. That is the way to preserve peace for myself. If I were to rely upon military strength, I might look' out for speedy annihilation; and if my people were to desert me and go in a body to some other state, the calamities that would come upon me would be no laughing matter." So he cut off young Meng's feet, and sent him back to Lu.

Then all the Mengs, father and sons, smote their breasts and railed on old Mr. Shih. But Mr. Shih said, " All who are lucky enough to hit the right moment prosper; those who miss it are ruined. The methods you adopted were the same as those of my own sons; it is only the results which were different. This was because you missed your opportunities, not because you acted unwisely. Besides, the principle of mundane affairs is not invariably right, while events do not invariably turn out wrong. What was used yesterday is rejected to-day, and what is rejected to-day may perhaps be used to-morrow; but the question whether such a thing is used or rejected is no criterion as to whether it is right or wrong. You may hit upon your opportunity, and come just in the nick of time; but it is never certain that things will turn out in your favor that must depend on a man's own shrewdness. If he is not shrewd enough, though he be as learned as Confucius and as accomplished as Lii Shang, he will be unsuccessful, whatever course he may adopt."

Then the Mengs, casting off their resentment, said, with recovered good-humor, " We see it all now! You need not repeat your words."

Guard Your Own Frontier

Duke Wen of Chin once started to attend a conference of the feudal princes, the object of which was to organize an attack on the State of Wei. On the journey his Minister, Kung-tzu Ch'u, was observed to cast up his eyes and laugh. " What are you laughing at? " demanded the Duke. " I was laughing," replied the Minister, " about a certain neighbor of mine. He was escorting his wife on her way to pay a visit to her parents, when he spied a pretty girl picking mulberry-leaves for silkworms. Delighted at the reconnoitre, he stopped to talk to her, when, happening to turn his head, he saw somebody else paying attention to his wife. That was what I was laughing to myself about."

The Duke understood the hint. He did not proceed any farther, but led his soldiers back; and they had not arrived in their own state when news reached them that an enemy had come during their absence and attacked their northern frontier.

Moderation Is The Best Policy

An elderly man lay dying, and as he felt his end drawing near, he called his son to him, and said, " The King has sought to load me with honors, but I have consistently declined them. When I am dead he will seek to confer honors upon you; but mind what I say accept no land from him which is worth anything. Now, between the States of Ch'u and Yueh there is a bit of ground that is of no use to anybody, and has, more-over, a very bad reputation; for the people of both Ch'u and Yueh believe it to be haunted. This is a kind of property that you may retain forever." Soon after this the man died, and the King offered a beautiful piece of land to his son. The youth, however, declined it, and begged for the bad piece. This was granted to him, and he has never lost possession of it to this day.

The Folly of Being Righteous Over-much

There was once a man named Yuan Ching-mu, who, during a journey, fainted with hunger on the road. An old robber-chief called Hu-fu Ch'iu, seeing him in this condition, brought out a kettle of soup and fed him; and when the traveler had swallowed three mouthfuls he recovered so far as to be able to open his eyes. Then, gazing at his deliverer, he said, " Who are you? " "I am Hu-fu Ch'iu," replied the robber. "What! " exclaimed Mr. Yuan, " why, you're a robber, aren't you? How is it you have given me food? My sense of rectitude forbids me to accept your hospitality." Whereupon he knelt with his two hands upon the ground and retched. He was unable, however, to vomit what he had eaten, but coughed and choked so violently that he fell flat down and expired. Now, it is true that Hu-fu Ch'iu was a robber, but his food had been honestly come by; so that to refuse to eat food because it is given by a robber, who only may have stolen it, is to lose both the substance and the shadow.

The Elixir of Life

Once upon a time it was reported that there was a person who professed to have the secret of immortality. The King of Yen, therefore, sent messengers to inquire about it; but they dawdled on the road, and before they had arrived at their destination the man was already dead. Then the King was very angry, and sought to slay the messengers; but his favorite Minister expostulated with him, saying, " There is nothing which causes greater sorrow to men than death; there is nothing they value more highly than life. Now, the very man who said he possessed the secret of immortality is dead himself. How, then, could he have prevented your Majesty from dying? " So the men's lives were spared.

Doing Evil That Good May Come

There was once a man in Hantan who presented a live pigeon to Chientzu at dawn one New Year's Day. Chientzu. was delighted, and rewarded him liberally. A visitor asked him his reason for acting thus. "Because," said Chientzu, " it gives me an opportunity of releasing a captive bird; and to set living creatures free on New Year's morning is a special manifestation of mercy." The visitor replied, " But if the people know that your Excellency is so fond of setting birds at liberty, they will vie with each other in catching them to begin with, and numbers of the birds will die. If your object is to save their lives, would it not be better to forbid the people to catch them at all? First to catch them, in order to let them go afterwards, is surely to destroy the just proportions of good and evil."

Then Chien tzu acknowledged that his visitor was right.

A Youthful Anti-Teleologist

There was a wealthy man of Chi, named T'ien Tsu, who daily fed a thousand people in his own mansion. Among them was one who reverently presented his host with a fish and a goose. T'ien Tsu looked at the offering and sighed. " How bountiful," he exclaimed, " is Heaven to man! It gives us the nutritious grain for food, and produces birds and fishes for our use." All the guests applauded this pious sentiment to the echo, except the young son of a certain Mr. Pao, a lad of twelve years old, who, leaving his back seat and running forward, said

"You would be nearer the truth, Sir, if you said that Heaven, Earth, and everything else all belonged to the same category, and that, therefore, nothing in that category is superior to the rest. The only difference which exists is a matter of size, intelligence, and strength, by virtue of which all these things act and prey upon each other; so it is quite a mistake to say that one is created for the sake of the others. Whatever a man can get to eat, he eats; how can it be that Heaven originally intended it for the use of man, and therefore created it? Besides, we all know that gnats and mosquitoes suck our skins, and tigers and wolves devour our flesh; so that, accord-ing to your theory, we were ourselves created by Heaven for the special benefit of gnats, mosquitoes, tigers, and wolves! Do you believe that, pray? "

The Three Rules of Life

Once upon a time there were three brothers who went abroad to study ethics. On their return their father said to the eldest

"Well, and what do ethics consist in? "

"They teach me," replied his son, "to cherish my own health and life, and to regard fame as of secondary importance. "

"And what have they taught you? " inquired the father, turning to his second son.

"They teach me to kill myself, if necessary, in order to achieve fame," was the reply.

"And you? " said the father to the youngest.

"They teach me to preserve both body and fame intact," replied the lad.

Now, here you have three different theories all proceeding from a recognized authority. Which of them is right, think you, and which wrong?

CHAPTER 11. TAOIST HERMITS

THE tendency of nearly all religions in the direction of asceticism is proved by the existence, in almost every quarter of the globe, of hermits. A desire to flee from the cares and enticements of the world, to shun the face of one's fellow-man, and to devote oneself entirely to the contemplation of the unseen constitutes, in most instances, that frame of mind which impels its subject to abjure the claims of family and friendship and all that makes life sweet. With the growth of enlightenment and the rationalistic spirit, the hermit-race has gradually been dying out. Early in the Middle Ages the anchorite was a recognized institution a sort of " irregular " in the Church militant, yet one who very often came in for the highest honors of saintship. But it was not the hermit of poetry on whom the approval of the Church was principally bestowed. That variety represented the aesthetic rather than the ascetic type of anchoretics. He wore a very fine, full beard and flowing robes of serge. He lived in a charming grotto, adorned in picturesque fashion with a skull, a crucifix, and an enormous book, and slaked his thirst at the mountain rill which invariably babbled past his door. The hermits of whom saints were made were of a very different cut. They generally went naked, and affected the peculiarities of Nebuchadnezzar during the seven years in which that hapless monarch was afflicted with lycanthropy.

They slept in beds of nettles, in marshes reeking with miasmata and swarming with foul reptiles. They lacerated their skins, already covered with sores and smarting with the bites of insects. Cleanliness and comfort were loathed by them as crimes, dirt and misery being regarded as the highest indications of internal holiness. These men were reverenced in by-gone days as saints of the purest ray; and the honor in which they were held was perfectly compatible with times when physical phenomena, such as earthquakes and disease, were attributed to the action of demons. We in the nineteenth century, of course, can see where the mischief lay in the case of these unfortunates. They were really raving lunatics, and at the present day would have been consigned to the restraints of an asylum. In China the hermit-race has never reached quite such an abyss of degradation as in Europe. Indeed the old Taoist and Buddhist mystics of whom we read, and specimens of whom we may even see around us now, were rather interesting characters. They generally chose for their retreat some rocky glen shut in by mountains, sheltered from the burning sun by the thick foliage of trees, and surrounded by every natural feature which makes a landscape lovely. There they passed their lives in that state of mental vacuity and freedom from interest in mundane matters which is the nearest approach to the summit of virtue and bliss. That summit in the articles of the Buddhist Church is called Nirvana. The Taoists look forward to very much the same condition. Their idea of happiness is, after all, a very wise and very pure one. Perfect indifference to love and hate the annihilation of all passions, desires, and even preferences no striving, or wishing to strive nothing but absolute apathy and profound insensibility to those things which, painful or pleasurable, tend to wear out the bodies and souls of men; such is the Taoist heaven. It is a return to the pure, original, self-existent nature of men, which has been despoiled and injured by contact with worldly matters. How infinitely higher, this, than the wretched superstitions which debased the self-tormentors of the Middle Ages! And there are a few of these Taoists yet to be found men who are almost entirely uncontaminated by the follies and impostures of modern popular Taoism, and who may be said to represent the true apostolic succession in the Taoist Church. In certain instances some old worthies, who have been dead and gone for centuries, are believed by the simple mountaineers of China to be still alive.

Far away in the mountain-range which stretches from Peking across the provinces of Chihli and Shantung there is one very sacred peak, called the Mount of a Hundred Flowers. It is covered with wild flowers, and its bosky dells are said, and with some truth, to be the lurking-place of wolves and panthers. There, according to the legend, live, partly embedded in the soil, certain ancient Taoist hermits. By a long course of absolute conformity with nature they have attained to immortality, and are now in the enjoyment of unearthly bliss. To use a Taoist phrase, their faces are washed by the rains of heaven, and their hair combed by the wind. Their arms are crossed upon their breasts, and their nails have grown so long that they curl round their necks. Flowers and grass have taken root in their bodies, and flourish luxuriantly; when a man approaches them they turn their eyes upon him, but do not speak. No wild beast ever attacks them, for they are in harmony with all nature. Some of them are over three hundred years old; others are not much over a century; but all have attained to immortality, and some day they will find that their bodies, which have been so long in wearing out, will collapse from sheer withdrawal of vitality, and their spirits be set free. This is all fanciful and fabulous enough; but it is undeniable that that indifference or aversion to vulgar objects of desire which characterizes the true Taoist has laid China under many a debt of gratitude. The votary of the Naturalistic philosophy does not always become a hermit any more than the Christian always becomes a priest. He is often in the world, and occupies high offices of state. But circumstances make no difference in him. He is always the same, while living in mean and dirty lane and drinking from a gourd, as he is in the palace itself, the trusted Minister of a monarch. In this position he retains the same incorruptibility, the same indifference to power, that he has when living in obscurity. China has had many such Ministers, and she is rightly proud of them. Emperors and princes are said to have gone in person to solicit the services of some stern recluse whose fame had reached their ears, and to have been unsuccessful in their suit. The delineation of such characters forms a bright page in many a volume of dusty Chinese lore, and they are now held up to the reverence and imitation of the statesmen and scholars of the day.

CHAPTER 12. A TAOIST PATRIARCH

ALTHOUGH there is no country in the world in which official position and emoluments are more highly thought of than in China, there are, on the other hand, but few countries where they are more despised by certain schools of thought. The ideal man of Confucius was, first and foremost, an officer or Minister of State; and this conception has lived and flourished among the Chinese down to the present day. As a recoil, however, from the worldliness of the Confucian standard, we have the bright ideal of the Taoists, who look upon wealth and honors as illusory, and see the true Sage rather in him who abandons himself to quietism, contemplation, and the culture of his natural endowments. One of the most illustrious representatives of this persuasion was the patriarch Lit Tsu, about whom many curious stories are told, and to whom is attributed a very original and abstruse commentary upon the Tao T& Ching. Now it must be remembered, at the outset, that a great many of the fairy tales and legends familiar to all children are common to many countries. Mr. W. E. S. Ralston is well known as an indefatigable investigator of what may be called the science of comparative romance, and while his public story-tellings are crowded with children as delighted and spell-bound as if they were witnessing their first pantomime, he can write as learnedly in the Nineteenth Century about Cinderella or Puss in Boots as Max Mliller upon the science of language. One of these stories common to so many lands is that of Eip Van Winkle, the Chinese prototype of whom was a person called Wang Chih. Another is that of the King who put his head into a basin of water and took it out again, but in that brief second lived a long, chequered, and laborious career, rose from poverty to wealth, married, had a family, suffered disgrace, and was reduced to penury and old age.

The Chinese counterpart of this fabled monarch who was, if we remember rightly, a Persian is the illustrious sage of whom we are now writing. It is said that early in life Lii Tsu was animated by ambition, and longed to distinguish himself in the affairs of state. In this he was opposed by the wise counsels of a Taoist philosopher, who expatiated to him on the vanity of earthly things. It was not, however, until a very remarkable dream occurred to him that he was induced to give up his design. Entering an inn one evening, he ordered some rice for his supper, and while it was being cooked fell asleep. Immediately he commenced a long and adventurous career. He thought he rose high in office, passing through all the proper grades, until, when at the pinnacle of greatness, he incurred the imperial displeasure, and was disgraced. Waking with a start, he found that his rice was just ready; and the lesson he laid to heart was, that, for so unsatisfactory a career, which, in spite of its wearisome prolongation, really only lasted a few minutes, it would be foolish to surrender the truer pleasures of indifferentism. He therefore abandoned his high schemes, cheered his heart with copious libations of wine, and de-voted himself to the practice of what may be called the convivial phase of Taoist philosophy. Numbers of disciples followed in his footsteps, convinced that the world was very vain; and from this time Lli Tsu became a shining light of the school whose doctrines he had embraced. His mystically conceived interpretation of the great Taoist classic we have already referred to; but what gave him the widest celebrity he enjoyed was his wonderful talent in working the planchette. He became, in fact, a sort of planchette professor. There are very few of our readers, we suppose, who have witnessed a planchette stance in China. The board is suspended over a tray of clean sand, and through a hole in it hangs a pencil. Incense is burnt, prostrations are performed, and the passing spirit is invoked. Then the planchette begins slowly to wave to and fro, and the pencil traces characters in the sand, which are of a somewhat obscure and oracular signification. A capital description of afu luan, or planchette stance, is given in the novel P'm Hua Poo Chien, or " Precious Mirror of Choice Beauties," a translation of which appeared in the China Review a few years ago. Through the medium of the planchette Lli Tsu was enabled to purvey much highly-prized information, and his success in the art was such that he is invoked to this very day in Peking, and probably else-where, whenever the native mediums can be prevailed upon to give a stance. Among the most valued revelations vouchsafed through the mediumship of Lli Tsu were directions with regard to the cure of diseases. In fact, his fame became so great in this department of spiritual-istic art, that he has since been canonized as the Patron of

Medicine, and temples are erected to his honor in all the provinces of China. There are four in the capital one near the Jesuit Observatory, called the Lu Kung T'ang, close by the shrine built in, commemoration of the great Jesuit, Adam Schaal, by the Emperor Shun Chih; one just outside the Front Gate, called the Lii Tsu Tien; and two others, both of which are known as Lii Tsu T'sz. There is also a sanctuary dedicated to him in the Temple of the White Cloud, the great stronghold of Taoism, out-side the western wall. On the whole, we should say that Lii Tsu succeeded in acquiring far more fame as a soothsayer and mystic than he would have done had he contented himself with less transcendental studies and risen to be a humble magistrate. There are people in the world not unlike him now; and though we do not suppose that future generations will canonize Madame Blavatsky, or build temples to her coadjutor the quondam editor of the Hong-Kong Daily Press, both persons enjoy an amount of fame, or notoriety, that would never have fallen to their share had they stuck to more common-place pursuits. Spiritualists and mystery-mongers flourish to-day much as they did in China a thousand years ago; and, albeit that comparisons are odious, we cannot help remarking that they do not seem to have improved. There is often a grubbiness about the fingernails of professional mediums, and a certain shakiness about the proper use of the eighth letter of the alphabet, which go far towards counteracting the effect upon one's mind of their most astonishing performances; whereas our old friend of the T'ang dynasty was a person of undeniable erudition and most cultured tastes, and could lay claim, besides, to a very high position in the philosophic school he joined. Jargon as his poetry upon the " Cultivation of the Pure Essence " may sound to us to-day, it represented to the scholars of his time a distinct and fashion-able phase or craze of philosophy and speculation, to the pursuit of which many eminent and pure men devoted their entire lives, and which exercised a profound influence upon more than one Emperor of China.

CHAPTER 13. THE PEACH AND ITS LEGENDS

THE peach-gardens of China are a fair sight in all the glory of their springtide bloom, when the trees are laden with blossoms of delicate pink and white and the air sweetened with their rich fragrance. The Chinese, in celebrating their admiration for flowers, give a high place to the blossoms of fruit, which English poets appear generally rather to ignore. Bouquets in English houses do not include these beautiful specimens of nature, which are so favorite an ornament in the libraries and reception-rooms of well-to-do Chinese. The peach is held in special honor in the so-called Flowery Land, and much attention is paid to its cultivation. There are three sorts of peach-trees grown in China the dwarf, the shrub, and the full-sized tree. Of these the dwarf-peach is perhaps the most highly prized in point of beauty and perfume. It is remarkable for the size, wealth, and color of its blossoms, and is divided by Chinese florists into eighteen different species. It does not fructify, and is valued only for its peculiarity of form and the rich fragrance of its flowers. The shrub-peach grows to the height of four or five feet, and is much found in the imperial gardens, where it is placed, with that true eye to effect characteristic of the Chinese, on the margins of pools and the acclivities of those effective pieces of rockwork which form so prominent a feature in artificial landscapes. Peach-trees also form a very beautiful feature of many natural landscapes in China, and were celebrated during the Sung dynasty by the great historian Ssii-ma Kuang, who in some charming verses described the eye of the spectator as being guided by a colossal garland cf peach-blossoms, connecting the numerous villages that were dotted over the spreading plains of Lo-yang. The neighborhood of the Hsi-hu, or Western Lake, near Hangchow, was famous for its wealth of peach-trees, and the greatest care has always been bestowed upon their cultivation. The fruit of the full-sized tree is handsome, though somewhat poor in flavor. Its shape is varied, some specimens being fully spherical, others prolate, others a curiously oblate spheroid called by foreigners " flat" peaches while others again are pointed and even hooked. The same diversity prevails in the color of the pulp, the fruits varying from white and pale green to rich ruby, orange-yellow, and marbled tints.

The peach is said to have reached China in the first instance from Persia, Thibet, Samarcand, and Harni, and to have existed here at any rate for upward of two thousand years. The Emperor Wu Ti of the Han dynasty was presented by his courtiers with a number of foreign seed-lings for his garden; the belles lettres of all the great dynasties abound in allusions, poetical and otherwise, to the beauty of its flowers, while histories record the fact that peach-trees or their fruit formed part of the tribute brought to the capital of China by ambassadors from, abroad. It would be deemed curious by those who have studied native literature and systems of thought if the peach had not been laid under contribution by the poets and mystics of the country. As a fact, it plays a prominent part in both poetry and philosophy. By some writers it is regarded as an emblem of longevity and marriage. Of course this does not mean that it is the only emblem of either which exists. Longevity is also symbolized by the stork, and conjugal harmony by the music of lutes and bells, the strings of a guitar, and other figures of a like fanciful description. It is the well-known Ode on the Princess's Marriage in the Book of Poetry, according to Dr. Legge's translation, which seems to have originated the metaphor that has been so great a favorite ever since:

" Graceful and young the peach-tree stands;

How rich its flowers, all gleaming bright; This bride to her new home repairs; Chamber and house she'll order right."

The Taoists, too, attribute occult virtues to the peach. Mr. Mayers, quoting from the Huang Ti Shu, or books of the imperial magician known as the Yellow Emperor, him-self a disciple of the still more mystical Kuang Ch'eng-tzu, tells us that on one occasion two brothers, named respectively T'u Yu and Yu Liu, who had power over disembodied spirits, passed the ghostly legions in review beneath a peach-tree, and having bound all those who worked evil against mankind with scarlet withes, threw them as food to tigers. In memory of this it was customary for officials on the last day of the year to have figures cut in peach-wood mounted upon reeds, and to paint the likeness of a tiger upon the doorway as a talisman. At present, adds Mr. Mayers, the names of the two brothers are pasted on the entrance doors of Chinese houses on New-Year's Eve, to guard the dwelling from harm. Peaches, too, figure largely in Chinese fairy tales and mythology, and formed part' of the banquet prepared by the Royal Mother of the West when she paid a visit to the Emperor Cheng, better known as Shih Huang Ti; while a peach-garden was the scene of one of the most celebrated events in Chinese history, when the Oath of Brotherhood was taken between the three heroes who played so important a part in the historical romance of the "Three Kingdoms." There are many other interesting details connected with the peach-tree in Chinese literature, but we have no space to enlarge upon them. Some pundits aver that, properly speaking, the peach is an emblem, not of longevity, but of death; while Western theorists have attempted to connect it with the Tree of the Knowledge of Good and Evil, whose fair fruit presented so fatal a temptation to our mother Eve. It seems, however, certain that, according to ancient writers, peaches were not admissible in sacrifice, that those with double kernels were a mysterious but unfailing poison, and that the premature fructification of one species of peach-tree was a harbinger of national calamity. All this may be very interesting, but it is not practical. We will conclude with two facts which have the merit of being both. The best manure for peach-trees, according to Chinese horticulturists, is snow; and a cold decoction of pig's-head, poured about the roots and into the trunk itself, is a sure remedy for the insects which prey upon it.

CHAPTER 14. TREE AND SERPENT WORSHIP

IN spite of the many praises that have been lavished upon the Chinese for the comparative purity of their religions, it is nevertheless a fact that some of the lowest forms of superstition are to be found in Chinese popular worship. In saying this we do no injustice to the higher developments of the various national religions. We are not unmindful of the pristine monotheistic worship which prevailed in China centuries before Confucianism was known. We do not refer to the Worship of Ancestors, the belief in Feng-shui, or even the baser developments of the systems of Buddhism and Tao. But we presume that in every country there may be found those who, irrespective of the religion they profess, have hewn out of their individual consciousness ideas unrecognized by their own sacred books, and adopted as objects of worship things which were never contemplated as such by the framers of the religion in question. We have known, for instance, of an Irish Catholic servant being found in the kitchen, on her knees, worshipping the moon; and not the bitterest Protestant will venture to affirm that Popery even in its extremest forms has any room in its pantheon for the lunar goddess. And so in China; here, irrespective even of that form of Nature-worship of which we find traces in every issue of the Peking Gazette, where sacrifices are ordered to the Spirits of the Hills and Woods, and which may be found in the very earliest records of the Chinese, still exists an active, though quite unauthorized, system of adoration, the objects of which are, manifold and indiscriminate.

For instance, tree-worship may be found in China, as distinct in its character as that which existed in the olden days of Britain, when the chief Druid cut the sacred mistletoe from the hoary oak with a golden sickle. The favorite deity, or numen, of this worship is identified with the banyantree or sung shu, and his title is the Banyan Prince. It is affirmed that age has much to do with the divinity or " spiritual efficacy," to use the Chinese term, of this noble tree. The older it grows, the more it increases in spirituality, and the greater honor is paid to it. The chief seat of its worship is said to be Amoy, and some doubt exists whether it is worshipped in any other place. The peach-tree, again, is held in considerable veneration, it having been asserted that no Chinese will venture to burn its wood, lest the spirit which inhabits it should visit his displeasure upon them by an attack of madness. This tree, as we have already seen, is regarded as the symbol of longevity and marriage bliss. It occupies a prominent position in the mysticism of the Taoists, and the Fairy Mother of the West is said to have had one remarkable specimen in her garden which bore once only in three thousand years. Another tree which is superstitiously esteemed in China is that called the wutung shu, identified by Williams with the Elaococca, verrucosa. This is said to occupy a position in this land analogous to that of the oak in England. It is the national tree of China; it is much admired for its stately appearance, as well as for the lightness, durability, and fineness of its wood, and venerated as being the chosen roosting-place of the mysterious phoenix or feng huang, whenever that august bird condescends to pay a visit to the country. It is common enough in Japan, where its wood is used for boxes. But trees are not the only objects of this quasi-worship. Serpents are held sacred too, and are connected in the Chinese mind with the famous deity known as Hsiian T'ien Shang Ti, or Supreme Euler of the Somber Heavens, who is generally represented as using one as a footstool. It is not more than twelve years ago that Li Hung-chang himself fell prostrate before an insignificant water-snake, beseeching it to intercede with the great River Dragon to prevent another overflow of the Yellow River. " Five serpents," wrote an cbserver, about the same time that this truly pitiable spectacle took place, "of very large dimensions, such as are found sometimes among the mountains, and which are said to be over a thousand years old, are worshipped in Fukien with very great reverence. These are believed to have the power of transforming themselves into human shape when they have some fell purpose to execute on man. I have known a case where thousands of men and women have gathered round a serpent that had been killed by the roadside, and have worshipped it for nearly a month. The worship stopped only when it was found that the report of its efficacy to heal disease, &c., was untrue." Tortoises and turtles also enjoy an amount of reverence above most other crawling things; indeed, tortoise-worship may be said to have a somewhat extensive literature of its own, and dates back as far as 2900 years before the Christian era. Hedgehogs, too, have a faint aroma of sanctity about them, though we never heard that porcupines were similarly favored; while even rats and mice are regarded with more reverence than they deserve by a few misguided polytheists. We confess to some feeling of surprise at having been assured that the members of that most respectable sect of native teetotallers, the Tsai-li Hui, or Fellowship of Reason, are addicted to these foolish forms of worship. There is no doubt that the Fellowship has decidedly degenerated during the last few years, both in ethical purity and reputation; but it is to be hoped that a veneration for vermin is not reckoned among the signs of its decadence. Perhaps the most dreaded of the brutedeities in China is the fox, which has the power of transforming itself into the likeness of a beautiful woman, and so deceiving the unwary. This superstition is probably universal, and was made use of in the Peking Gazette about a year ago in order to screen some faithless eunuchs suspected of complicity in stealing certain objects of value from the imperial palace. Fox-myths, in fact, are to be found well-nigh the whole world over, and nowhere are they so deeply rooted in the minds of the people as in China and Japan. It is the favorite plea of some gay Lothario who has not come home overnight, and presents himself haggard and pale the following day to his anxious family, that he was un-lucky enough on his way home the previous evening to meet and be deluded by a " fox."

CHAPTER 15. THE SOPHISTS OF CHINA

THE philosophers of Greece and the philosophers of China are all more or less familiar even to those whose reading on such subjects is superficial. Everybody of ordinary education knows something, at any rate, of Socrates, Plato, and Aristotle; and most people, at all events in China, have a rough acquaintance with the names of Confucius, Mencius, and Lao-tzu. But while the great teachers who have founded schools of thought have now a world-wide fame, the empirics who opposed them in their day have fallen into something very much like oblivion. And yet the Sophists did good service. Superficial prattlers though they were, confessedly arguing for the mere love of argument, and playing with logic much as a clever conjurer plays with peas and thimbles, it cannot be denied that they encouraged the exercise of independent thought, and afforded considerable assistance in bringing the art of ratiocination to perfection. Their very sophisms afforded material for true philosophers to work upon, and the exposure of their clever fallacies was a favorite and by no means unproductive pastime even among those whose object was more to discover truth than to juggle successfully with words. A study of Plato's Dialogues is all that is necessary to prove the justice of this assertion, for it is to Sophists that we owe some of the finest exhibitions of dialectical skill that the Greek philosophers have bequeathed to us.

Now, just as there were Sophists during the golden age of philosophy in Greece, so were there Sophists, or " garrulous quibblers," as the Chinese call them, during the golden age of philosophy in China. And, as we shall prove, the two classes of men bore a very striking family resemblance to each other, even to the point of advancing almost the same theories and attempting to prove the same paradoxes. Most of our readers are no doubt familiar with the famous fallacies which the Greek Sophists loved to fabricate. " That is my dog. That dog is a father. Therefore, that dog is my father." " If, when you speak the truth, you say you lie, you lie; but you say you lie when you speak the truth; therefore in speaking the truth you lie." " Bread is better than nothing. Nothing is better than Elysium. Therefore bread is better than Elysium." Such were the word-quibbles in the production of which the sophistical quacks of Greece delighted about the time of Socrates; and when we turn to the corresponding period in China we find very much the same phenomenon existing here. There was one very famous Sophist named Hui Shih, who is attacked in a spirited and lively style by Chuang-tzii, himself regarded as a Sophist by the orthodox followers of Confucius. " The works of Hui Shih," says his critic, " are numerous and extensive; he has published a great collection of books. But his doctrines are unpractical and contradictory, and his words do not hit the mark; he says just what comes uppermost, without regard to accuracy, affirming that that which is unsurpassably great, and outside which there is nothing, is the Great Unit; and that that which is infinitesimally small, and inside which there is nothing, is the Atom. He says that the whole universe may be filled with matter even though there be no foundation for anything to rest upon; that heaven is no higher than the earth; that a mountain is as level as a pool; that sunset is the same as the meridian, in that one is the result of the other; that life comes from death, and death from life; that general resemblance is different from resemblance in details, and that this detailed resemblance should there-fore be called a difference, while the final resemblances and differences in the universe only amount to saying that the differences are less than the resemblances." Hui Shih is said to have looked upon all this as a very fine performance, about which all his fellow-Sophists delighted to talk and argue. These men would undertake to prove a variety of absurdities for instance, that there is no heat in fire; that the eye does not see; that a wheel does not triturate the ground; that when you have arrived at the farthest extreme there is nothing to prevent your going farther still; that there is hair upon an egg; that if the half of a stick a foot long be cut off every day, it will take ten thousand generations till there is nothing left. Chuang-tzii condemns all this as so much foolish, wordy babble, saying that the Sophists would argue with each other in a circle ceaselessly, puzzling people's minds to no purpose, and simply bent on showing off their own cleverness in disputation. His criticism on the arch-Sophist Hui Shih is dignified and to the point. "He talks away about everything without reflecting; the more he talks the farther he is from finishing. If he were to confine his attention to one thing only, it would be well enough; then he might be said, by his additional reverence for truth, to have almost attained to it. But the man is incapable of thus setting his mind at rest; he diffuses his mental powers abroad over everything without getting any satisfaction; he just acquires a reputation for controversial skill, and nothing more. Alas for the talents of Hui Shih! He employs them lavishly enough, yet reaps no advantage; he pries into everything, but never thinks of penetrating to the root of anything; he is like a body which runs after its own shadow in hopes to catch it up and stop it." It is difficult to realize that there used actually to be men in this stolid, conservative country, this stronghold of platitudinarian orthodoxy, to whom such a description was applicable. Yet here is the proof of it; and not only were their methods analogous to those of the Greek Sophists, but the theories they advanced were very similar too. The arguments of the Sophist Gorgias on the mysteries of existence remind one very curiously of the speculations which Chuang-tzii puts into the mouth of the God of the Northern Sea. The aim of Gorgias is to prove that nothing exists; that if anything does exist, it cannot be an object of know-ledge; and that if even anything exists and can be known, it cannot be imparted to others. If anything is, says Gorgias, as quoted by Sextus Empiricus, it must be either being or non-being, or even at one and the same time both being and non-being. All these cases are impossible; for a non-being cannot be, because it is the opposite of being; and therefore, if the latter is, the former cannot be; because if it were, it must be at the same time being and non-being. Chuang-tzu's North-Sea God is similarly paradoxical and abstruse. " What is said to exist," he argues, " is so spoken of because it does exist; and, if so, there ' is nothing in the universe that does not exist. Similarly, what is said not to exist is so spoken of because it does not exist; and, if so, there is nothing in the universe which is not non-existent." This follows close upon the enunciation of a theory which is not without its bearing upon both speculative and practical mathematics. The argument is, briefly, as follows: " Subtlety is the occult part of the minute. Be a thing subtle or gross, it seems to me that it must have a form. A formless or unsubstantial thing cannot be distinguished as gross or subtle, discriminate as minutely as you will. What can be spoken of is the gross or palpable part of an entity; what can be imagined only is its subtle part or essence; but I take it that what is neither gross nor subtle can neither be talked of nor imagined." Some time ago there died, at Peking, the greatest Chinese mathematician of the present century. His name was Li Shan-Ian, and he was Professor of Mathematics at the T'ung Wen Kuan. But he differed from the mathematicians of Europe in this respect, that he denied the non-existence of a point. A point, said Professor Li, is an infinitesimally small cube; and in saying so he only reproduced the theories put into the mouth of the sophistical God of the Northern Sea, two thousand years ago, by Chuang-tzii.

CHAPTER 16. PORTENTS

THE prevalent belief in China respecting the connection between physical phenomena and political events has been productive of at any rate one good result. It has induced the Chinese to keep rigid and, in a measure, accurate records of all events of a striking nature in both astronomy and meteorology, and these cannot but be of value to historians and scientific men alike. If a comet is said to have appeared on a certain day in a certain portion of the heavens, a simple astronomical calculation will at once guide the student of Chinese history to the discovery of some important date which may give the required clue to many a disputed point in the science of chronology. Similarly the record of-geological up-heavals, over-flowings of the Yellow River or the Yang-tzii, and such-like disturbances, places a valuable key in the hands of those who study the land of China from a physical or scientific standpoint. It may be left to curious and speculative minds to range through the dim corridors of Chinese history and try to find the corresponding political event of which the physical occurrence was supposed to be the portent. Such a compilation would be more interesting, perhaps, than useful; in any case, the task does not come within our province. Let us content ourselves with recapitulating some of the more important natural events that have occurred in China during the past two thousand years. Many of these ap-pear at first sight to partake of the apocryphal; but there is no doubt that much that appeared miraculous, and therefore portentous, in the days of Chou, Tsin, and Han was explicable enough, had there only been the requisite amount of natural philosophy at hand to bear upon it. For instance, we read of " red rain " having fallen in the neighborhoods of Nanking and K'ai-fe'ng Fu in the years 300 and 1336 A.D., when the Western Tsin and Yuen dynasties held sway. The water which fell is said to have stained cloth with the color of blood; and even in our own day, some seven or eight years ago, the same phenomenon was reported as having occurred in certain districts of Kiang-si. The explanation of this is probably as simple as that of the red snow mentioned by Aristotle, and observed in recent times in the polar and alpine regions. Black rain as black as ink fell, according to native chroniclers, during the reign of Hung Wu, the first Emperor of the Mings; and the river Yang-tzu is credited with having suddenly assumed a crimson hue on more than one occasion. These phenomena, it must be confessed, are not so easy of explanation. It is possible that they may have grown out of some metaphorical expression too deep to be understanded of the people; though there is no reason why critics who believe in a similar metamorphosis anciently recorded of the river Nile should hesitate to accept a story which attributes the same marvel to the Yang-tzii.

The principal scourges to which China seems to have been subject, about which there can be no doubt, are famines, droughts, inundations, and the ravages of insects. These are said to have been of constant and almost regular recurrence. Earthquakes, though apparently not doing any great mischief, except in one instance when the marble pillars of the Emperor's palace were thrown down in the reign of Hsiao Wu Ti, of the Eastern Tsin dynasty, appear to have occurred more frequently than is generally supposed to have been the case in China. Far greater are the ravages that have been caused by storms. These have constantly destroyed the crops of entire districts in a few hours, and are described as violent in the extreme, having been frequently accompanied with thunderbolts and showers of destructive hail. Indeed, it seems wonderful that the unfortunate people ever reaped any harvests at all, when we read the list of forces arrayed against them. If there were no inundations, sweeping away the produce of their fields, to say nothing of the houses in which they lived and occasionally the men themselves, there was pretty sure to be a drought; or if not a drought, a swarm of grasshoppers or of locusts would devastate the plains, selecting, as, with a sort of infernal instinct, such creatures do, the richest and most fertile districts as their prey. The sufferings of the people in such fatal years are said to have reduced them frequently to cannibalism. They preyed upon each other; they fed themselves on corpses. On three occasions an army of rats invaded the country. In one instance these insatiable vermin, travelling from one place to another, attempted a passage of the Wei river, and were fortunately drowned, their carcasses choking up the banks of the stream for several days after their destruction. On the other occasion, however, they were more successful. Myriads of the creatures appeared in the neighborhood of Nanking from the Hu-kuang provinces. They are said to have crossed the brooks and rivers in their course during the night by making themselves into a moving bridge, each animal seizing the tail of the one in front of him with his teeth, and so swimming across; and on arrival at the other side they threw themselves upon the crops and devoured them. Another time they effected the passage of the Yellow Kiver. Among the minor plagues of China, in times past, are recorded thick yellow fogs, described in terms that would do full justice to the November fogs in London; excess of snow in winter; cold, biting winds in the summer months; violent gales, sometimes so charged with dust as to render it impossible to distinguish a man two paces off; hailstones as large as a man's fist; groanings and rumblings underground, and under the waters of the Yellow River; and an occasional landslip. In the year 5 of Cheng Te of the Ming dynasty we read of a rain of earth, which was no doubt a dust-storm of preternatural violence, and on various other occasions of the appearance on the ground of dew as sweet as sugar to the taste. Only two years ago we heard of " summer snow " having fallen near Soochow, and the terror of the people in consequence. It is not often that we hear of pestilence, although in the reign of the last Ming Emperors one occurred of such severity that it is said there were not enough survivors to bury the dead, and that a few years earlier the roads were blocked up with corpses; all of which is no doubt greatly exaggerated. Still, it would be difficult to point out which of the Ten Plagues of Egypt has not visited the Chinese, according to their own account, in one form or another, and each such visitation is regarded by them as a separate and distinct indication of the displeasure of Heaven.

CHAPTER 17. FEATHER-BRUSHES

THERE is, perhaps, nothing for which an educated Chinese feels such keen appreciation as what is called a kutien, or historical allusion, wherever or in whatever shape it may present itself. It would be a mistake to suppose that the kutien is only found in literary compositions, although the more elegant and accomplished the writer the more fully adorned will be his essay with references to the events of old as found in the early essayists and poets of China. Just as the naturalist may see in the fully developed organ of an animal the evolutionary product of the embryo which existed in that animal's remote ancestor thousands of years ago, so will the Chinese scholar recognize in a fan or trinket the descendant, degenerate enough, per-haps, but still legitimate, of some forgotten progenitor of the past. It needs no unusual erudition even in Western life, for instance, to see in our modern habit of nodding to an acquaintance a relic of the complete .prostrations that were performed in ancient times, or in the gold-topped cane a civilized form of the ponderous bludgeon once wielded by our forefathers in Scandinavia. Now there is no commoner object in any house in China, foreign or native, than the feather-brush. It is not very ornamental, nor is it so practically useful, perhaps, as the homely cotton duster used by the ingenuous housemaids of England. Its principal value to the Chinese " boy " lies in the fact of its being a regular and unfailing means of squeezing his master to the extent of at least half a dollar or so a month. That, however, by the way. Even when not thus misused, it occupies what may be called a subordinate, if not menial, position in the household. But it has a history an ancestry. There was a time when the feather-brush or its remote progenitor, to speak more accurately had not been put to the base use of dusting furniture in the remarkably imperfect manner practiced by the A-choys and A-lings of modern days. It bore a part, and a very honorable part, in the ancient chivalry of China, being no less than a recognized standard for the mustering of soldiers to battle. An allusion is made to it by Chuang-tzu, the St. Paul of Taoism, two hundred years before Christ, who tells us that when the great military leader Sun, standing on an eminence which overlooked the plain, waved on high his plume of feathers, the men of the State of Ying rushed with one accord into the field and put themselves in battle array. It was, in fact, an ancient military signal, and used, perhaps, much as a flag is used to-day, as a sign for mustering; a bell being struck where now we brandish the flag of truce. There is something strange in the fact of an instrument so honorable being degraded from the battle-field to the boudoir; but the poets of China view the matter hi a vastly different light. It appears to have been a certain Empress who first laid her fair hand upon this old emblem of chivalry, and appropriated it to the use of the " inner chambers; " and high compliments were paid Her Majesty on the occasion by the carpet-knights and versifiers of the Court. But the task of doing so must have taxed the poetic resources of these gentlemen to no ordinary degree. Truth must out; and we are bound to confess that this pretty little bit of history is some-what tarnished by the reason assigned for the imperial depredation. The fact seems to be, that the Empress wanted something to switch away the insects which infested her apartments. We must not be too severe upon Her Majesty. Our own kings and archbishops swarmed with vermin centuries after the Chinese Empress, in desperation, apparently, at the lively condition of her floors, laid hands upon the martial semaphore and turned it into a weapon of defense against the hopping hosts by which the palace was invaded. Then it became a fashionable article of use and ornament, and a lively trade in the feather-brush sprang up, ably fostered by the Government. It was made generally of actual feathers, and this kind was, and is now, used for dusting furniture. Other sorts, however, were made of horsehair, and these were often placed in the hands of sick persons to wave about and prevent gnats and mosquitoes from annoying them as they lay in bed. It is even possible to see people at the present day walking about and laying about them right and left at their minute assailants. The writer once spent some weeks in the monastery of a certain Buddhist priest, a portly, full-fed abbot, who was never seen without a bright-green horse-tail, which he used constantly to keep his saintly person free from flies. Indeed, the graceful waving and manipulation of a feather-brush or horse-tail is cultivated as an art, and forms part of the stock-intrade of many a Chinese petit maitre. But the rami-fications of this subject are too numerous to be followed out in detail on the present occasion. We might describe the use to which the instrument is put as a head-dress; for there are pictures to be seen in which an actual feather-brush is represented as worn on the top of the head, very much in the same way as a soldier wears a plume. The digression, however, would lead to others, and we must forego it. We will only add that the feather-duster has been made of use on several occasions to point a moral, if not adorn a tale, by Chinese moralists, imperial and other. "The superior man renews himself day by day; " " The sage incessantly shakes the dust of the world from off him; " " The purity of the soul can only be preserved by perpetual care; " such are some of the virtuous if somewhat platitudinarian aphorisms which have been taken from the writings of the ancients, and playfully used by modern essayists to reflect on brooms and feather-brushes all the grace and dignity which cluster round the pages of classic lore.

CHAPTER 18. THE SEVEN WONDERS OF COREA

THE love of the marvelous, which forms so distinguishing a characteristic of all Eastern and a few Western nations, recently led a Japanese editor to regale his readers with a vivid account of the wonders of Corea. We are no longer told of golden sarcophagi and royal tombs bursting with inexhaustible treasures. That fable seems to have died out, and in its place we are assured that Corea is a land where Nature, and not art, has played some of her strangest freaks. The Seven Wonders of the Old World were all the works of men. The Seven Wonders of Corea are natural or, as we suppose we ought to say, supernatural. It is a beautiful and fertile land, and it would, perhaps, be strange if no myths were found to be associated with the mountains and forests and rivers which diversify its aspect. The graceful superstitions of classic Greece find but few analogues in the Ear East. There is nothing in the mythology of China to compare with them in point of imagery or aesthetic beauty. The naiads and dryads which played at hide-and-seek amid the bosky dells and woodland scenery of the Peloponnesus may be said to have had a few distant relations in the mythology of Chinese fairy-tales, but the relationship was exceedingly remote. There is not wanting, however, even there, in those prosaic Eastern lands, much in the way of folk-lore that is worthy of attention, especially when the legends are of such a nature as to attract the traveler, and induce him to visit the scenes of the alleged marvels himself. Briefly, the Seven Wonders of Corea are as follow. The first is a certain hot mineral spring near a place called Kinshantao, the healing properties of which are believed to be miraculous. There is no necessity to wait until an angel troubles the water. Its virtues are in constant vigor, and so great are they that they have never failed in efficacy within the memory of man. No matter what disease may afflict the patient, a dip in these healing waters will prove as sure a cure as the bath in Jordan did to leprous Naaman. Therefore, the spring is believed to be divine, and is spoken of accordingly. The second wonder is also connected with water. There are two springs, situated at a considerable distance from each other in fact, there is almost the breadth of the entire peninsula between them. These have two peculiarities. They are arranged, apparently, on the principle of the " littleman-and-his-wife " of those cottage barometers which are still seen in primitive parts of England. When one is in, the other goes out; or, in plainer words, when one is full, the other is empty; and the Coreans seem to believe that, somewhere deep in the bowels of the earth, there is a mysterious tide, which ebbs and flows with marvelous rapidity at stated intervals of time, filling one spring while it empties the other. But the strangest part of the phenomenon is, that the water is so strongly sweet that whatever is cooked in it, no matter how bad it may be of itself, immediately acquires a most delicious taste. The third is called Cold-wind Cavern. This is a cave somewhere in the mountains, in which a mysterious wind blows perpetually a wind so cold as to pierce to the very bones, and so strong that the most powerful man is unable to stand against it. There is something like this to be found in the Western Hills near Peking. Among the ruins of an old temple on the hillside there is a little cave, quite open to the air, and at the farther end of it a hole, opening apparently into the earth, up which rushes a strong blast of cold wind. The entire cave is several degrees colder than the surrounding atmosphere, and the line which divides the two temperatures is very precisely denned. The fourth wonder of Corea is the Ineradicable Forest. This is a large grove of pine-trees, which sprout again directly they are cut down. It matters not what injury is done to the root; the tree may be hacked to pieces or burnt with fire nothing will avail to destroy it, but up it will sprout again in no time, like a phoenix from its own ashes.

The fifth wonder is more wonderful still. This is the Floating Stone, and a temple has been reared in its honor, called the Fou Shih Miao. In front of the temple stands, or appears to stand, the extraordinary stone. It is of great bulk, and a sort of irregular cube in shape. To all appearance it is resting on the ground, and perfectly free from all supports on any side. But if two men, standing at opposite ends of it, hold each the opposite ends of a thread, they will find themselves able to pass the thread wider the stone without encountering any obstacle! In other words, the stone is actually hovering a little way above the earth, and the miracle can be tested in the way described by anybody who cares to pay the priest a trifling sum for the privilege of doing so. The sixth wonder also consists of a stone, but a stone of a more practically useful nature. It is called the Warm Rock very flat and smooth, and forms the summit of a hill upon which there is a pavilion or kiosque for the benefit of travelers. Here they may rest and pass the night. However cold the weather may be, there is no stove, nor any need for one; the stone on which the rest-house stands diffuses its wonderful and benign warmth through every room in it, and the poorest may bask in its comfort. About the seventh wonder we believe that some slight uncertainty exists. There are two objects which are both entitled to the honor. One is simply a relic of Sakya " Julai " the Buddha who thus comes in the form of a small chest or case of exquisitely fine workmanship. This is to be seen in a temple somewhere near the sea. The other is far more extraordinary, and we think there should not be a doubt of its claim to " wonder "-ship. It is a drop of the sweat of Buddha. Around the large temple where it is enshrined, for thirty paces square, not a blade of grass will grow; there are no trees, no flowers; the very birds and animals desert it, instinctively recoiling from profaning with their foot-falls a plot of ground so holy. The association of ideas is not particularly happy, for the more natural impression would be that the presence of a relic of so benign a personage would have had a genial and fertilizing effect, and instead of a bare blank patch we should have looked for a lovely oasis, gay with lotuses and summer flowers, and full of the song and gambols of those innocent creatures, the protection of whose helplessness forms so distinctive a feature of the gentle teachings of Julai.

CHAPTER 19. CHINA'S GREATEST TYRANT

CHINA may justly be said, in many ways, to be the country of pretensions. There are few things in which the Chinese do not claim pre-eminence, and it is this habit of self-complacency which renders them so very much averse to being enlightened on those points on which they habitually are found wanting. The belief in their own infallibility cannot but be a standing obstacle to the progress of the people in all departments where it prevails, and the difficulty of getting a Chinaman to acknowledge that he is beaten in an argument is but another phase of the same phenomenon. It is a sufficient answer, for him, that, however useless or hurtful a given practice may be, it is the " custom " of the country; and the belief that all the customs which have descended from generation to generation are, for that very reason, incapable of improvement, renders him a very hopeless subject to deal with.

A very few illustrations will, we think, suffice to prove the justice of this remark. In no country, for instance, are morals more highly esteemed as a basis of public administration and private conduct. Nothing could be more unexceptionable than the theories on which the government of the country is professedly carried on.

Foreign writers have over and over again applauded the Chinese for resting all their rules of life on right reason, and bringing to the test of principle, rather than to that of material welfare or advantage, their general policy of action. In spite of this, China is one of the most miser-ably misgoverned countries in the whole world. There is, perhaps, no place where peculation is rifer, or more unblushingly carried on. Considering, for instance, the unrivalled estimation in which literature and education are held by both governors and governed, it is astounding to read in the official gazette the gross impositions which are practiced every year at the public examinations. Then the innocent are being constantly plundered by the rich and powerful, and although false accusations, made with a view to extorting money, do sometimes recoil upon the guilty parties, it too often happens that the only recompense received by the victim takes the form of an honorable burial for his corpse. The high position accorded to agriculture in China might naturally lead us to look for corresponding results in the fruits and vegetables that are cultivated, and to some sound principles as actuating the Chinese farmer or market-gardener in his work. But what is the state of matters here? China scarcely produces a fruit worth eating. The apples are soft and woolly, the pears not nearly so toothsome as a good turnip, the peaches are full of worms, and all, fruits and vegetables alike, are inferior, tasteless, and poor. The Chinese laborer has no idea of manipulating the ground. He contents himself with scratching its surface, and then deluges it with liquid manure. Of what may be called agricultural chemistry he never heard; still, he fancies that he has no more to learn, for has not the soil of China been dealt with in the self-same manner for centuries, and could he be so unfilial as to improve upon the methods of his forefathers? The Chinese have acquired some celebrity in point of manual skill. They will carve wonderful balls of ivory one inside the other, and expend no small amount of time and ingenuity in the production of articles of taste. But is there a locksmith in China who can pick a lock without spoiling it, or make the commonest appliance in wood or metal which shall compare with the work of a European artificer, or do what it is intended to do? It seems that the farther we go in our observation of Chinese capabilities, in whatsoever direction, the more essentially inferior we find them. The fact is, that, having reached a certain stage of development, the Chinese have rested content, and have never progressed since. If we accept Mr. Herbert Spencer's definition of Progress, that it is the evolution of the heterogeneous from the homogeneous, we must conclude that the Chinese have no experience of progress themselves at all. , Their thought, as a nation, is essentially homogeneous. The slightest divergence towards the heterogeneous is shunned and execrated as incipient heresy. They never ask the why or the where-fore of a fact; suffice it for them that such a thing exists that such a custom is followed, such a theory held and it would never occur to a Chinese to inquire into the reason of it, or to test its truth. Innovations are regarded with suspicion almost amounting to horror; and no arguments have any force to a Chinese mind in proving the elementary and insufficient nature of the methods so long in vogue. It is, indeed, undeniable that the Chinese are bound hand and foot by custom. This is often amusingly exemplified in little every-day matters. A high military mandarin, handsomely appareled, comes riding by on a filthy, spavined little horse that was never combed, perhaps, since it was foaled. To the natural question of a foreigner, "Why don't you groom your horses? " the reply comes, prompt and conclusive, " It is not our custom." Tell a farmer how he may render a naturally unfruitful soil fertile, or improve the flavor of his fruits, or achieve greater results at the cost of less labor by the use of finer implements; he will only stare, and tell you it is not their "custom." Ask a school-master why he forces tiny children to learn by rote a number of abstruse books he does not pretend to understand himself, and why he does not explain those which are capable of explanation; whether he does not think a child would be more benefited by learning something of the world in which he lives than by gabbling over the meaningless formulae of the Yih Cking, and be better fitted for the business of life by a little knowledge of arithmetic than by a parrot-familiarity with the conversations between Mencius and King Hui of Liang; he will raise his eyebrows in amazement, and contemptuously reply that such is not their " custom." No real progress can result from such petrifaction of the intellect; a fossil cannot grow. And the disease, as we have pointed out, exists in every department of life: in education, in government, in mechanics, in agriculture, in society. It will cost a mighty effort to free the Chinese from these bonds and ligatures, which have held them in durance vile so long. Naturally utilitarian, they seem to have been despoiled of all power of putting their utilitarianism into practice, and to fall back, in a shiftless way, upon " custom " as their final court of appeal in everything. There is a movement now, as we all know; but at present it is confined to a very few persons who have had the benefit of foreign intercourse and education, and it will be long before it spreads over the masses in the interior of China.

CHAPTER 20. THE FLOWER -FAIRIES: A TAOIST FAIRY-TALE

"At close of day my cottage door

Is barred by the wind and rain; The blossoms fall in a crimson shower No denizens of my maiden bower

But willow-leaves, remain; In sweet disorder they lie strewed,

While zephyrs and breezes toss; And never shall gardener's besom rude Among their rosy ranks intrude,

As they lie on the verdant moss."

Introduction

According to a certain delightful Chinese story-book, called Rare Events in Ancient and Modern Times, which has afforded us many a pleasant hour of relaxation in the midst of graver studies, there flourished, in the T'ang dynasty, a retired scholar whose name was Ch'ui Hsuan-wei. He was one of those amiable recluses who, though professedly misanthropic, are by no means averse to such pleasures as appeal to their peculiar tastes an Epicurean, if you will, certainly not a Stoic, but a man who, keeping aloof from the madding crowd, sought no other companionship than that of his books and flowers. He was never married; the presence of another human creature would have taken the edge off the exquisite flavor of his enjoyments. Even his servants lived outside, and no one was admitted on any pretext but that of urgent business. He loved to pore over those deep, bold volumes of Taoist philosophy which Lao-tzu, Chuang-tzu, and the other masters of that school have bequeathed to an ungrateful posterity, and which are now regarded by the bigoted Confucianists as the embodiments of all that is heterodox and wrong; but his dearest pleasure was in the cultivation of his magnificent garden, to the laying out of which he had devoted thirty years of his voluptuous but innocent existence. His mansion stood surrounded by flowers by a splendid wilderness of flowers gleaming with all those gorgeous colors which only skilful culture can produce, and flourishing on all sides with a luxuriance past conception. In this floral paradise he reigned alone and supreme. He tended his precious flowers with the solicitude of a nurse and the homage of a devotee; while the only sorrows that ever reached him were such as resulted from the blighting of a geranium or the death of a favorite rose.

Having lived for many years in this state of philosophic indolence which is extolled by Taoist writers as the summit of all obtainable happiness and wisdom an event occurred which seriously interrupted the noise-less tenor of his way. It was " blue night." The moon shone with unexampled splendor, pouring its silvery effulgence over the garden, and spiritualizing every twig and leaf with liquid lustre. Absolute quiet reigned in the little paradise; not a breath of air was heard; and the philosopher was utterly unable to tear himself away from the bewitching influences around him. As he stood, silent and absorbed, a shadow seemed to flit among the flowers. It was a bluish shadow, and it appeared to be advancing stealthily, as if afraid of being seen. The philosopher strained his eyes and rubbed them, to make sure that it was not a dream. Suddenly the figure of a woman, dressed in a long robe of pale blue, emerged from among the flowery thicket, and moved slowly towards him. By this time the good man was transfixed to the spot with awe. Collecting his senses as best he could, he gasped out an inquiry as to who his mysterious visitor was; but still on she carne, silently and noiselessly, saluting him courteously with her graceful head as she approached.

"Who are you? " burst out the philosopher at last. The spell was broken, and he was himself again.

"My dwelling is not very far from yours," replied the Lady of the Azure Kobe, opening a pair of vermilion lips and disclosing two rows of teeth as white and glistening as jade. " As I was passing on with my attendants to visit a relative, I felt a longing to rest a while in this beautiful garden of yours; but," added the maiden demurely, " I did not feel quite sure whether you would permit me to do so."

Hsuan-wei thought that it was altogether the most extraordinary thing that had ever happened to him; but such was the fascination of his visitor that he consented with delight. The princess for such she seemed to be overwhelmed him with thanks and retired; and in a few minutes returned, bringing with her a bevy of the loveliest girls that ever blessed the eyes of sinful man. The philosopher looked attentively at them in the pale, bright moonlight. Some were carrying flowers, others willow-boughs; all were of the most exquisite and seductive beauty, and of surpassingly voluptuous grace; but no two were in any way alike. On they trooped, filling the moonlit garden with fair forms; while the bewildered recluse gazed wonderingly at the strange scene, marveling within himself whence they had all come. At last he recollected himself sufficiently to invite them to enter his pavilion; and when they were all seated he found that he could restrain his curiosity no longer.

"Ladies," he said, " I cannot express my delight at your arrival, unexpected as it is; but I do beg you to tell me at least what your names are, and what relative it is that you are in search of, that you have suddenly invaded my poor domains with your bright presences in the very dead of night."

Then arose a maiden in a green robe, and announced that her name was Aspen. Pointing to one in a white robe, " And hers," she said, " is Plum; the one in a purple garment is named Peach; " and so she went on, presenting them one after another, till she came to a little girl in a crimson robe, whose name, she said, was Pomegranate. " But although we have all different names," added the maiden, " we are all sisters, and all live together. Now the Lady Wind, who is our maternal aunt eighteen times removed, said some days ago that she was coming to visit us; but she has never done so; and as the moon is unusually brilliant to-night, we sisters are going to visit her instead. So we thought that, as you have always been such a dear friend and protector to us, we should like to pay you a call on our way; and here we are, you see! "

Hsuan-wei was just about to make a suitable reply when in came the Lady of the Azure Kobe, and announced the arrival of the Lady Wind. This caused a tremendous flutter among the girls, who all hastened out to welcome her. The philosopher stepped on one side, where he could peep at what was going on without being seen. When the ladies of the many-tinted robes had all made their obeisance, one of them said

"We were just on the way to visit you, but this kind host detained us " which was a very artful way of putting it. " We never thought you were so near at hand. However, we have met, and that is the purpose we both had."

"I have been coming to see you for a long while," replied the Lady Wind, " but I have had a great deal to do lately. This is the first time I have had any leisure at all, and you see that I have come at once."

"It is a clear and glorious night," rejoined the girl; " stay and rest with us a while, and we will keep your birthday." Then, turning to the Lady of the Azure Robe, she begged her to procure some wine.

"But may we stay in this place? " inquired the Lady Wind.

"Why not? " replied the lady who had introduced herself by the name of Aspen. " The owner is a kind and worthy man, and the place itself is charming."

"But where is the owner? " asked the new arrival.

Then Hsuan-wei started out of his hiding-place, and, lifting his eyes, beheld the Lady Wind. Her form was graceful, and had a certain gauzy, floating appearance, like a gossamer; but her words were cold, like the breath that plays among the leaves of a forest; and when Hsuan-wei stood near her a chill struck him to the bone, so that he shivered from head to foot. However, he invited her into the pavilion, where the attendant sylphs had set out materials for an exquisite repast. He placed the Lady Wind in the seat of honor, and all the others took their ranks in order. In a twinkling the table was covered with delicious viands and jars of fragrant wine as luscious as the purest honey. The moon increased in splendor, till the room was as bright as day; rich perfumes rose into the air, sweet and heavy, permeating the persons of the revelers; host and guests drank to each other repeatedly; cups and goblets were mixed together on the table, presenting a scene of most luxurious confusion. At last, when the fumes of the wine were beginning to take effect, a sylph in a red robe filled a huge goblet to the brim and presented it to the Lady Wind, saying, " I have a song to sing to you." Upon which she broke forth as follows:

"The gauzy robe, worn carelessly,

Displays the charms within, Pink as cosmetic's artful dye

On lip and cheek and chin; But ah! the bloom will fade away,

The ruby tint grow pale; The winds of spring last not for aye

Who would their loss bewail.

The singer's voice was sweet and winning, but the listeners seemed to have no great relish for the burden of her song; whereupon a sylph in a white robe presented another goblet to the Lady Wind, saying, " I have also a song, which I will let you hear."

"She is pure as the priceless jade, whiter than driven snow; Luminous as the lovely moon shining on flow'rs below; Sighing and singing a sorrowful song, as the sweet spring zephyrs die

Who would reproach them with more than a murmured 'Adieu! ' as they fly?
And so when her flowery beauty, like all around, decays, She sighs and smiles unconsciously, and dreams of the bygone
days."

The strains of this song were somewhat melancholy; indeed they were almost harrowing. Now the Lady Wind, if the truth must be told, was of a very flighty and frivolous disposition; and, what was w6rse, she was very fond of wine, and had drunk so many cups that she became quite ungovernable, and began to act in a most extravagant and silly way. When, therefore, she had listened to these two songs, she exclaimed

"How is it that, on this auspicious occasion, when we are all enjoying ourselves, and delighting in the beautiful view, you sing such sorrowful stuff as this? Besides, the meaning is too obscure for anybody to understand; it's an insult to all the company! "

Whereupon she condemned the two unfortunate song-stresses to pay forfeit by drinking a large cup of wine apiece, and said that they would have to sing again. But as she was handing them the cups, it was proved only too plainly that she had taken too many herself; her hands shook so that she could not grasp them securely, and suddenly she lost her hold of them altogether. Crash they went, and the wine flowed all over poor little Pomegranate. Now little Pomegranate was very young and very pretty, and had always been very fond of gay clothes. On this occasion she had on a brand new embroidered crimson robe, which she was naturally very anxious to keep from wine-stains, as the slightest drop would spoil the color; and now she was covered with it from head to foot! Unfortunately, too, she had had a little more than was good for her already; and when she saw her dress ruined, she flushed with anger, and cried

"Sisters! you are all for courting this aunt of ours, eighteen times removed; but I am not afraid of her, and you may just court her for the future by yourselves."

Then she got up and left the room. The Lady Wind flew into a terrible rage, and exclaiming, " That little girl has found the wine too much for her, in daring to insult me so," she gathered up her robes and prepared to depart. All the sylphs implored her not to go away, but without avail. Then they tried to calm her anger, saying, " Pomegranate is very young, and just now is not quite herself; pray forget what she has done, and to-morrow we will bring her to beg pardon." As, however, nothing would appease the Lady Wind, they accompanied her to the door, and off she flounced in high dudgeon towards the east. Then the sylphs trooped back, and, taking a graceful leave of their entertainer, moved towards a place where the flowers grew thickest, and disappeared.

Up sprang the philosopher, and gave chase. But in his hurry his foot slipped, and he fell sprawling upon his back; and when he picked himself up again there was not one of them in sight. Then he sat down and began to think seriously over what had happened. Could it have been a dream? He was sure he had not been asleep. Were they ghosts? Surely not; their robes were too beautiful, their utterance too distinct, for any-thing evil. And yet, supposing them to be human beings, how could they have disappeared so suddenly, without leaving so much as a shadow behind them? It was an impenetrable mystery, so far; and the good sage was utterly perplexed. Then he went back into his pavilion, and not a sign of the late revelry was visible; his chairs and tables stood decorously in their accustomed places, unsullied by the remains of fruit or the dregs of wine; all that he noticed was a subtle odor, a faint sweet fragrance different from anything he had ever perceived before.

But the next night, as he was strolling thoughtfully among his flowers in the clear moonlight, he suddenly found himself once more surrounded by his elfin friends. Where they came from he never could find out; it seemed as though they had sprung out of the ground, or been materialized from the sweet aroma of the flowers. At first they seemed not to perceive him, for they were all busily engaged in urging little Pomegranate to beg pardon of the Aunt Wind. Pomegranate, however, was inexorable. " Why should I go supplicating that horrid old woman? " she cried, with flushing cheeks. " If there's likely to be any mischief, let us ask the dear old gentleman to protect us; what need we be afraid of then? " At this suggestion all the sylphs were quite enraptured, and turning to their kindly host, they explained the whole affair. " You see," said the spokeswoman, " that all we sisters live in your garden, and every year we are injured by malignant gales, so that we never feel at ease; we often ask our aunt, the Lady Wind, to treat us kindly and protect us; but now, alas! Pomegranate has mortally offended her, so we cannot count upon her any more. So, dear, kind guardian, we appeal to you; and if you can help us in our extremity, we shall be very grateful."

"But what power have I to help you? " asked Hsuan-wei, more puzzled than before.

"We don't want you to do anything very difficult," replied little Pomegranate. " All you will have to do is to prepare a crimson flag embroidered in gold with the sun, moon, and stars, and then hoist it to the east of the flowers at daybreak on the first morning of each new year; then we shall feel quite safe. As regards the present year, New Year's Day, of course, is past, so please do it on the 2ist of the present moon at dawn instead, when there is just the faintest breath of east wind; then there will be no fear of any recurrence of what happened yesterday."

"That is easy enough," replied the sage politely. "You may certainly rely upon my doing what you ask." Then they all thanked him with one voice, producing a concert of the most melodious music in the world, and said they would never forget his goodness. But no sooner had they finished speaking than off they started as fleetly as if they had wings, waving a smiling adieu to the bewildered philosopher as he panted after them with-out the smallest chance of being able to catch them up. Suddenly he felt a puff of fragrant wind in his face, and all the fairies simultaneously disappeared.

The next day he set to work, and prepared a splendid flag, in accordance with little Pomegranate's request. On the 2ist of the moon he rose before daylight, and, sure enough, there was a little breath of east wind blowing; so he made haste to run it up, and then awaited the result. He had not long to wait. In less time than it takes to write it, a tremendous hurricane sprang up which shook the very earth; the air was filled with whirling dust and flying stones; all the forests in the neighborhood were injured, and huge trees torn up by the roots. In his garden, however, everything was calm and still; not a single flower so much as trembled. Then the truth of the whole mystery burst upon Hsuan-wei. The enchanting girls he had been entertaining were the spirits of his own flowers; the little maiden in the crimson robe was nothing but a bud of red pomegranate; and the flighty, excitable lady whom they called their aunt eighteen times removed was the Goddess of the Wind! That evening, as soon as the moon was up, all the fairies came garlanded with peach-blossoms and plum-blossoms, tc tender their thanks to their preserver. " We know," said one of them, " that we cannot make you any adequate return; but we have brought you these blossoms, which, if you will eat, will confer upon you the gift of everlasting youth. Take them, then, dear friend; long may you live to be the guardian of our race, and then our own lives will be long and happy too! " So the philosopher took the blossoms, and ate them; when suddenly his face grew young again, the wrinkles disappeared from his brow, his complexion became fair and delicate, and he felt a new strong current of energy coursing through his veins. Soon afterwards he attained to a knowledge of the True Way, and shared the immortality of the Genii.

The Story

Now I daresay, remarks our author, that all you gentlemen look upon what I have written about flower-fairies and the Goddess of the "Wind as so much incoherent nonsense. I grant that they are things which nobody in the world appears ever to have seen or heard of, and that they are not mentioned in any historical records or classical writing; but strange and supernatural as they are, the world is full of them, though only a very small proportion of them find their way into books; so when they do occur it is not a matter to be wondered at.

Now in the reign of Jen Tsung, of the Sung dynasty, there lived at a village in Kiangnan an old man named Tsiu Hsien, who belonged to a literary family and possessed a few acres of land. His wife was dead, and had left him without children. He spent his whole life in the cultivation of a handsome flower-garden, for flowers were his very special hobby. He loved them as he might have loved his children had he been blessed with any. He was an indefatigable collector of rare specimens and exotics, which he valued far more than any jewels; and whenever he passed any gay gardens, during his constant rambles, he would insinuate himself into them with a benignant smile, whether he were invited or not. If the flowers were familiar to him, he would trot out again; but if they were at all unique, nobody would be able to drag him away the whole day long. People said that he was flower-mad. If he met with any for sale he always bought them, whether he had any money or not; and when he had none about him, he would just strip off his coat and give it to the seller in payment. Of course he was often terribly taken in. His mania being notorious, the flower merchants asked of him the most exorbitant prices; while some rascals would even stick cut flowers into a flowerpot, and impose upon him with a rootless plant. But nothing would cure him of his infatuation, and eventually he found himself master of a superb pleasure-ground, full of his choicest favorites. It was surrounded by a bamboo-fence grown all over with red, white, and yellow roses, clematis, almonds, rose-mallows, touch-me-nots, cocks'-crests, sunflowers, golden lilies, white lilies, pinks, carnations, princes'-feathers, white butterflies, night-falling goldmoneys, camellias, peonies, and a host of others. When they were all in full bloom, they looked like a great screen blazing with a mass of different colors; and by the time one began to fade another opened. The path leading to the house was bordered with bamboos, and the house itself was surrounded by the rarest plants. An eternal spring reigned in this delightful spot. Here flourished the watersprite flower as clear as ice and exquisitely pure as jade; the moutan, with its heavenly fragrance and royal tint; pear-blossoms as white as moonlight, peach-blossoms ruddy as the sun, tea-flowers more precious than pearls, and roses in a blushing cloud.

It was not long before the fame of this wonderful garden spread over all the country side, and people came flocking every day to get a furtive peep over the stone wall which ran around it. No annoyance, however, occurred until one afternoon, when the recluse was sitting, as usual, in the midst of his little paradise. Suddenly he looked up, and saw a coarse, disagreeable face peering over the top of the wall. Then a hand was thrust rudely forward, and grasped a beautiful rose of peculiar delicacy. The old gentleman hemmed two or three times, and cast glances of indignation at the intruder; but that personage was the son of an official of some small rank, and disdained to notice the anger of so obscure an individual as Tsiu Hsien. At last, however, the old man could contain himself no longer.

"This humble place is mine, Sir," he said, with as much politeness as he could command; " it is not worth the attention of your worship. I beg you will not demean yourself by entering; you can see the flowers equally well from rather a greater distance."

"You old fool," was the young mandarin's reply, " haven't you lived near me long enough to know my name? What do you mean by not wanting to let me see your flowers? "

Then he began to pick flowers right and left; and the unfortunate owner stood by in a grievous state of indignation, yet did not dare to remonstrate. His unwelcome visitor showed no signs of moving; on the contrary, he jumped down into the garden, and then bawled to his servants on the other side to go home and bring some wine. This increased the distress of poor old Tsiu, and emboldened him to enter another protest against the outrage.

"Indeed, Sir," he said, trembling with agitation, " there is no room in my snail-shell of a house fit for your worship to sit in; let me beg you, when you have seen enough, to return to your own mansion and drink there."

"No room? " retorted Chang, pointing to a cozy nook; " that place will suit me very well."

"Nay," said the old gentleman, " that place is far too dirty; your worship can certainly never sit there."

"If that's all," replied Chang, " I can sit upon a bit of carpet; so don't you trouble yourself about me."

Just then his servants came back, carrying all the materials for a luxurious picnic. A piece of cloth was spread upon the ground, and Chang and two or three of his friends, who had now joined him, squatted down and began to play at gamble-fingers, making a most intolerable noise. Chang enjoyed the whole thing immensely, and stared with delight at the old gentleman, who sat scowling helplessly by. Then a vile idea entered his wicked head.

"Here, you old idiot," he roared, with his mouth full of meat and his face all flushed with wine; " you're not worth a place in the corner of my eye, and yet you seem to know something about flowers. Take a cup of wine, and let us drink together! "

"Drink it yourself," said the old gentleman haughtily; " I never touch wine."

"Look here," continued Chang, too tipsy to notice the slight, " I have taken rather a fancy to this garden of yours; what do you say to selling it? "

"Sell my garden! " shrieked the old man, as a pang of rage and terror shot through his heart; " why, it's my very life; you don't know what you're asking. Sell my garden! No, Sir; I will not sell it. I tell you my garden is my life, and I will never part with it."

"Your life, indeed! " retorted Chang scornfully. " Look here; I mean to buy it, so you had better make up your mind to sell at once. And I'll tell you what; as you have nowhere else to live, buy you into the bargain, and then you can stay here and look after the place for me. Well, what do you say? "

Then all the others chimed in. " Why, there's a stroke of luck for you! " they cried; " why don't you thank his worship for such a gracious offer? " But the old man had grown numb and powerless under the insult, and his lips refused to move.

"What a brute of an old fellow this is! " exclaimed Chang. " Why don't you answer me, Yes or No? "

"I have already told you No," replied the victim, with as much firmness as he could muster; " why do you ask again? "

"Bosh! " was the polite rejoinder. " Now look here; if you dare to say i No ' again, I'll have you arrested. I can do it, mind; so look out for your own skin. I'll give you one more chance."

Tsiu became speechless with grief and indignation. There seemed no hope for him at all. Then he thought his best plan would be to tide over the immediate difficulty by temporizing; for Chang was a man of influence, and just then he was very tipsy; the great thing was to get rid of him as soon as possible. So, repressing his wrath by a violent effort, he replied

"If your worship really wants my garden, we will speak about it in a day or two; it is not a matter that can be settled hastily. Come, gentlemen, you have business; do not let any considerations of politeness detain you longer."

So saying he rose, in the hope of effecting a general move. His plan was successful, and everybody swore that his proposition was very reasonable. Then Chang and his associates staggered to their feet, while the attendants cleared away the mess they had made, and sauntered slowly towards the gate. Tsiu was in an agony of fear lest they should commit further depredations, and took care to walk between them and the flower-beds. Chang, however, went on ahead, and soon began to climb a piece of rockwork to pick some flowers that had struck 'his fancy. The old man rushed after him in terror. " Although these flowers are but useless trifles," he panted, " your worship cannot think how much labor is required in the course of a year to produce as many as you see; is it not a grievous pity to spoil them so? If you pick them, they will fade in two days at the very farthest; why should your worship do such mischief? "

"Pooh! " bawled Chang roughly; " what mischief am I doing, pray? You are going to sell me the whole affair to-morrow; so, you see, your flowers are virtually mine now. Supposing I were to pull every one of them up by the roots, what business would it be of yours? "

Then he made as though to thrust Tsiu away; but the old gentleman stood his ground manfully, saying, " You may kill me if you like, for I am but an old man; but you shall not pick my flowers."

"This is a most abominable old fellow," struck in the parasites. " His worship has but taken a few worthless buds; what does he mean by kicking up such a row about it? Do you think, Sir, that you are going to frighten us away? "

Then they all made a general rush upon the flowers, picking them by scores, and throwing them in shocking confusion upon the ground. The poor old fellow's rage was inexpressible; his cries of anguish rose to heaven. He relinquished his hold of Chang, and risked his life in trying to put a stop to the cruel massacre; but he was overpowered by numbers, while his flowers flew like hail about him. " You pack of cut-throat thieves," he cried, in a paroxysm of despair, " have you no honest calling, that you must come here to insult and injure me? Ah, what value is my life to me any longer? " And with that he butted his head furiously against Chang, who, being shaky on his legs, measured his length upon the ground. Then all the bullies, crying " Shame! " rushed up to avenge the fallen hero. Among them was an elderly man, who, seeing that their victim was already far advanced in years, and fearing that serious mischief might be done, attempted to dissuade them from further violence. He assisted Chang to rise; but Chang was beside himself with drink and fury, and, rushing forward like a mad dog, he struck off all the flowers that remained upon their stems and strewed them all over the place. And even then he was not satisfied, but crushed them to pieces with his feet.

Meanwhile the unhappy Tsiu was beating the earth and calling vainly upon Heaven, rolling all over the ground in impotent frenzy. By this time, however, the cries and shrieks of the combatants had reached the neighbors, who came flocking in, and were aghast at the scene of ruin and desolation, and the strange sight of so many lubberly fellows attacking a feeble old man. They immediately put a stop to the spoliation, and asked what it was all about. Some of them, who were the tenants of Chang's father, were inclined to take the part of Chang. At last, however, they managed to get the bully out of the garden-gate. " Tell that old thief he'd better make me a present of the garden, roared he, by way of a parting salute; " then we'll consider the affair settled. But if he says so much as half a ' No, let him look out for his skin." Of course, the neighbors saw the wretch was drunk, and paid no attention to his tipsy nonsense; so, having seen him well off the premises, they came back and tried to comfort poor old Tsiu. But his soul refused to be comforted, and he lifted up his voice and wept. Indeed the case was past all help, and there was nothing for the neighbors to do but to leave him in his misery and return to their several homes.

As they went back their conversation naturally turned upon the events of the afternoon. One man said that it served the old fellow right for locking up his garden and never allowing anybody to see the flowers, and that he had no one but himself to thank for it. But this view of the question excited the indignation of the others, particularly of one man, who retorted with more candor and abruptness than the first speaker at all relished. " Don't talk such arrant nonsense," he blurted out. " There is an old proverb which says that if you cultivate a garden for a year, you will enjoy the flowers for just ten days. People are fond enough of looking at them, but who thinks of the long drudgery that was necessary to bring them to such perfection? Just think, now, what years of toil this poor old man must have de-voted to his hobby to produce such a magnificent show; why should you be angry with him for loving his garden and taking pride in it? " To this nobody was able to reply, and so the subject dropped.

Meanwhile the unfortunate old Tsiu sat, weeping and disconsolate, in the midst of his fallen treasures. Tenderly he picked them up, and talked to them, saying, "O dear flowers, I have loved you all my life; you never lost a petal or a leaf before. Who could think such sad misfortunes were coming on us all today? " Then he fell to sighing and bemoaning himself afresh; the crushed, bruised blossoms lay strewn in sad disorder on his lap; to-morrow, perchance, he would be driven out of his lovely garden altogether.

"What are you crying about, Mr. Tsiu? " suddenly inquired a sharp, clear, pleasant little voice at his elbow. Tsiu turned his head, not a little startled, and beheld, close by him, a lovely and elegant girl of about sixteen summers. He had no idea who she was, or how she had got in; but there she was, and she looked very much indeed as though she meant it.

"Who are you, my little girl? " replied Tsiu, wiping his eyes; " and what has brought you here? "

"Oh, we are near neighbors I and my family," re-joined the girl, in her sweet, sharp voice, which acted like a tonic upon the old man's unstrung nerves. " I've heard that you have the finest moutanflowers to be seen any-where, so I thought I should like to come and look about me a bit. But what is the reason of all this ruin and desolation I see? Who has been murdering all your flowers like this? "

At the mention of his moutanflowers Tsiu very nearly broke down again; but he mastered his emotion, and told the cheery little girl all about the outrages of Chang To his perplexity, however, she only laughed; she didn't seem to pity him a bit.

"So that is it, is it? " she replied, with a pretty smile. " Now, wouldn't you like to be able to stick all these flowers on their stems again? "

"Don't jest with me, little girl," said Tsiu reproach-fully; " I am in no humor for a joke. Who ever heard of such a thing as putting dead flowers on their stalks as they were before? "

"Don't you be so conceited and so sure, as though nobody in the world could do anything that you can't," retorted the child again, with her silvery, saucy laugh. " It so happens that my ancestors were in possession of a secret by which even that wonderful thing might be done; and I don't know but what I might be able to accomplish it myself."

Then old Tsiu began to prick up his ears. " No, but really, little girl," he said, " is there such a secret? "

"Why should there not be, really?" replied the saucy girl, mimicking his earnest tones. Then Tsiu made her a low bow, and said

"If, my child, you are indeed able to perform this miracle, the old man's obligations to you would be such as he could never hope to repay. See, here is a full-blown rose; operate on this one to begin with."

"Don't bow to me like that," replied the little girl; " but go into the house and fetch me a bowl of nice fresh water." Up jumped old Tsiu with wonderful alacrity, turning the thing over and over in his mind as he walked along. He procured the water, and came trotting briskly back again; but where was the little girl? She had disappeared; but every flower was on its stem again, as fresh, as blooming, as full of life as ever not one was lying bruised upon the ground his favorites were all restored!

The old man could hardly believe his eyes. His delight was more extravagant, even, than his grief had been. He ran from flower to flower, and from bed to bed, stroking and fondling the pretty blossoms, and congratulating them upon their happy restoration. Their colors were deeper and more brilliant than ever; a spell seemed to have passed over the whole garden. Formerly all the flowers on a single plant were of the same color; but now they were all diversified red flowers had become purple, pale flowers had become vivid, and five different hues blazed in splendid contrast where there had been only one before.

When he had given full vent to his joy, he went in search of the delightful little girl who had wrought this charming miracle. He thought she must be hiding somewhere among the flowers; but there was not the slightest trace of her she had vanished altogether, with-out leaving so much as a shadow behind. It seemed impossible that she should have gone far, however, so he made for the garden-gate, feeling sure that she would be just outside. But he found it securely bolted, and not looking at all as though anybody had just gone through. Whereupon he opened it, and, sure enough, there was nobody in sight but two old cronies of his, Mr. Yii and Mr. Shan, who were watching a fisherman drying his nets. When they saw Mr. Tsiu come out, they rose and made him a low bow, saying, " We have just heard of the outrage perpetrated upon you by that fellow Chang, but we were in the field at the time, and not able to come before to inquire about it."

"Don't mention the matter," replied Tsiu. " I was, certainly, the victim of that rascal's malevolence; but owing to the timely aid of a dear little girl, who suddenly made her appearance like an angel from heaven, and by some wonderful means restored every one of my flowers, everything is all right again. But she has gone off as suddenly as she came, without waiting to be thanked; pray, gentlemen, did either of you see which way she took? "

The two old men listened to this story with astonishment. "How is it possible," they said, "that flowers once cut should be refixed? Who was this wonderful girl, pray? And how long is it since she disappeared? "

"Just now," replied Tsiu eagerly; " not a minute ago. You must have seen her go out of the gate."

"We have been here a considerable time," said the old men, " and we have seen no girl; nobody has come out of the gate at all."

When Tsiu heard that, the conviction suddenly flashed upon him that his little benefactress must have been a fairy, and not a human child at all. As he was pondering the affair, his two friends began to question him about it, and he told them the whole story from beginning to end; whereupon they exclaimed, " But how is such a miracle possible? Let us both come into your garden and see it with our own eyes."

So Tsiu ushered them in, and they walked round and round, the excited proprietor never ceasing to repeat, " Oh, it was a fairy. Yes, it must have been a fairy. Human beings cannot work such wonders." Then he burnt a large quantity of fragrant incense, and kotowed in gratitude to Heaven, while his two old friends said, " Yes, it must have been so. This is the recompense of your sincerity of heart and your unconquerable love of flowers. Now, to-morrow you must invite Chang and his rascally associates to come here and see the marvel with their own eyes, that they may be made thoroughly ashamed of themselves."

"Nay, nay," said Tsiu; " not I, indeed. Men of their stamp are like vicious dogs, which, when they are seen at a distance, must be avoided. Why should I go out of my way to ask them here again? "

"You're right, you're right," nodded the two old fellows. Then Tsiu, who had never been in such spirits before, proposed a cup of wine in honor of the occasion; and the three friends sat drinking and hobnobbing till long after sunset, when the visitors got up to go away, leaving the old gentleman as happy and light-hearted as his previous visitors had left him miserable and sad.

The news of the prodigy spread like wildfire over the village, and next morning, as soon as it was light, the people came in crowds to see and hear all about it. They were not at all sure that Tsiu would let them in; none of them knew what a change had come over him since the visit of his fairy benefactress. He had not slept the whole night, but had sat in his garden in the still moonlight meditating upon the events of that most eventful day. Suddenly the thought flashed across him that perhaps all this had happened to him because he had been a little mean and selfish in never permitting anyone else to enjoy his garden with him, and he considered how different it might have been if he had had rather more of the liberal, kindly, generous spirit of the fairies. So the next day he flung open his garden-gate, that anybody might come in who wished to, and gave a kindly welcome to the first visitors who presented themselves. The news that the place was free to everybody passed from mouth to mouth, and the long-closed garden was soon filled with a respectful, wondering, and enchanted throng.

And now we must return to Chang, who had as yet heard nothing of the way in which his mischief had been mended. His rage had not cooled with the hours. " The old rascal butted me with his head yesterday," he said; "'shall I have no revenge? I am going to him now, this very minute, to demand possession of his garden; and if he says no, I'll get together a lot of men and make them cut down every stick in the place."

"Don't be afraid of his refusing/' replied his friends; " his garden is so close to your own house, you've got him in your power. Only don't destroy any more flowers, or you won't have any left to enjoy yourself."

"Pooh! " said Chang; " they'll bloom again next year, won't they? Come, let us be off at once; it's not polite to keep the old man waiting."

Then they all got up and started; but as they were just going out of the door, a man, seeing whither they were bound, said

"What, haven't you heard the news? There has been a descent of fairies in Mr. Tsiu's garden, and all the flowers are joined on to their stalks again. And there's what is more wonderful than that, too; for people do say that the flowers are far finer than they were at first that five colors may now be seen where there was only one before! "

This startled Chang considerably; but he soon re-covered himself, and took refuge in disbelief. " As though it was likely," he said scornfully, " that that old thief should have such luck! Besides, how is it that no one ever heard of fairies coming before, but only when the flowers had been destroyed? It's all a flam, to keep me from going again. He wants to make out that he's under supernatural protection, in order to scare me off! "

"What your worship says is exactly to the point," chimed in the parasites. In a short time they arrived at the garden-gate, both leaves of which were flung open, while the garden was full of visitors, who all had the same marvelous story in their mouths. But all this only hardened Chang's purpose, and he swore, loud enough to be heard, that if the fairies were there even then, he would still seize upon the garden. At last, however, after following a winding path, he found him-self at the scene of his outrages of the day before, and then he saw that everything he had heard was true. Not a sign of devastation was visible; every flower bloomed upon its stalk: and there was something strange about their appearance the more one looked at them the more beautiful they seemed to grow, till at last each flower bore a mysterious resemblance to a smiling human face.

Then Chang was chopfallen indeed; ay, and he was frightened too. But even this had no effect upon his resolution. He cast a cold, malicious glance around him, and then a thought of hideous wickedness came into his head. " Come, let us be off," he said to his associates, abruptly; "there's nothing to be done here."

"What! " exclaimed the parasites, " go away without insisting on the garden being given up to you? "

"Hush! " was the reply; " I have just thought of a splendid plan." Here they passed out of the gate, and began walking along the road again. " I am not going to say one word to old Tsiu, good or bad; but to-morrow his garden will be mine."

Then they all pressed him to tell them what his intention was, and he proceeded as follows: " You know," he explained, " that there's trouble at Pei-chou. A fellow named Wang Tseh is after some seditious business, and is driving the people mad with his pretended sorcery ^and magic. The Privy Council have accordingly sent dispatches round to all the districts and departments in the empire, instructing the authorities to put down unflinchingly all manner of heterodox and illicit doctrines that may be current among the people, and to arrest all persons suspected of the black art. The Governor here has offered a reward of three thousand strings of cash to anybody who will give evidence that will lead to the arrest of the ringleaders; so to-morrow I mean to go and lay information about this affair in Tsiu's garden, and send my servant Pa to accuse him of being a magician and seducing the people. He won't be able to stand the examination by torture; he'll confess, and then hell be put in prison and his garden confiscated. When it is put up for sale, who will dare to buy it? It will just fall into my hands, and the three thousand strings as well."

"Superb! " exclaimed the other wretches, in a chorus of exultation. " The idea is splendid. Waste no time, but set to work at once."

So Chang hurried into the city, and drew up an indictment in due form. Next day he sent his servant with it quite early, selecting this particular man Pa because he was on good terms with all the people, besides being his own right hand in villainy. The magistrate was on the look-out for sorcerers, and found no difficulty whatever in believing a story to which the entire country-side was witness. He therefore made out a warrant of arrest, and dispatched an officer with Pa to take Tsiu into custody. Chang was in high feather, and distributed largess lavishly among the yam6n runners, following them at some short distance, that he might enjoy the scene. The poor old man was walking, as usual, in his garden, and paid no attention to the crowd of people whom he saw approaching, thinking they were visitors like the rest. But he was soon undeceived. They suddenly set up a wild halloo, rushed for-ward in a body, and pinioned his arms securely. The old man was horribly frightened, and cried, " Why, what fault have I committed? What is my crime? I do beseech you, gentlemen, to explain." Then they all bawled out in concert, abusing him for a wicked old sorcerer and rebel; and without allowing him to say a word in his defense, dragged him violently towards the gate. When the neighbors witnessed these proceedings they came flocking together in amazement, and asked what was the matter. " Matter! " retorted the leader of the gang; " do you still ask what is the matter? He's a vile old rebel, and you are every one of you inculpated in the affair." This startled the simple people not a little, and they one and all made off as fast as they could in all directions, fearing lest by some means or other they too should be involved. A few of Tsiu's friends, however, followed him at a distance. Chang remained behind with his parasites, and as soon as the garden was clear they took formal possession of it. They then searched in every nook and corner to see that there were none of Tsiu's people hidden away anywhere; and finding that nobody was left, they locked the garden-gate and trooped off to the magistrate's.

On their arrival they found that the officers had taken old Tsiu into their charge, and had made him kneel down on the stone pavement in front of the inner entrance. The jailers, who had been heavily bribed by Chang, had got their implements of torture in readiness, and were anxiously waiting to commence operations. Just then the magistrate came in, and the examination began.

"What place do you belong to, wizard? " bawled the " father-and mother-of-his people," roughly. " What do you mean by coming here and corrupting honest folk with your sorceries? and how many confederates have you? "

These words sounded to Tsiu like a sudden explosion of gunpowder in the dark, and he did not know what to reply. At last he said

"The insignificant magi is a native of the village of Chang-lo; he is not a wizard, and does not come from anywhere else; and he knows nothing of any sorceries."

"What! " roared the magistrate; " will you deny that only the day before yesterday you conjured a number of broken flowers on to their stems again? What do you call that, pray, but the black art? "

When Tsiu heard that, he knew directly that Chang was at the bottom of the whole affair; so he began at the beginning, and told the magistrate everything that had happened from the time of Chang's drunken out-rage to the visit of the beneficent little fairy. But the magistrate, whose nature prompted him to take a distorted and one-sided view of everything, would not believe a word of it.

"A very ingenious tale, indeed," he said, with a brutal laugh. " How many men, do you think, are there not who would be only too glad to be visited by fairies in their distress; and to how many do the fairies come? Do you suppose it was your tears and sobs that brought her to your help? Pray let us know her name; she surely didn't make off without telling you who she was. And you really think you are going to take us in with this? Don't trouble yourselves to accuse him further," continued the mandarin to the bystanders; " he most certainly is a wizard. Quick, now, with the press-boards! "

The words were hardly out of his mouth when all the jailers rushed off to get the instruments of torture, with the ferocity of wolves and tigers. They soon came hurrying back like a swarm of bees, and grasping the old man violently, laid him by the heels, pulled his legs apart, and were just about to apply the torture when the magistrate was seized with a sudden fit of dizziness. He felt his eyes become dim; his head seemed to go round, so that he could no longer hold, himself erect; indeed he nearly toppled off his bench. He therefore ordered the adjournment of the case till the next day, and told the jailers to put a cangue, or wooden frame, on Tsiu's neck, and lead the unfortunate man back to prison, guarding him strictly in the meantime. Tsiu was accordingly marched back, weeping and bemoaning his sad fate, and followed by a crowd of gaping spectators. On his way he saw Chang. " Sir," he exclaimed, " I never injured you when you came into my garden the day before yesterday, nor have I committed any fault against you to-day; why do you pursue me with this relentless cruelty, and try to take my life? "

Chang made no reply, but turned on his heel and walked off, accompanied by his confederates. Then Tsiu's two old friends, Shan and Yii, came up to him and asked him how he fared, saying, " Never mind the false accusation you are now suffering under; tomorrow we and all your neighbors will rally round you, and personally bear witness to your innocence." " May it indeed be so," said Tsiu; " then everything must come all right." Then his jailers turned round and bullied him, saying, " You condemned criminal, you, you do nothing but weep; don't you know you've got to walk? " So Tsiu restrained his tears, and entered his dungeon. All the neighbors brought him food and wine; but they could get no farther than the prison doors, and the jailers, instead of giving it to the old man, kept it and gobbled it up them-selves. At last night came on; and then it really seemed as though his woes had reached their crisis. He was made to lie down upon what was called the " prisoners' bed " a diabolical contrivance on which all the prisoners were packed close together, and fitted up with heavy beams and ropes so disposed that each man lay under a crushing weight and tightly lashed to the ground; not a muscle could be moved, not a wrist or ankle turned; a living man was just as powerless as a corpse. " Alas, alas! " groaned Tsiu, in his bitterness, " I know not what fairy it was who restored my flowers; yet this wretch makes it an excuse for his persecutions. O fairy, dear fairy! if you have any pity for me, do for me what you did for my poor flowers, and save my life! Help me in this, and I will renounce all my family, give up the world, and enter the True Way! "

No sooner were the words out of his mouth than he espied, in the dim distance, a faint advancing figure. It was, indeed, no other than his fairy benefactress. Tsiu uttered a wild cry of joy and hope. " Fairy, dear fairy," he exclaimed, " if it is really you, extricate me from the dreadful position I am in! "

"Are you so very anxious to escape? " replied the girl, with a smile. Then she stretched forth her hands; and lo! the manacles with which old Tsiu was bound fell clanking to the ground. Up he sprang, and knocked his head three times upon the floor in speechless gratitude. The first thing he did when his transports of joy were over was to ask the fairy who she was. " I am the Protectress of Flowers," replied she, " at the Emerald Pool in Fairyland, where the Royal Mother reigns. I love you because you love flowers; that is the reason I have been assisting you. Now everything that has happened to you came through Destiny; it was your fate, and could not be avoided. Tomorrow all your miseries will end! The Spirit of Flowers has taken a strict account of all Chang's villainies, and made a full report of them to God; and God has deprived him of the measure of his years, and is keeping great tribulation in store for his confederates. Continue the cultivation of your heart for a few years longer, and then I will visit you once more for your ever-lasting good."

Tsiu bowed his head again in wondering gratitude. " And what method am I to adopt," he asked, " for the cultivation of my heart? "

Then the fairy proceeded to explain how, by continuing to love and care for flowers, his heart would undergo a process of constant renovation; and how, by feeding on certain species, and drinking the dew of heaven, he would gradually bring about the sublimation of his body, and eventually attain to the immortality of the genii. Tsiu prostrated himself for the third time; and when he raised his head the fairy visitor was gone. But looking upward, he saw her hovering in mid-air and waving her hand in sign that he should follow her.

Tsiu accordingly pulled himself together and began to 'clamber up the wall of the prison-yard. When he had got half-way he felt his strength beginning to fail; but he made a tremendous effort, and managed to scramble on to the top. No sooner had he gained this point of vantage, however, than he heard a deafening noise below; every gong in the place was being banged, and shouts were raised on all sides that one of the prisoners had escaped. This put Tsiu into a dreadful state of trepidation; his hands grew numb, his legs shook, and all of a sudden he tumbled violently off the wall, struck his head upon the ground, and awoke!

He was still in the prison; the whole thing had been a dream. But as he lay on his hard couch he reflected seriously about the matter; he turned it over and over in his mind, and tried to find out the meaning arid interpretation of it; arriving at last at the satisfactory conclusion that everything would end happily, and that he need give himself no more anxiety at all.

When Chang saw that the magistrate treated Tsiu as a wizard, he was immeasurably delighted. " Ah," said he, chuckling, " the old wretch was always after some-thing or other which nobody could understand. Well, to-night he'll sleep on the prisoners' bed, and I shall enjoy myself in his garden." " Yes," replied his friends; " the day before yesterday it belonged to him, and now it is your worship's; so it is only proper you should enjoy it to your heart's content." "Eight you are," shouted the hero; so, without further delay, they started off, telling the servants to bring a supply of wine and eatables after them. The neighbors were greatly incensed when they saw the party arrive, but no one dared to speak. Mean-while Chang and his friends proceeded to the summer-house; but when they got there, and looked round, what was their astonishment to see not a single flower upon its stalk! There they lay, strewed about just as they were when Chang had cut them off; broken and bruised and spoilt. At first nobody could speak for amazement. Chang, how-ever, soon recovered himself. " It is evident," he said, "that the old conjurer has been at his tricks again; if not, how could there be such a change in half a day? It surely can't be the fairy again! " This happy thought was speedily capped by one of the hangers-on. " The old fellow knew that your worship would come to enjoy the flow-ers again," said he; " and therefore he had recourse to this trick to put you out of countenance." " Well," said Chang, " if it be so, let us enjoy the fallen flowers." So saying, he spread a carpet on the ground, sat down, and laid himself out to make the most of things. He gave a couple of bottles of wine to his trusty servant Pa, and they all ate and drank till sunset, by which time they were more than half-drunk. Suddenly, how-ever, a tremendous gust of wind arose; it swept violently across the garden, gathered up all the scattered flowers, and blew them on to their stalks again! Then, in the twinkling of an eye, every flower was transformed into a beautiful girl, a little over two feet high, each of whom, in apparent obedience to successive puffs of wind, visibly increased in size. At last they appeared in a great gleaming group of exquisitely lovely fairies, dressed in bright parti-colored robes. All the intruders were so dazed with their beauty that not one of them could utter a word; when suddenly a girl in a crimson robe began to speak as follows:

"Sisters, it is now more than ten years that we have lived here in peace and happiness, thanks to the care and cultivation of good old Mr. Tsiu. Who ever imagined that this mad slave would come to suffocate us with the vulgar odor of his presence, and violate us with his venomous hands? And then he throws Mr. Tsiu into prison for being a wizard, because he is scheming to swallow up his garden! But we have now got our enemy before our eyes; what is to hinder us, sisters, from combining our strength and giving him the thrashing he deserves? Nay, it is our duty; first, out of gratitude to our old friend for his goodness; secondly, to revenge ourselves for the injuries and insults that have been heaped upon us. Is there any reason why we should refrain? "

Then all the other fairies cried with one voice, " You are right! You are right! Let us set about it at once, before any of them have time to escape." Whereupon they all pulled down their long sleeves to serve as whips, and flourished them till the cold produced was like that of a piercing wind which cuts to the very bone. By this time the intruders had taken the alarm; and with the cry, " They're devils! they're devils! " a general stampede took place, everybody looking out for himself, and forgetting all about the plates and dishes on the ground. Some tumbled over the stones; others had their faces torn and scratched by the branches of trees; and no sooner had a man scrambled to his legs than down he fell again. At last, after a series of misfortunes, they came to a dead stop; and, on reconnoitering their ranks, they found that Chang and Pa were missing. Just then the wind stopped, and the heavens grew black; so they all made the best of their way home, barely escaping with their lives holding their heads, and skulking off like rats. When they reached their own doors, and were just able to draw their breath again, they got together a number of stalwart laborers, whom they provided with torches, to go in search of the two missing ones. Arrived at the garden, the men soon heard a sort of moaning under a large plum-tree; and bringing a light to see what it was, they found the servant Pa, who, having tripped over the trunk of the tree, was lying there with a broken head, utterly unable to rise. Two of them, accordingly, picked him up and carried him home, while the rest hunted all over the garden to find Chang; but all was silent not a sound was to be heard nor a form to be seen. They discovered, however, to their amazement, that the moutanflowers were blooming again as brilliantly as ever; not one was on the ground. Then they came to where the plates and dishes had been left; and there they were, all in the greatest possible confusion, while the wine was spilt in every direction at which they all put their tongues out in astonishment. Some of them set themselves to clearing the things up, and the others resumed their search for Chang. But not a sign of him did they discover. " How can such a thing be possible? " they exclaimed; " the garden is not a large one, and yet we've been round it four or five times without finding so much as his shadow. Surely the wind can't have blown him away, or the devils of girls devoured him? " So they had no alternative but to go home for that night, and postpone further search for him till the next morning.

Just as they were about to pass through the gate, however, they met another batch of men coming in with lanterns, among whom were no other than the two old gentlemen, Mr. Yii and Mr. Shan. They had heard of all these strange doings, and how Chang had been spirited away; but they knew not whether it were true or false, so they had come to see for themselves, and a party of neighbors had come with them. When, therefore, the two old men inquired of the laborers they met coming out, and found every particular confirmed, they were speechless with amazement. "Well, well," they replied, " you go away; we will search the garden ourselves." So they pottered and peered about, but of course discovered nothing; whereupon they both uttered an ejaculation of helpless perplexity, and went out again. " There is nobody in here," said they to the people who were still waiting outside; " let us lock the gate securely and come away."

The villagers, having lost their headman, were like a serpent that has lost its head; they knew not how to act; so they all replied, ' As you please, gentlemen, as you please; we will do exactly as you tell us." Just as they were on the point of dispersing, however, a laborer who had been peering about with his lantern suddenly cried out, " His honorable worship is found! "

A general rush took place, the people all scudding together like a gust of wind. " Isn't that his silk muffler," continued the man, "hanging on that locust-tree?" "To be sure it is! " cried everybody. " Then its owner cannot be far off." So the man continued to pry about near the wall, and before he had gone far he uttered an exclamation of horror; for there, sure enough, was Mr. Chang or all that could be seen of him with his head stuck hard and fast in a dung-pit!

Yes, there he was; recognizable only by his clothes, as his face was invisible, and his legs pointing upwards to the sky. The laborers rushed forward, and, in spite of the horrible stench, pulled the body out of the hole, and washed it in the nearest ditch. The two old gentlemen, recognizing in the bad man's fate the just retribution of Heaven, went home, and the others quietly dispersed. Meanwhile the news had reached Chang's family, and they prepared a coffin and a shroud, and consigned the dishonored corpse to its last resting-place. By this time the villain Pa had died of the wound in his head, and such was the end of these two wicked men.

Next morning the magistrate, who had recovered from his sickness, took his seat upon the bench, and prepared to go on with the case. But the first thing he heard was, that the accuser was no more; and then all the facts of the occurrence were made known to him by the officers of the court. The magistrate was overwhelmed with astonishment, and could hardly believe his ears; but the story was confirmed by the two old gentlemen and over a hundred of the neighbors, who all came to bear their testimony. Then the magistrate was delighted to think that he had been prevented from applying torture to an innocent man, and, sending for old Tsiu, he told him he was free. He also posted a proclamation out-side the garden-gate, warning everybody against daring to touch the flowers, or trespass in the domain on any pretext whatever. So Tsiu and his friends went in a triumphal procession back to the garden, where they found the moutanflowers blooming more splendidly than ever; and all the neighbors gave the old gentleman a banquet of wine, to cheer him after his sufferings; after which he invited them in his turn, and the feasting was kept up for several days on end.

From this time forward Tsiu began to follow the directions of the flower-fairy. He lived entirely on flowers, and abjured the use of cooked food altogether. Soon his hair, which had been white with age, turned black again; the wrinkles in his face disappeared; his complexion became as fair and fresh as that of a beautiful boy. At last, as he was sitting one radiant summer's day among his flowers, a warm, sweet wind began to blow; the air filled with clouds, bright with all the colors of the rainbow; white storks, the emblems of longevity, disported themselves in the sky; lovely melodies came floating on the breeze; and a faint, rich perfume was wafted into his nostrils. Raising his eyes in wonder, he saw, approaching from above, a bevy of fairy maidens carrying waving flags, in the midst of whom was the Flower Goddess. " Come," she said, " your period of probation is finished. I have reported your good deeds to God, and He ordains that you shall be raised to the ranks of the genii as Guardian of the Flowers, with power to bless all who love them, and punish all who violate their purity." Then the whole lovely vision rose solemnly into the air, and Tsiu, gazing after it, rose too; and all the flowers in his garden, seemingly endowed with life, accompanied their beloved master; who, looking back as he sailed upward through the sky, raised his hands and continued waving an adieu to his old friends on earth until he arrived in heaven, and was lost sight of for evermore.

The End
Of
Leaves from My Chinese Scrapbook

Biographies of Immortals

By

Lionel Giles

1. INTRODUCTION

READERS of *Gulliver's Travels* may remember that on his way to Japan the hero of that work came to the Kingdom of Luggnagg, where he first heard of the existence of certain remarkable individuals called struldbrugs. They formed but a small part of the population, and were distinguished at birth by a red circular spot on the forehead which was an infallible sign that they would never die. Struck with wonder and delight, Gulliver began to dilate on the happiness which he felt sure must be the lot of such fortunate creatures, delivered by the continual apprehension of death. But he was soon disillusioned on discovering that the struldbrug's immortality was not accompanied by that perpetuity of youth, health, and vigor which alone could make life tolerable. Indeed, when he was brought into the presence of a few struldbrugs, his reaction was one of extreme disgust at the ghastliness of their appearance. Still, he was naturally interested in such an unexampled phenomenon, and hoped to learn more on the subject from the accounts given by Japanese authors. However, the shortness of his stay in Japan and his ignorance of the language prevented him from pursuing his inquiries.

That was a great pity; for the Japanese, having been in touch with the civilization of China for many centuries, could really have told him things about the "immortals" of that country which would have reawakened all his enthusiasm. These immortals were indeed vastly superior to the struldbrugs in that they could remain forever exempt from both physical and mental decay. By the Chinese they were called *hsien*, a word which in its written form is a character composed of two pictographic elements, "man" and "mountain"; thus it appears that the name was originally applied to men who had retired from the world in order to live a hermit's life in the mountains. Their activities were mostly confined to the gathering of certain herbs and roots which, when eaten, would not only cure disease but also rejuvenate the body and lengthen life far beyond its normal span. Chief among such plants was the *ling-chih* or "magic fungus", believed to contain vitalizing elements of marvellous efficacy. We are told that an aged man once dug up something like a human hand, very plump and pink. He boiled and then ate it, whereupon his teeth and hair sprouted anew; his strength returned, and his complexion became like that of a youth. A Taoist who met him said: "The thing you ate was a fleshy *chih*. Your longevity will equal that of the tortoise and crane." We also hear much about cassia or Chinese cinnamon; *shu*, a species of Atractylis with a root resembling ginger; pine resin, which according to the standard Chinese pharmocopoeia "renders the body light and prevents the onset of old age"; and peaches, the fruit of immortality, which grew in the garden of Hsi Wang Mu, the Western Queen Mother, who dwelt in the K'un-lun mountains.

The eccentric behavior of the typical hsien, and the seclusion in which he lived, led to the weaving of many legends round him. He was often credited with all kinds of supernatural powers besides the indefinite prolongation of life: thus, he might be able to evoke rain, wind, thunder and lightning, have spirits at his beck and call, pass unharmed through solid matter or fire, effect a transformation of his bodily shape, move with incredible speed, or even appear in several places at once. It is not surprising, therefore, that the hsien cult is soon found in close association with the amorphous system of Taoism, which seems to have existed in some form before the time of Confucius, and was always ready to assimilate any new movement dealing with what was strange or miraculous. No precise date, however, as to the origin of the cult can be extracted from the Taoist writings of the Chou dynasty. Lao Tzu in the *Tao Te Ching* speaks of the man possessed of Tao as enduring forever: "By maintaining the unity of body and soul, can you not escape dissolution?" And in another mystic passage: "He who has grasped the secret of life will be safe from the attack of buffalo or tiger. . . And why? Because he has no spot where death can enter." Such sayings, vague though they are, may have opened the way to a belief in the possibility of attaining actual immortality. Chuang Tzu goes a little further when he describes "a spiritual being dwelling on a mountain, whose flesh was smooth as ice and skin as white as snow; he was gentle and submissive as a young girl, ate none of the five cereals but inhaled the wind and drank the dew; soaring above the clouds, he drove a team of flying dragons and roamed beyond the limits of this world." And elsewhere he more than hints at a regimen of the soul and body which will keep death at bay.

Lieh Tzu, who revels in the marvelous, tells of a man who was seen passing through solid rock and floating in the midst of flames, but who when questioned was unable to give any explanation of these feats. Lieh Tzu himself brought his mental passivity to such a pitch that he became wholly unconscious of what his body was resting on, and was borne this way and that by the wind. But the passage which most closely foreshadows the later conception of hsien occurs in his description of the five Islands of the Blest:

"The towers and belvederes built upon their heights were all made of gold and jade, the birds and beasts living there were all spotlessly white.
Trees of pearl and coral bore thick masses of flowers; their fruit was delicious to the taste, and those who are thereof knew neither old age nor death.
The inhabitants all belonged to the race of demi-gods and immortals, and in countless numbers they would fly across to meet one another
within the space of a single day or night."

Here we have the earliest known occurrence of the character for *hsien*, though the "immortals" thus designated are more like what we should call fairies than human beings who have won immortality through their own endeavors.

It is true that in a less exalted mood Lieh Tzu also writes as follows: "That which has life must by the law of its being come to an end; and the end can no more be avoided than the living creature can help being alive. So that he who hopes to perpetuate his life and to shut out death is deceived as to his destiny." But enthusiasts were content to ignore any such warning as this. To them it seemed only natural that Tao, the ultimate principle of the universe, being itself everlasting, should be able to impart the same blessing to its creatures; that is to say, if the whole human personality could be brought into complete harmony with Tao, it might be expected to share in its immortality. Thus, the great question came to be, how to achieve this harmony, or as the common phrase went, how to "attain Tao". Generally speaking, a twofold process was considered necessary: (1) cultivation of the mind, with Tao as the model: quietude, passivity, gentleness, self-effacement were the main characteristics to be aimed at; (2) a gradual refinement of the bodily substance by means of physical exercises, dieting, regulation of the breath, and the taking of appropriate drugs.

All these methods were practiced, more or less, by aspirants to hsienship, but as time went on, more and more importance was attached to the swallowing of a special drug, or elixir, which could make one immortal on the spot, without further trouble. The secret of its preparation has not been revealed to us in full, but we do know that cinnabar, or red sulphide of mercury, was an essential ingredient. Long before the theory of the transmutation of metals led to the beginnings of alchemy in China, instances are recorded of cinnabar having been used as food by hsien of the primitive type: one Ch'ih Fu, for example, is said to have succeeded in becoming completely rejuvenated after dosing himself with a mixture of refined cinnabar and some kind of stone which had been fused in a crucible. Other minerals generally used in compounding the elixir were realgar, copper carbonate, sulphur, mice, sal ammoniac, nitre, and ochre. But cinnabar heads the list as the most important of all, and the reason is not far to seek, for from it is obtained by sublimation the unique metal mercury or quicksilver (i.e. *living* silver), which is so volatile that it seems to be actually endowed with life. The making of pure gold, either for its own sake or as the basis of a life-prolonging potion known as gold-juice, was also a prime object with Chinese alchemists, and this too was produced in some mysterious way by means of cinnabar. The process is mentioned but not described by Li Shao Chun, the first alchemist about whom we have reliable information.

Once the quest for immortality had got well under way, the number of officially recognized hsien increased rapidly. It was felt that any eminent Taoist ought to be included in their ranks, and consequently the list of immortals was swelled by the addition of numerous magicians, philosophers, statesmen, physicians, and so forth, to say nothing of various legendary figures of the past such as the Yellow Emperor and His Wang Mu. Some difficulty must have arisen at first in the case of historical personages whose claim to immortality was rendered dubious by the fact that their deaths had been publicly recorded; but this could be met by the circulation of a report that their coffins had been opened and found empty, except perhaps for a sword or a slipper or some other article of clothing.

At least one great Taoist teacher appears to have been canonized in spite of himself. This was Ch'iu Ch'ang-ch'un, who in his old age was summoned to the court of Jenghiz Khan. When questioned about the secret of longevity, he replied that the essentials were a pure heart and few desires, whereupon Jenghiz exclaimed: "God has sent this venerable hsien to awaken my conscience!" But, strictly speaking, he was no hsien at all, for he openly declared that there was no such thing as a drug of immortality, and his death was followed by no startling resuscitation. Yet he was duly enrolled in the list of immortals. Even a high moral standard was not always regarded as essential for a hsien. As an example we may take the wealthy Fan Li, who helped the King of Yueh to overcome the once powerful State of Wu in 473 B.C. Renowned for the his cunning and aptitude for intrigue, he may fitly be termed the Machiavelli of his day. After a diplomatic triumph in Yueh he migrate to Ch'i, where he amassed great riches. But again he refused to tempt fortune too long, and finally settled down in Lan-ling, where he became a millionaire for the third time. According to the Taoist version of his career, he then took to selling drugs, attained hsienship, and was seen and recognized by successive generations of mortals.

Taoism was largely a reaction against the sober outlook and strict moral discipline of the Confucianist system, which may account for the general tendency of hsien to treat life rather as a huge joke than as a serious problem. The life-story of the famous poet Li Po, dubbed "the banished hsien", reflects this carefree, bohemian mentality. Much of his time appears to have been spent in roaming over the country and in frequent carousals with a number of choice spirits whose thoughts were centered less on the elixir than on wine. One of these coteries was known as the Six Idlers of the Bamboo Brook, another as the Eight Immortals of the Wine-cup. Different accounts are given of Li Po's end. The Old T'ang History says bluntly that his last illness was brought on by excessive drinking, but the popular tradition is that he was drowned one night from a boat while making a drunken effort to embrace the reflection of the moon. Even this is rejected by the Taoist fraternity in favor of the more acceptable legend that he was borne up into the sky on the back of a whale.

As the number of hsien multiplied, it was found convenient to divide them into classes according to their habitat, as follows: (1) celestial hsien: those who ascend ot their abode in heaven;; (2) terrestrial hsien, who either from insufficient merit, personal inclination, or, as some say, by taking half a dose only of the elixir, remain on earth for an indefinite period without growing any older; (3) aquatic hsien, or hsien of the watery element—purely *yin* or feminine, without any admixture of *yang* or the masculine principle; (4) divine or spiritual hsien, demi-gods who dwell on the Isles of the Blest or in the Paradise of His Wang Mu. Another classification omits the third group and introduces two others: the human hsien, ascetics who have been able to subdue all earthly passions and lusts of the flesh, but have not yet attained immortality; and the demonic hsien, bodiless phantoms who lead a spectral existence, flitting restlessly hither and thither. But neither of these groups can be regarded as hsien in the usual acceptation of the term, and the distinction between celestial and terrestrial hsien is the only one of real significance.

The Chinese have taken their immortals very seriously, and a literature of almost incredible bulk has grown up around them. A considerable portion of the huge Taoist Canon consists of works dealing with their lives, teachings, and multifarious activities. And in the great encyclopedia *T'u Shu Chi Ch'eng* we find biographies of well over a thousand hsien, drawn from various sources and arranged in order of date. Of separate collections, the earliest is the *Lieh Hsien Chuan*, which contains tersely worded notices of 72 persons of every rank and station, ranging from purely mythical beings to hermits, heroes, and men and women of the common people. Its reputed author is the statesman and Taoist scholar Liu Hsiang, who lived from 77 to 6 B.C. For several reasons, this attribution will not pass muster, but there is some internal evidence to show that part of the book at least must have been written during Liu Hsiang's lifetime. Another work of a similar kind, but rather more expansive and stylish in composition, is the *Shen Hsien Chuan*, by the famous writer and adept Ko Hung, more about whom will be found on page 97. Lastly, we may mention a very popular compilation, also entitled *Lieh Hsien Chuan*, made by the Taoist monk Huan-ch'u of the Yuan dynasty, a thousand years after Ko Hung. This contains 55 biographies with illustrative woodcuts. In a few cases an account of the same hsien is given in more than one of these books, and Lao Tzu appears in all three.

Several other sources have been laid under contribution in the following pages, including some of the official dynastic histories; these are more sober as a rule in their treatment of facts, yet they do not refrain from reporting many a fantastic tale of magic. It has been thought best to make the arrangement of this selection as far as possible chronological, though dates are often uncertain. It will be remembered, of course, that the very nature of a hsien exempts him from the ordinary limitations of time.

2. ABBREVIATIONS

C.H.F.C. = *Chin hua fu chih*: Topography of Chin-hua Prefecture.
C.S. = *Chin shu*: Chin dynastic history.
C.T.S. = *Chiu t'ang shu*: Old T'ang dynastic history.
F.S.T. = *Feng su t'ung*: Popular traditions (2nd cent. A.D.).
H.H.C. = *Hsu hsien chuan*: Supplementary biographies of hsien (T'ang Dynasty)
H.H.S. = *Hou han shu*: Later Han dynastic history.
H.W.T.N.C. = *Han wu ti nei chuan*: Legend of the Han Emperor Wu (3rd cent. A.D.?).
K.S.C. = *Kao shih chuan*: Biographies of Scholars (Chin dynasty).
K.T.S.C. = *Kuan ti sheng chi*: Historic vestiges of Kuan Ti, God of War.
L.H.C. = *Lieh hsien chuan*: Biographies of hsien (3rd cent. A.D.?)
L.H.C. (H.C.) = *Lieh hsien chuan (by Huan-ch'u)*: Biographies of hsien (Yuan dynasty).
L.H.C.C. = *Lieh hsien ch'uan chuan*: Detailed biographies of hsien.
L.T.S.H.C. = *Li tai shen hsien chuan*: Biographies of hsien through the ages.
N.H.H.C. = *Ning hai hsien chih*: Topography of Ning-hai District.
P.P.T. = *Pao p'o tzu*: Taoist practices. By Ko Hung (4th cent. A.D.)
P.W.C. = *Po wu chich*: Record of strange events.
S.C. = *Shih chi*: Historical Record. By Ssu-ma Ch'ien (1st cent. B.C.)
S.H.C. = *Shen hsien chuan*: Biographies of hsien. By Ko Hung (4th cent. A.D.).
S.H.F.C. = *Shao hsing fu chih*: Topography of Shao-hsing Prefecture.
S.H.T.K. = *Shih hua tsung kuei*: Literary Miscellany.
S.K.C. = *San kuo chih*: Dynastic history of the Three Kingdoms.
S.K.C.Y.I. = *San kuo chih yen i*: Historical novel of the Three Kingdoms.
S.S.C. = *Sou shen chi*: Book of marvels (4th cent. A.D.).
T.M.C. = *T'ung ming chi*: Events of the reign of the Han Emperor Wu.
T.P.K.C. = *Tai p'ing kuang chi*: Fabulous tales (10th cent. A.D.).
T.S.C.C. = *T'u shu chi ch'eng*: General Encyclopaedia (A.D. 1726).
T.Y.C.J.C. = *T'ang yeh chen jen chuan*: Life of Yeh Fa-shan.
Y.C.C.C. = *Yun chi ch'i ch'ien*: Taoist extracts (11th cent. A.D.).

3. REMOTE ANTIQUITY

HUANG AN

HUANG AN was a native of Tai Chun and became an official messenger at that place. He said to himself: "My condition in life is too mean for me to live in the society of others." When studying, he held a whip for self-castigation and carried a thorn in his bosom to keep him from drowsiness .... He was in the habit of eating cinnabar, and his body was red all over. In winter he wore no furs. He used to sit on a spirit tortoise, two feet broad, and to those who asked him how many years he had sat there he answered: "Long ago Fu Hsi caught this animal when he first invented fishing-nets, and gave it to me. I have sat on its back so long that the shell has become quite flat. The tortoise fears the light of sun and moon, and puts out its head only once in two thousand years. This I have seen it do five times already since I have been sitting here." When Huang An wandered about, he carried the tortoise on his back. Men of that time called him "An of the Myriad Years". T.M.C.

MA SHIH HUANG

Ma Shih Huang was a horse doctor in the time of the Yellow Emperor. He knew the vital symptoms in a horse's constitution, and on receiving his treatment the animal would immediately get well. Once a dragon flew down and approached him with drooping ears and open jaws. Huang said to himself: "This dragon is ill and knows that I can effect a cure." Thereupon he performed acupuncture on its mouth just below the upper lip, and gave it a decoction of sweet herbs to swallow, which caused it to recover. Afterwards, whenever the dragon was ailing, it issued from its watery lair and presented itself for treatment. One morning the dragon took Huang on its back and bore him away. L.H.C.

PO SHIH SHENG

Po Shih Sheng was a pupil of the Venerable Chung Huang. In the days of P'eng Tsu [a Chinese Methuselah] he was already more than two thousand years old. He had no longing to ascend on high, but aspired to nothing more than a long life on earth. Gold-juice he regarded as the best of all drugs, but as his family was poor he could not obtain it. So he kept pigs and sheep, and after ten years or so had amassed a fortune of ten thousand pieces of silver, which enabled him to buy the drug and swallow it.

It was his habit to boil white stones and use them as food. This led him to make his abode on the White Stone Mountain, and thus he acquired the name of Po Shih Sheng (Master White Stone). Sometimes he would eat dried meat, and sometimes too he would abstain from all cereal food.

He was able to walk as far as three or four hundred *li* (about 130 miles) in one day. His appearance was that of a man of thirty. When somebody asked him why he did not wish to fly up to heaven, he replied: "I'm not at all sure I should enjoy myself as much in heaven as I do in this world." L.H.C. (H.C.)

WU KUANG

Wu Kuang lived in the time of the Hsia dynasty. His ears were seven inches long.

He was fond of playing on the lute, and fed on garlic roots. When T'ang ofYin was about to smite Chieh, he approached Wu Kuang for counsel, but the latter said: "It is no affair of mine." T'ang asked from whom he should seek advice. -- "I do not know."--"What about I Yin?"--"He who employs force must endure mortification. I do not know that it can be otherwise with him."

When T' ang had overcome Chieh, he offered to hand over the administration of the Empire to Wu Kuang, saying: "The wise proffer counsel to it, warriors rally to it, good men abide in it. That is the way of the ancients. Why do you, Sir, not rally to it? I wish to make you my chief minister." But Wu Kuang refused, saying: "To abandon one's sovereign is not righteous; to kill other men is not humane. That others should encounter the difficulties and I enjoy the benefits is not just. I have heard that one should not touch the emoluments of unrighteousness, nor occupy an official post in a wicked generation. How can I, then, accept any honor for myself? I cannot bear to witness such things any longer." Thereupon, taking a stone on his back, he threw himself into the Liao river, and disappeared for over four hundred years. In the reign of Wu Ting he appeared again, and Wu Ting wanted to make him his minister. He declined, and when Wu Ting went to seek him in his chariot and attempted forcible measures, he fled into the. Fou-liang mountains, and afterwards wandered away over the Shang-fu range. L.H.C.

4. CHOU DYNASTY (1122-249 B.C.)

LU SHANG

LU SHANG was a native of Chi Chou. He was born possessing the intuition of a sage and the capacity of foreseeing life and death. From the disorderly conditions prevailing under the rule of Chou Hsin, he fled to Liao-tung, where he remained in seclusion for forty years. Then he wandered westward to the realm of Chou, and found in the Nan Shan, another retreat. There in a stream called P'an he angled with rod and line for three years without catching a fish; and the people of those parts all told him that he had better stop fishing. But Lu Shang replied: "This is something quite beyond your comprehension." And at last he did succeed in catching a large carp, with a military seal in its belly.

Meanwhile, King Wen of Chou dreamt that he had found an inspired sage; and hearing of Lu Shang, he came in his chariot and took him back to the capital. When at last King Wu smote Chou Hsin, Lu Shang wrote a book entitled *Secret Counsel* in over a hundred sections. He used to eat marsh fungi and earth-marrow.

After the lapse of two hundred years he announced that he was about to depart this life. And so it came to pass, but there was trouble in the land, and his coffin remained unburied. Later on, when his son Chi came to fulfil the funeral rites, no corpse was found in the coffin, which was empty but for a jade seal and six bamboo tablets of manuscript. L.H.C.

YU TZU

Yu Tzu [Jade philosopher] was fond of studying the classics as a youth, and King Yu of the Chou dynasty gave him an official post. He did not take it up, however, but exclaimed with a sigh: "We who are born into this world let the days of our life slip away one by one, death looming ever nearer as the day of our birth recedes further into the past. Yet all we crave for is wealth and honor, and we have no idea how to nourish the stream of life itself. As soon as our allotted span is exhausted and our breath fails, we die. Then, when we are merely dust and ashes, how shall we benefit by the rank of prince or marquis, or by stores of gold and jade piled mountain-high? Only by translation as a hsien can one hope to avoid dissolution." Accordingly, he became the disciple of Ch'ang Sang Tzu, who initiated him into all his arts.

He would place a bowl of water between his two elbows and blow upon it, whereupon a brilliant red light would shoot up from the water to a height of ten feet. This water he used for medical purposes, giving it to the patient to drink if the disease was internal, or washing him with it if it was external. In every case the cure was instantaneous.

In the end, he climbed to the summit of Mount K'ung-t'ung [in Honan] and rose up to heaven in broad daylight. S.H.C.

TU TZU

Tu Tzu ["Master Calf"] was a native of Yeh. As a young man, he used to gather fir-cones and *fu-ling* on the Black Mountain to diet himself with. For several hundred years he alternated between robust youth and old age, good looks and ugliness, so that he came to be recogl1ized as a hsien. His usual round took him past the establishment of the vintner Yang Tu, whose daughter sold wine in the marketplace. Her eyebrows met in the middle, and her ears were long and delicate. These marks were considered extraordinary, and everybody declared that she was a celestial being.

Now Tu Tzu, while he was leading a yellow calf along the road, happened to meet Yang Tu's daughter, and was so delighted with the girl that he arranged to keep her as his handmaid. She, therefore, went out in Tu Tzu's company to gather peaches and plums. They would spend one night away and then return with a number of sacks full of fruit. People in the town tried to follow and keep a watch on them, but although they went out of the gate together, still leading the calf, no runner was able to overtake them, and there was nothing for it but to return. The couple continued to frequent the market-place for thirty years or more, and then they departed.

They have been seen at the foot of Mt. P'an selling their peaches and plums in winter. L.H.C.

CH'ANG JUNG

Ch'ang Jung was a Taoist of Ch'ang-shan, who called himself Yin Wang Tzu. His food was the root of the wild bramble, and he spent his life roaming about the country. Though seen at intervals during more than two hundred years, his complexion remained that of a man of about twenty. From certain plants he was able to extract purple which he used to sell to dyers. Any money that he got he would give to widows and orphans. Thus he lived for generation after generation, and the shrines put up in his honor were ten thousand in number. L.H.C.

CH'I LUNG MING

Ch'i Lung Ming was a native of Hun-t'ing. At the age of twenty, when searching in a pool, he found a young dragon, in shape resembling a house-lizard, with more than ten heads. He gave it food and kept it in a hut thatched with straw. Soon after the dragon was fully grown it disappeared. Some fifty years later the hut was washed away by a flood, and its owner left the locality. One day he returned to Hun-t'ing riding on the dragon, and shouted to the inhabitants below: "I am the grandson of Feng Po-ch'ang.

If the people in this place do not remove to a distance of five hundred li, they will perish." Those who put faith in the warning all went away, while the others regarded it merely as a piece of devilry. But in the eighth moon a flood actually did occur, in which thousands of persons lost their lives. L.H.C.

HSIA CH'IU CHUNG

Hsia Ch'iu Chung was a native of Ning [in South Manchuria], where for over a hundred years he was a seller of drugs, the people merely regarding him as an instance of ordinary longevity.

His hut was shattered by an earthquake, and dozens of dwelling-houses in the same village were destroyed in the flood that followed. Chung himself perished; whereupon some people came and threw his dead body into the river, afterwards proceeding to appropriate his drugs and offer them for sale. But ere long they found themselves confronted by Chung in person, who was wearing a fur robe. The culprits who had stolen his drugs and disposed of his body were terrified, and prostrating themselves at his feet begged for mercy. Chung, however, said: "I am only vexed that you have caused people to know me for what I am. I must depart." Subsequently he served as an express messenger under the barbarian King of Fu-yu, in which capacity he revisited Ning. Throughout the northern regions he was known as the banished hsien. L.H.C

LAO TZU

Lao Tzu was a native of Ch'en.

His surname was Li (Plum), his personal name Erh (Ear), and his "style" Po-yang. His mother gave birth to him while leaning against a plum tree. He was able to speak as soon as he was born, and pointing to the plum tree said: "I take my surname from this tree." Though born in the Yin period, he became Palace Secretary under the Chou dynasty. He made a practice of nourishing his vital essence, his great aim being to absorb strength without dissipating any. In due course he was made Custodian of the Archives, a post which he held for more than eighty years--the Shih Chi says, for over two hundred years. His contemporaries called him the Noble Recluse, and his posthumous title was Tan (Flat-eared). When , Confucius came to Chou and visited Lao Tzu, he recognized him as an inspired sage and took him as his Master.

Later on, when the virtue of Chou had fallen into decay, he mounted a chariot drawn by a black ox and departed for the land of Ta Ch'in.

When he passed through the Western Barrier, the Warden of the Pass, Yin Hsi, received him with honor, knowing that he was a saintly man, and persuaded him to write a treatise, which was no other than the *Tao Te Ching* in two parts, one roll to each. L.H.C.

Confucius paid a visit to the Chou State in order to question Lao Tzu on matters of ceremonial. The latter replied, saying: "Those about whom you speak are men whose bones have all turned to dust, and whose words alone survive. Now, when the princely man finds his opportunity, he rides in a State chariot; if he fails to find his opportunity, he goes on foot in humble guise. I have heard it said that a clever merchant, though possessed of great hoards of wealth, will act as though his coffers were empty; and that the princely man, though of perfect moral excellence, maintains the air of a simpleton. Abandon your arrogant ways and countless desires, your suave demeanor and unbridled ambition, for they do not promote your welfare. That is all I have to say to you."

Confucius went away, and said to his disciples: "I understand how birds can fly, how fishes can swim, and how four-footed beasts can run. Those that run can be snared, those that swim may be caught with hook and line, those that fly may be shot with arrows. But when it Comes to the dragon, I am unable to conceive how he can soar into the sky riding upon the wind and clouds. To-day I have seen Lao Tzu, and can only liken him to a dragon." S.C.

I for my own part think it only natural that, if Lao was a spiritual being of celestial origin, he should have appeared in some form in each successive generation, exchanging his honorable rank for a humble condition, sacrificing his ease and freedom in order to subject himself to toil, turning his back on the pure serenity of paradise in order to come into contact with the defilement of the world, giving up his celestial office and accepting inferior rank amongst men. S.H.C.

During the reign of Wen Ti [I79-I57 B.C.] of the Han dynasty Lao Tzu went by the name of Kuang Ch'eng Tzu. The Emperor sent an envoy to question him, but the Sage replied: "Tao is worthy of veneration, and the virtue it manifests is highly to be prized. It is not meet that these things should be inquired about from a distance." The Emperor then ordered his carriage, went to visit him, and said:

"Within the universe there are four great powers, of which the sovereign is one; and even though you are a man of Tao, you are still my subject. If you are unable to bend low, how shall you be exalted? It is in my power to bestow poverty and abasement as well as riches and rank."

By way of reply, the Sage clapped his hands and, remaining in a sitting posture, slowly levitated into mid-air like a rising cloud, until he hovered motionless in celestial space, some thousand feet above the earth. There was a pause, and then he looked down and spoke: "Poised thus between heaven and earth, having my abode in neither, nor belonging to the race of mortals, how can I be subject to your sovereignty, and how can your Majesty cause me to be rich or poor, of high or lowly station?" Understanding came to the Emperor, and descending from his carriage, he made humble obeisance. The Sage then presented him with a copy of the two holy books.

Not a generation passes but Lao Tzu appears. Throughout the past eons of human existence he has ceaselessly exercised powers of conversion. For ever in the boundless ages to come he will continue to exist; sometimes visible, sometimes invisible, but always mysterious to mortal men. His transformations are without end; his achievements in bringing salvation to beings both of heaven and earth are too many to be told. L.H.C. (H.C.)

FU LU

Where Fu Lu originally came from is not known; but he constantly stayed at Chii [in Shantung], and wandered about among the temples along the sea-coast. In one temple he Id three hsien gambling for melons. Seeing Fu Lu, they bade him bring them a few dozen yellow and white melons, and then told him to shut his eyes. When he opened them again, he found himself in the island of Fang-chang, which lies to the south of P'eng-lai.

Afterwards, when he revisited Chu, he brought out a quantity of pearls and jade and other precious things which he had taken from Fang-chang, and offered them for sale. Time went on, and one day he appeared in reddish brown garments with shaven head and all the look of an old man. On being questioned, he said that he had been convicted of stealing objects from a temple. A few years later, however, he resumed his youthful appearance and his hair grew long again as it was in the days gone by. L.H.C.

MU YU

Mu Yu was a native of Ho-p'ing village, south of Chli-lu [in Hopei]. His mother was poor and of humble station, and followed the profession of a midwife. She attended on a lady at her confinement, and when the child was born it opened its eyes and, looking at its mother, burst out laughing. The mother was much alarmed, but that night the midwife dreamed that she saw a personage in a large official cap with a red kerchief, watching over the child, who said: "This boy is the Controller of human destiny. In requital for your kindly services he will cause your son Mu Yu to attain hsien-ship." The woman believed and treasured up this promise in her heart; and afterwards, when she gave birth to a son, she gave him the name of Mu Yu. When the other boy, whom she had helped to bring into the world, had reached the age of fifteen, a carriage and horses came to fetch him away in the night; and as he passed the woman's house he called out: "Mu Yu! Mu Yu! Come and drive my carriage for me." So they both went off together.

More than twenty years later, a stork would come every morning with a fish two feet long in its beak and deposit it at the woman's door. The latter said nothing about it, but used to sell the fish. This continued for thirty years, when the bird ceased to appear. Mu Yu's mother attained the age of a hundred before she died. L.H.C.

KU CH'UN

Ku Ch'un was a native of Yo-yang [in Shensi], and held an official post in the reign of the Eniperor Ch'eng Ti (32-7 B.C.)

Stricken with disease, he died to all appearance, except that his body did not grow cold. His relatives carried out the funeral ceremonies and went into mourning, but they were loathe to nail up the coffin. Three years later, Ku Ch'un reappeared, sitting upon the parapet of one of the town gates, and still wearing his cone-shaped official hat. Consternation prevailed among the townsfolk. His relatives came to bring him home, but he would not go with them. They opened his coffin, and found grave-clothes but no corpse. For three days and nights Ku Ch'un remained where he was. Then he transported himself to Ch'ang-an [the capital] and took up a similar position above the Heng Gate. As soon as his people heard of it, they went after him and tried to get him to return. Again he departed, and took refuge on Mt. T'ai-po. A shrine was then built for him on the mountain, to which he would come from time to time and stay for the night. L.H.C.

SHEN HSI

Shen Hsi was a native of Wu-chun [in Kiangsu] who studied Tao in the land of Shu [Szechwan]. He achieved the power of dissipating calamity, curing disease, and bringing succour to the common people, but knew nothing of the drugs of immortality and their use. His virtue found favor in the sight of God, and was duly recorded by the spirits of heaven.

Hsi and his wife, the lady Chia, were returning on one occasion from a visit to their daughter-in-law when they encountered three chariots, one drawn by a white deer, another by a green dragon, and the third by a white tiger. There were thirty or forty mounted attendants in scarlet livery, armed with lances and swords, who filled the roadway with pomp and glitter. They inquired if he was Shen Hsi; and the latter, who knew not what to make of this astounding apparition, replied: "I am; but why do you ask?" One of the men on horseback said: "Shen Hsi has deserved well of the people. Tao is ever present to his mind, and from earliest infancy his conduct has been free from blame. But his allotted span is short, and his years are approaching their close. So Huang and Lao [the Yellow Emperor and Lao Tzu] have sent down three hsien officials in these chariots to escort him to heaven" ...

Presently the three hsien came forward in their feather robes, with staves of office in their hands, and bestowed on Hsi a tablet of white jade, a green jade suit of mail, and a set of red jade characters, which he could not understand. After this ceremony he was borne off to heaven, his ascension being witnessed by a number of field-laborers in the vicinity, who did not know what to make of it. For a little while here came a thick mist, and when it cleared away the whole company had disappeared; all that remained were the oxen which had drawn Hsi's carriage and which were now grazing in the fields. Someone recognized the animals as belonging to Hsi, and informed his family. His disciples, fearing that their master had been carried off to the hills by evil spirits, searched for him in every direction for a hundred *li* around, but in vain.

Over 400 years later, Shen Hsi unexpectedly revisited his native village and sought out one of his descendants named Huai-hsi. This man said he had heard his elders speak of a certain ancestor who became a hsien and disappeared, never to return. Shen Hsi stayed with his kinsfolk for about a month, and told them of his experiences when he first went up to heaven: "Though I was unable to see God himself," he said, " I saw Lao Chun [" Prince Lao", i.e. Lao Tzu] seated on the right-hand side. The attendants instructed me not to make any formal acknowledgments, but simply to take my seat in silence. The celestial palace seemed to be composed of an insubstantial, luminous haze; shot through with an indescribable variety of colors. There were hundreds of attendants, mostly female. In the gardens grew trees bearing gems and jade, and all the different kinds of chih plant in great profusion. Dragons and tigers gambolled in our midst, and a tinkling sound was audible, like that of bronze ornaments hanging round a bell, the origin of which I could not discover. The walls shone with a bright glow, and were covered with magic charms.

" Lao Chun was about ten feet in height. His hair hung loose, and he wore embroidered garments. His whole person radiated light. After a while, a bevy of fairy maidens brought in a golden table with jade goblets and set it before me, saying: 'This is the divine elixir: whoso quaffs it shall be exempt from death. If you and your wife each take a cup, endless longevity will be yours.' After the draught we were to make an obeisance but proffer no thanks; and when we had drunk, they brought us two dates as large as hens' eggs, and five-inch slices of dried meat. 'Return for a time,' they said, 'to the world of mortals, and go on curing the diseases of the people. Whenever you wish to ascend on high, write out this charm and hang it on the end of a pole, and we will come to fetch you.' So saying, they handed me a charm and a fairy prescription; and anon I fell into a drowse from which I awaked to find myself on earth. Many times have I had occasion to test the efficacy of this charm." S.H.C.

5. CH'IN DYNASTY (246-207 B.C.)

AN CH'I SHENG

THE Master An Ch'i was a native of Fu-hsiang in the district of Lang-yeh. He used to sell drugs on the shore of the Eastern Sea. His contemporaries all called him Old Father Thousand Years. When the First Emperor of the Ch'in dynasty made a journey to the East, he sought an interview with An Ch'i, and lingered talking with him for three days and three nights. The Emperor bestowed on him vast quantities of gold and precious jewels; but on his departure An Ch'i left his gifts in the pavilion of Fu-hsiang, together with a letter saying that he considered himself sufficiently rewarded with a pair of red jade slippers, and adding: "After the lapse of a few years look for me on the island of P'eng-lai." The First Emperor lost no time in sending out to sea an expedition numbering several hundreds of persons, led by Hsu Shih and Lu Sheng. They never reached P'eng-lai, because they encountered violent storms which caused them to turn back. Shrines in honor of An Ch'i have been set up in about a dozen places along the sea shore near the Fu-hsiang pavilion. L.H.C.

MAO NU

Mao Nu [" Hairy Woman "], whose style is Yu-chiang, has been seen by hunters on Mount Hua-yin for many generations. Her body is covered with hair. She professes to be one of the ladies from Ch'in Shih Huang's palace who, during the troubles that attended the downfall of the Ch'in dynasty, became a wandering fugitive and took refuge on the mountain. There she encountered the Taoist recluse Ku Ch'un, who taught her to eat pine-needles. In consequence of this diet she became immune from cold and hunger, and her body was so etherealized that it seemed to fly along. For over 170 years the mountain grotto in which she makes her abode has resounded to the thrumming of a lute. L.H.C.

6. FORMER HAN DYNASTY (206 B.C.-A.D. 24)

YIN SHENG

YIN SHENG was a beggar boy who lived under a bridge spanning the river Wei at Ch'ang-an. He used to take up his stand in the market-place and beg from those who did business there. On one occasion, disgusted by his importunity, they bespattered him with filth. Yet, when he appeared in his place again, his clothes were in their normal condition and showed no trace of dirt. The authorities, getting wind of the affair, had him arrested and thrown into chains; and yet he continued to beg in the market-place. Being again arrested, and threatened with the death penalty, he left the city. But the houses of all those who had bespattered him collapsed in ruins, killing some dozen people. Hence the jingle which is current in Ch'ang-an:

" If you meet a beggar boy, give him a drink,
Or your house will fall down before you can wink." L.H.C

CHANG LIANG

One day, when Chang Liang was sauntering over the bridge at Hsia-p'ei [near Soochow], an old man clad in a coarse serge garment crossed his path, and deliberately let one of his shoes fall under the bridge. Thereupon he turned to Liang and said: " My child, run down and fetch my shoe for me." Liang, taken aback, felt half inclined to beat him for his impudence, but forbearing on account of his age, he went down and brought up the shoe. "Put it on my foot," said the old man. Having already fetched the shoe for him, Liang knelt down and did as he was bid. With his shoe on once more, the old man went away chuckling, while Liang stared after him in utter amazement. However, he had not gone far before he turned and came back, saying: "My child, you are teachable. Meet me here at dawn in five days' time." Though he thought this very strange, Liang assented, and at dawn on the fifth day he went to the rendezvous; but the old man was already there, and said angrily: "Why do you come late when you have an appointment with an old man?" And he departed, telling Liang to meet him in the early morning five days later. On the fifth day Liang was there at cock-crow, but the old man was again before him, asked angrily why he was late, and went away telling him to come very early five days later. This time, Liang went before it was midnight, and the old man arrived very soon after. "That's as it should be," he exclaimed, well pleased; and producing a manuscript he said: "Read this, and you may become the teacher of princes. In ten years' time you will begin to rise, and after thirteen years, my child, you will see me: a yellow stone lying at the foot of Mount Ku-ch'eng in Chi-pei--that is I." Then he departed, saying nothing further, and was not seen again. When daylight came, Liang examined his book and found it was T'ai Kung's *Art of War*, which he studied constantly until he knew it by heart.

Thirteen years later, Liang was accompanying the Emperor through Chi-pei when, at the foot of Mount Ku-ch'eng, he did actually see a yellow stone, which he took home with him and treated with extraordinary honor .... Being afflicted with many physical ailments, Chang Liang now began practicing regulation of the breath and abstained from cereal food. But when the Emperor died, the Empress Lu, out of pure kindness, strongly urged him to eat, saying: " Man's life on earth is like a white colt passing a crack: why torture oneself in this manner?" Thus the Marquis of Liu [as he had then become] had no option but to obey: he took some food, and eight years afterwards he died. S.C.

When the Marquis of Liu died, he was buried on the Dragon's Head Plateau. During the rebellion of the Red Eyebrows [at the close of the Former Han dynasty] his tomb was broken open, but only a yellow stone pillow was found, which by a sudden transformation flew away like a shooting star. No corpse nor clothing was to be seen, but a certain *Book of Plain Words* was recovered, and also several chapters of a military treatise. T.P.K.C.

T'AI SHAN LAO FU

The real names of T'ai Shan Lao Fu (" The old Gaffer of Mt. T'ai ") are not known. When Wu Ti of the Han dynasty was on a hunting expedition in the cast, he saw an old man hoeing the ground near the roadside, round whose head there was a halo of light several feet in breadth. This astonished the Emperor, and he stopped to question him. The old fellow appeared to be about fifty years of age, but his face was fresh-colored like a boy's, and his skin was unusually smooth and clear. Asked by the Emperor what Tacist method he had employed to this end, he replied: "When I was 85 years old, my body was decaying fast and death was at hand; my hair was white and my teeth were gone. Then I met one possessed of Tao who taught me to abstain from cereal food, to eat nothing but *shu* (Atractylis root) and drink nothing but water. He also made me a magic pillow, stuffed with 32 ingredients ... I practiced this regimen, and lo! my age was turned to youth; black hair grew again on my head, new teeth filled the place of those that had gone; I was able to travel 300 *li* in one day. Your servant has now reached the age of 180."

The Emperor, having received this prescription for longevity bestowed upon him jade and silk. The veteran afterwards retired into the fastnesses of Mount T'ai, only returning to his village at intervals of five or ten years. When 300 years had elapsed, he returned no more. S.H.C.

LI SHAO CHUN

Li Shao Chun was a native of Ch'i. When the Emperor Wu was summoning magicians to Court, Shao Chun had acquired from the Master An Ch'i the art of transmuting cinnabar in the furnace, but his family was poor and he was unable to procure the necessary drugs. So he said to his disciples: "Old age is approaching, and the money I earn is insufficient to supply my wants, even though I should labor with all my strength in the fields. Now, the Son of Heaven is addicted to Tao, and I wish to go and see him. I pray you to compound the drugs for me, so that my ambition may have free scope." They did so, and Shao Chun presented the drugs to the Emperor, saying: "Cinnabar may be transmuted into pure gold, and the latter when swallowcd will enable one to rise to heaven as a hsien .. ." The Son of Heaven treated him with honor and respect, and gave him innumerable presents.

Shao Chun once attended a banquet given by the Marquis of Wu-an. Among the company was an aged man, over ninety years old. Shao Chun inquired his name and said: " I recognize that old man because I saw him as a child going for a walk with his grandfather." Whereat those present were much astonished. On another occasion, Shao Chun was able to identify an old bronze vessel which he saw in the imperial palace: "That vessel," he said, "was kept by Duke Huan of Ch'i in his sleeping-chamber." Accordingly, the Emperor examined the characters incised thereon, and found that, as he had said, it was an ancient vessel of the Ch'i State ...

Having secretly manufactured the elixir, Shao Chun said to the Emperor: "So long as your Majesty cannot make an end of pride and extravagance, and renounce the allurements of the senses; while smiting and killing go on unchecked, and the passions of joy and anger are not overcome; while in your dominions there are spirits that are not submissive, and in the market-places there are executions and bloodshed, the great secret of the celestial drug cannot be mastered ... " Soon after, Shao Chun fell dangerously ill. The Emperor went to see him, and commanded an attendant to take down from his lips the secrets of his art; but he died before the task was completed. "Shao Chun is not dead," said the Emperor; he has only undergone a voluntary transformation." When he was put. into his coffin, the corpse suddenly disappeared, although the clothes in which he was wrapped were not unfastened, and remained there like the slough of a cicada. This increased the Emperor's wonder, and he regretted that he had not been more diligent in seeking out Shao Chun. S.H.C.

Shao Chun said to the Emperor Wu: "Sacrifice to the Furnace and you will be able to summon up the spirits. Having summoned up the spirits, you may transmute cinnabar into pure gold. When you have produced pure gold, make it into eating and drinking-vessels, and you will prolong your span of life. If your span of life is prolonged, you may behold the hsien who live on the island of P'eng-lai. When you have seen them, and performed the sacrifices to Heaven and Earth, then you will become immortal. That is what happened to the Yellow Emperor. Your humble servant once voyaged across the sea and visited An Ch'i Sheng, who gave me dates to eat as large as melons . An Ch'i Sheng is a hsien who wanders at will in P'eng-lai. When it is fitting, he makes himself visible to men; otherwise he remains invisible."

It was after this that the Son of Heaven first sacrificed to the Furnace in person, sent magicians over the sea to seek for the island of P'eng-lai, An Ch'i Sheng and the other immortals, and occupied himself with the transmutation of cinnabar and various other substances into yellow gold. S.C.

LIU AN

Liu An was Prince of Huai-nan under the Han dynasty. In those days the young feudal princes made a virtue of extravagance: they spent their lives in music, making love, and hunting with dogs and horses. Liu An, on the contrary, maintained a humble demeanor, paying respectful attention to the learned. Scholarship was his constant and beloved pursuit, and he also acquired proficiency in prophecy and magic.

Taoists from all parts of the country visited Liu An's abode, and among others, eight worthies whose beards and eyebrows were all hoary white. The door-keeper went first secretly and informed the Prince, who ordered him, as if on his own initiative, to put some puzzling questions to the newcomers. Accordingly he said: "Uppermost in our Prince's mind is a desire to seek the Tao that makes one live long without growing old; next, he wishes to find great scholars with a wide range of learning and intimate knowledge of abstruse subjects; and lastly, he wants lusty devil-may-care fellows whose strength is equal to the lifting of weighty tripods or attacking tigers unarmed. Now you, Sirs, are too old, and it is evident that you lack the magic means of warding off senility. How can you investigate profundities, or exercise control over things at a distance, thoroughly assimilate eternal principles, perfect your moral nature? As you are wanting in these requirements I dare not announce you to the Prince."

To this the Eight Worthies smilingly replied: "If his Highness dislikes our antiquity, we will become young." Scarcely had they spoken these words than they all turned into youths of fourteen or fifteen. Their coils of hair became black and silky, and their complexions like peach-bloom. The door-keeper, much amazed, went and told the Prince. Directly the Prince heard the news, he went, without putting on his shoes, bare-footed to welcome them, and conducted them up to the Terrace of Meditation on Hsienship, where he spread brocaded hangings over an ivory couch, kindled the Hundred Harmonies Incense, and placed before them tables of gold and jade.

The Prince paid them deference as if he were their disciple. Facing north, he made obeisance to them, saying: "I am a man of mediocre ability. Since childhood I have loved Tao and the virtue it manifests. Fettered with ordinary occupations and sunk in the depths of mundane affairs, I cannot escape from my trammels and shoulder my satchel in order to live in the mountains and forests. Yet morning and evening I hunger and thirst while meditating on the glories of spiritual life, and long to wash away my muddy sediment of mortality ... Earnestly I beg you Princes of Tao to pity and instruct me. Then, though now a crawling insect, I shall borrow the wings of a heron and be enabled to soar up into the sky."

Thereupon the eight youths turned into old men again and, addressing the Prince, said: "Although our knowledge is incomplete, and we possess merely the education of children, yet hearing that the Prince loves scholars, we have come to join him; but we have still to learn the Prince's mind and what it is he desires. One of us is able without effort to call up wind and rain, instantaneously to raise clouds and mists. He can trace lines across the land and they become rivers, and by scooping up the soil he can make mountains. Another of us can cause high hills to collapse, and the sources of deep springs to dry up. He can tame tigers and panthers, summon scaly monsters and dragons to appear, and press the spirits of heaven and earth into his service. Another of us can divide his personality and transform his shape, and is also able to become visible or invisible at will. He cam hide whole army corps, and turn midday into night. Another can ride the clouds and tread the empyrean, cross the sea and walk upon the waves. He can go in and out where there is no crevice, or travel in a breath one thousand li. Another can enter flames unscathed and plunge into water without a wetting. He is invulnerable by sword or shaft. He feels no cold in winter frosts, nor does he sweat in summer heat. Another is capable of a myriad transformations: bird, beast, plant or tree--as the fancy takes him, he can become each or any of these. He can move mountains and bring rivers to a halt; he can transport a palace or shift a house. Another can boil mud into gold, or freeze lead into silver. He can fuse the eight minerals of the alchemist into a liquid from which pearls fly aloft in lieu of steam. He rides in a chariot of clouds with dragons for his team, and floats above the Great Purity.

Thou, O Prince, hast but to choose which of these powers thou desirest."

The upshot was that the magic drug was duly prepared, but the Prince did not yet proceed to swallow it. Before ascending to heaven he met some of the hsien nobility. Having had but little practice in doing honor to others, and having seldom had occasion to perform the ceremonies of self-abasement, he showed some lack of politeness in his demeanor, talked in too loud a voice, and made a blunder in referring to himself as the Solitary One.

Thereupon the chief of the hsien nobles formally accused him of disrespectful behavior, and said that he ought to be expelled from their company. The Eight Worthies, however, interceded for him, and a milder penalty was substituted: he was condemned to be Keeper of the Latrines at the capital for three years, after which he was to become a hsien of the rank and file, ineligible for any official post, and merely exempted from mortality.

It is related by men who were living at this time that when Liu An and the Eight Worthies at last took their departure from this earth, the vessel containing the dregs of the elixir was left lying in the courtyard, and that the contents were finished up by the dogs and poultry of the establishment, with the result that they too sailed up to heaven; thus, cocks were heard crowing in the sky, and the barking of dogs resounded amidst the clouds. S.H.C.

KOU-I FU-JEN

Kou-i Fu-jen [the Lady Hook-wing] was a native of Ch'i. Her real name was Chao. As a girl she followed the Taoist doctrine of "purity".

As the sequel of an illness which kept her bedridden for six years, her right hand became permanently contracted and clenched. She took very little food and drink. The imperial soothsayers announced that the aura of a noble lady made its presence felt in the north-east, and advised the emperor to seek her out. She was summoned to Court, and found to be of surpassing loveliness. Wu Ti opened her clenched hand and found in it a jade hook, after which the hand remained open. In due course she conceived and bore the future emperor Chao Ti. Later on she was put to death by Wu Ti, but when the body was encoffined it did not grow cold, and diffused a fragrant odor for the space of a whole month. Afterwards, when Chao Ti came to the throne, he arranged for a reinterment, but nothing was found in the coffin except a silk slipper. L.H.C.

CH'I FU

Ch'i Fu was a basket-maker of Nan-chun [in the modern Hupeh], and dwelt in the mountains. There was constantly staying at his home a certain hsien from whom he bought melons. The latter taught him how to extract the active principle from melon-seeds; he kept a store of these together with the seeds of cassia fruit and berries of angelica, and after eating them in equal proportions for twenty years and more, was able to move at a flying speed, to scale high mountains, and to live under water. More than a century later he was dwelling on the summit of Mount Chueh. People called him the Old Man of the Valley, and he would talk to them about things that had happened in the course of his lifetime. L.H.C.

TUNG-FANG SO

Tung-fang So was a native of Yen-tz'u in P'ing-yuan, and lived for a long time in Wu [Kiangnan] as a schoolmaster. After thirty years or so, in the reign of Wu Ti, he sent in a memorial on the needs of the State, and was given an appointment at Court. By the time of Chao Ti, he was regarded by some of his contemporaries as an inspired sage, by others as a common fellow. His behavior showed such a strange combination of depth and shallowness, openness and reserve, that no one knew exactly when he was speaking from his heart or when he was merely jesting. At the beginning of the reign of Hsuan Ti, in order to escape from the disorders of the age, he threw up his post, laying aside his cap of state and quitting his official residence, and drifted away whithersoever chance might take him. Later on he was seen in Kuei-chi, selling drugs in the region of the Five Lakes.

The initiated had reason to suspect that he was really the Spirit of the Year-star [the planet Jupiter]. L.H.C.

Tung-fang So is commonly said to be the spirit of the planet Venus, and to have passed through a number of incarnations. In the reign of the Emperor Wu, men of virtue and learning were invited to Court, with the expectation of obtaining posts outside the regular system of promotion. Written applications poured in from every part of the Empire, but So presented himself in person at the Palace and made the following declaration: "At the age of twelve I lost my father, and was brought up by my elder brother's wife. At thirteen I was engaged in study, at fourteen I practiced sword-play, at sixteen I could repeat the Book of Odes, and at nineteen I was versed in the art of war as taught by Sun and Wu; moreover, I always observe the rule of conduct attributed to Tzu Lu.

Now I am twenty-three years old, over six feet in height, with eyes like swinging pearls and teeth like even rows of white shells. I am as brave as Meng Fen, active as Ch'ing Chi, honest as Pao Shu, faithful as Wei Sheng. Thus I am fully qualified to be your Majesty's chief minister."

Though So's words were lacking in modesty and extravagant in their self-praise, he was at once accepted as a man of heroic mould, and gradually rose high in the Emperor's favor. But he kept a troupe of singers and actors, and did not concern himself with State business. Liu Hsiang in his youth often questioned him about the prolongation of life, and found him full of shrewdness and insight. His own contemporaries all describe him as the prince of good fellows, and irresistible in argument. F.S.T.

At the age of three Tung-fang So was in the habit of gesticulating, pointing up to the sky, and talking to himself. One day his foster-mother missed him, and a year went by before he returned. She was greatly shocked, and said: "You have been away for a whole year. Is this how you care for me?" So replied: "I only went to the Sea of Purple Mud, where the water stained my clothes so that I had to go to the Yu spring to wash them. I left in the morning, and got back at noon: what do you mean by 'a whole year'?" His mother then asked him about the places he had been to.—"After I had finished washing my clothes," said So, "I rested for a bit in the Ming-tu-ch'ung Pavilion and took a nap. The King and his nobles fed me on red chestnuts and sunset-cloud liquor, and when I had eaten my fill I went into a sort of trance. Then I drank a small quantity of celestial yellow dew, and revived again. On my way home I came across an old tiger lying by the roadside, and returned riding on its back." L.T.S.H.C.

The Western Queen Mother once paid a visit to the Han Emperor Wu, and was received in the Nine-Blossom Hall. She bade her attendants fetch in seven peaches, each only the size of a pill, five of which she presented to the Emperor, and ate the other two herself. When the Emperor had eaten his peaches, he placed the stones on his lap, and when the Queen Mother asked why he kept them, he replied: "These peaches are so delicious that I wish to plant the stones." She smiled at this and said: "My peach-tree only bears fruit once in three thousand years."

Now, the Emperor and the Queen Mother were sitting alone together, and none of their suite were allowed to enter the apartment. But Tung-fang So had stolen into the corridor adjoining the Hall on the south, and was peeping at the Queen Mother through a window. She observed him, and said to the Emperor: "This young fellow who is looking through the window has come three times before and stolen these peaches of mine." The Emperor marveled greatly at this, and from that time onward people looked upon Tung-fang So as a divine being. P.W.C.

Wu Ti of the Han was travelling eastwards, and had not yet emerged from the Han Ku Pass when he came upon a monstrous creature blocking the way. Thirty or forty feet in length, its body resembled in shape that of a buffalo or an elephant. It had black eyes that blazed with light, and its four legs were so firmly planted in the ground that every effort to dislodge it was unavailing. All the courtiers were terrified, but Tung-fang So came to the rescue and asked for some wine to sprinkle over it; then, after some dozens of gallons had been used for that purpose, the monster gradually melted away.

The Emperor asked Tung-fang So to explain the phenomenon, and he replied: "This may be called the product of an atmosphere of sorrow and suffering. The spot on which we stand must have been the site of a dungeon under the Ch'in dynasty, or else the scene of the labors of a multitude of transported criminals. Now, wine has the power to banish grief, and that is why it was able to dispel this phantom."—"Oh, man of much learning," exclaimed the Emperor, "to think that your knowledge can extend as far as this!" S.S.C.

When about to die, Tung-fang So said to one who shared his abode: "In all the world there is none who knows me for what I am, save only Ta Wu Kung." After his death, Wu Ti sent for Ta Wu Kung and questioned him: "Do you know Tung-fang So?"—" No, I do not know him."—"What sort of things can you do?"—"I possess some skill in astronomy."—"Are all the stars included in the scheme of your calculations?"—"All are included," he replied."—"Alas!" said the Emperor, looking up to heaven with a sigh, "Tung-fang So has lived at my side for eighteen of those years, and I never knew that he was the Year-star." L.H.C. (H.C.)

One day, Tung-fang So bestrode a dragon and flew away. At the same moment a number of people observed him ascending from the north-west and, gazing upwards, were able to watch his flight. After a while, he was enveloped in a dense mist which made it impossible to see where he went. H.W.T.N.C.

FU CHU

The Master Fu Chu [Box-carrier] was a man of uncertain origin, but his speech seemed to indicate that he had lived in the old Yen State.

He always carried on his back a box of implements for polishing mirrors, and used to frequent the market-towns of Wu in order to exhibit his skill in this work. He charged one cash for polishing a mirror. Having inquired of his host if there were any sick persons in the place, he would produce a drug made up into purple pills and administer these. Those who took them invariably recovered. After he had been practicing in this way for some forty years or so, a great pestilence broke out, and whole families flocked to consult him. He gave medicine and saved thousands of lives, but would not take a single cash in return, so that the people of Wu recognized in him a man of spiritual purity. Afterwards he took up his abode on Mount Wu, and used to lower medicines down the side of a steep precipice for the benefit of those in the valley below. At last, having made up his mind to depart, he announced his intention as follows; "I am returning to the fairy island of P'eng-lai, and will send some magic water from the top of the cliff for you all." And true enough, one day a stream of white-colored liquid was seen trickling down rocks. People came and drank it, and many were cured of their diseases. In a dozen places shrines were erected in Fu Chu's honor. L.H.C.

HU TZU HSIEN

Hu Tzu Hsien was a fortune-teller of Kuan-hsia in Hall-chung [in Shensi]. When he had reached the age of a hundred odd, he made preparations to depart, and called to the wife of a certain wine-dealer, saying: "Get ready as quickly as you can! You and I must obey the summons of the Prince of Chung-ling [a ruler of the Immortals]." The same night, a hsien came to Hu Tzu Hsien, bringing with him a couple of straw dogs.

He and the lady of the wine-shop each mounted one of these steeds, which straightway turned into dragons and flew up Mount Hua-yin. Since then they have constantly been heard shouting from the top of the mountain: "Here we are! – Tzu Hsien and the old lady of the wine-shop." L.H.C.

WEN PIN

Wen Pin was a villager of T'ai-ch'iu [the modern Yung-ch'eng Hsien, Honan] who made his living as a vendor of straw sandals. He took a number of wives, turning them away after thirty years or so. At a later period, one of his former wives, who had now passed the age of ninety, saw Wen Pin again. He was still in the full vigor of manhood, and the old lady wept, and pleaded with him to take her back. Wen Pin excused himself, saying: "It wouldn't do; but could you perhaps meet me at the altar west of the village pavilion, at daybreak on the first of the first moon?" Accordingly, the old lady, accompanied by her grandson, travelled over ten *li* by night and sat by the altar waiting for Pin. In a short time he arrived and was greatly surprised to see her. –"So you really love Tao, then?" he said. "Had I known that before, I should never have sent you away." He then instructed her to swallow chrysanthemum petals, *ti fu* [*Kochia scoparia*, Schr.], certain epiphytes of the mulberry, and pine-seeds. Thus increasing her store of vital energy, she too became rejuvenated, and was seen for more than a hundred years afterwards. L.H.C.

7. LATER HAN DYNASTY (A.D. 25-220)

LIU CH'EN *and* YUAN CHAO

LIU CH'EN was a native of Yen Hsien [in Chekiang]. In the 15th year of Yung-p'ing in the Later Han dynasty (A.D. 72), he and his fellow-townsman Yuan Chao went up into the T'ien-t'ai mountains to collect herbs, but lost their way and could not get back. Thirteen days passed, and their hunger and thirst were extreme, when they saw a peach-tree growing on the mountain-side. They plucked the fruit and ate it, and then went down to drink from a mountain stream. Here they saw a freshly picked cabbage leaf come floating by, and afterwards a cup containing grains of sesamum. The two friends were overjoyed, feeling sure that there must be a human habitation close by. Crossing a hill, they passed into a large valley, where they came upon two maidens of surpassing beauty. One of the maidens addressed them by name and said with a smile: "Did you manage to get hold of that cup just now?" This filled them with astonishment, but the maidens went on to inquire merrily why they had been so long in coming, and invited them to their home. This was furnished with much magnificence, silken tapestries covering the walls. Richly attired waiting-women set before them a delicious meal of sesamum and goats' flesh. When they had finished, wine was handed round and a musical entertainment was given, lasting until midnight. Then they retired to rest, each in his own alcove.

After staying here for ten days, the two friends said they must depart, but were finally induced to remain for six months. The climate was mild and temperate, the birds singing as in one perpetual spring; but homesickness overtook them, and they begged hard to be allowed to return. The two fairy maidens said: "We got you to come here before retribution had fallen on the guilty."

Then they directed fairy attendants to escort them on their way with music and singing, and pointed out the road they had to follow. But when they got back to their native town, they found it in ruins, in which condition it had already lain for several generations. A surviving member of the Liu family was discovered, who said he had heard a story about a remote ancestor who had gone away into the mountains and never come back. The two men went again to look for the house where they had been entertained, but failed to find it. In the Chin dynasty, in the 8th year of T'ai-k'ang [A.D. 287], both of them disappeared altogether. L.H.C. (H.C.) *and* S.H.F.C.

LIU KEN

Liu Ken was a native of the capital, Ch'ang-an. Having taken his degree, he was given an official post; but subsequently he renounced a worldly career in order to study Tao, and retired into a cave situated on the edge of a sheer precipice. Winter and summer he wore no clothes; his body was covered

"You have the bodily structure of a hsien," he said, "and that is why you were able to see me. But at present your marrow does not fill your bones, your blood lacks heat, your breath is scanty, your brain is of insufficient bulk, your sinews are undeveloped, and your flesh is wasting away. Hence you cannot derive the proper benefit from drugs and breathing exercises. If your desire is for long life, you must treat these physical defects for a period of twelve years before you can begin taking the drugs that lead to hsienship. Now, the Way of the Hsien includes ascension heavenwards and treading on the clouds; roaming over the Five Sacred Peaks; the avoidance of death by means of dieting; release from the mortal part of the body and attainment of hsienship.

"For every aspirant of hsienship an essential thing is the assimilation of drugs. But some drugs are better than others, and there are several grades of hsien. He who is unversed in the mysteries of sexual intercourse, in the art of controlling the breath, and in physical exercises, as well as in the science of celestial drugs, can never hope to become a hsien. Of drugs, the most potent are the reverting cinnabar, nine times refined, and the gold-juice of the Great Monad. Anyone who swallows these will rise up to heaven forthwith, without any interval of days or months. Next in efficacy are such drugs as mica and realgar, which do not immediately confer the power of riding on clouds and driving a team of dragons, yet enable you to have spirits at your command, to assume different shapes, and to live for an indefinite time. After these come the vegetable drugs, which enable one to cure diseases, to rectify shortcomings, to preserve juvenility, to do without cereal food; and to strengthen the breath, although they cannot confer actual immortality. At the best, they will prolong life for a few hundred years, in other cases they will only fortify the natural constitution, and cannot be relied upon for long.

"If you are bent on attaining immortality, begin by getting rid of the three body-spirits. As soon as they are gone, you will gain fixity of will-power and freedom from passion and desire." According to a treatise which the stranger gave me, said Ken, these hidden spirits are in the habit of going up to heaven twice a month in order to report a man's sins and transgressions. Acting on this information, the Controller of Destiny deducts something from his allotted span and diminishes his length of years.

The ethereal spirit in a man's body is anxious to keep him alive, whereas these grosser spirits are anxious to have him die; for when he is dead they are dissipated into thin air and become ghosts, which can enjoy the flavor of any sacrifices that are offered to them.

I obeyed these instructions, prepared and swallowed the elixir accordingly, and was thus able to become a hsien. S.H.C.

CHANG TAO-LING

Chang Tao-ling was a native of the State of P'ei [part of Kiangsu and Anhwei]. He began as a student at the Imperial Academy, and made a thorough study of the Five Canonical Books. "Alas!" he exclaimed with a sigh, "all this study will not add to my span of life; "so he set himself to master the principles of longevity. Having acquired a copy of the Yellow Emperor's *Treatise of the Elixir refined in Nine Cauldrons,* he wished to compound the magic draught, and dissipated his fortune on drugs required for the purpose. His family being in a chronic state of poverty, he resolved to earn his livelihood by tilling the fields and breeding cattle; but these experiments failed through his lack of skill.

Hearing that the people of Shu [part of Szechwan] were simple, honest folk, easy to teach and convert, and that there were many celebrated mountains in that region, he departed thither with his disciples, and settled on the Crane's Call mountain, where he wrote a work on Tao in 24 parts. As the result of magical power bestowed on him by Lao Tzu, he now found himself able to heal the sick. Thereupon the people with one accord began to serve and venerate him as their Master, and the number of his followers amounted to tens of thousands. Straightway he appointed so-called Libationers, each of whom had a certain number of families under his control, while some carried out the functions of regular government officials. He also laid down laws and regulations whereby his followers had to contribute in rotation, according to circumstances, rice, silk, utensils, paper and writing-brushes, fuel, and various other articles.

He ordered the people to repair the roads, and punished defaulters by sending sickness upon them. Inspectors were sent round to see that bridges and highways were kept in good condition. The peasants were made to lop away brambles and drain cesspools; in short, there was no useful work to which they did not put their hand ...

Chang Tao-ling also tried to govern the people by appealing to their sense of shame, for he disliked inflicting punishment. He therefore made it a rule that sick persons should write down all the sins they had committed since they were born and cast these written confessions into a stream of water, vowing to the gods that they would sin no more, on penalty of death. The result was that all the people could count on a cure: if they unexpectedly fell sick, they would forthwith proclaim their misdeeds; thus on the one hand they obtained healing, and on the other were moved to shame and remorse, which deterred them from sinning again. Moreover, the fear of Heaven and Earth brought about a change of heart, and from that time forward all who had transgressed returned to the path of virtue.

In course of time Chang Tao-ling amassed much treasure wherewith to buy the drugs he needed in order to compound the elixir. When the elixir was ready, however, he only took half a dose, for he did not want to rise up to heaven immediately. S.H.C.

Chang Tao-ling, styled Fu-han [Pillar of the House of Han], was a descendant of Chang Liang (q.v.) in the eighth generation. He was over six feet tall, had bushy eyebrows, a wide forehead, a vermilion-colored pate, a prominent nose, a square chin, and green eyes with triangular orbits. A tapering projection like a rhinoceros horn protruded from his skull. His hands, when hanging down, reached below his knees. When crouching, he looked dragon-like, and in movement, like a tiger. His general aspect was stern.

He was born near the T'ien-mu [Eye of Heaven] mountain in the 10th year of the *chien-wu* period of the reign of the Han Emperor Kuang Wu (A.D. 34). To begin with, his mother dreamt that a giant came down to earth from a star in the Great Bear, and gave her a perfume distilled from certain fragrant herbs. On waking, she found the whole house filled with this strange perfume, which still pervaded the place after a month had gone by. Subsequently she conceived and became pregnant. On the day of his birth, yellow clouds enveloped the building, a purple vapour filled the courtyard, and the chamber in which he lay was irradiated with light, as from the sun or moon.

At the age of seven, Tao-ling had mastered the *Tao Te Ching* and the diagrams known as the plan of the Yellow River and the Scroll of the River Lo, having profoundly studied their mysteries. His character was wise and virtuous, honest and upright. Although he embarked on an official career, all his thoughts were centred in alchemy and the cultivation of Tao. He visited Shu, and falling in love with its deep valleys and lofty peaks, he lived as a hermit on the Hao-ming [Crane's Call] mountain.

Among his disciples was one Wang Ch'ang, who had practiced astronomy and was versed in the doctrines of Huang and Lao [the Yellow Emperor and Lao Tzu]. Together they engaged in alchemical research for the rejuvenating drug of the dragon and tiger, and in three years discovered it. Tao-ling was then over sixty, yet after tasting the magic potion he felt like a man of thirty. Accompanied by Wang Ch'ang, he retired to the Northern Sung Mountain, and there encountered a celestial envoy in embroidered robes who delivered the following message: "In a rocky cavern on the central peak are hidden two books entitled *The Esoteric Treatise of the Three Sovereigns* and *The Yellow Emperor's Classic of the nine times refined*

Elixir. Find and study these, so that you may learn how to ascend to heaven." After that, Tao-ling fasted for the space of seven days. On entering the cavern he heard a sound like the tramping of feet. He dug into the earth at that spot, and there, sure enough, he found the two books.

By means of spiritual meditation and a process of mental refinement he was now able to multiply his bodily form and to dissipate his shadow. Thus, at one and the same time he would be seen floating in his boat on the lake, reciting Taoist scriptures in the main hall, talking to his guests with his elbows on the table, and humming verses as he leant on his staff. This puzzled everybody very much.

"Your services should have qualified you to attain the ninth degree of purity, and to ascend on high as a hsien. I sent you into Shu merely to separate men and demons into their proper spheres, and thus prepare for your translation into the Pure Serene. Yet you slay an inordinate number of the demons; and, moreover, presume to raise the wind and rain, and to press spiritual beings into your service. You have darkened the light of day and polluted the void with the breath of slaughter--a deed inconsistent with the spirit of Tao that loves all creatures. God is about to punish your transgressions, and that is why I cannot approach you. You will retire to your place of abode and diligently work out your atonement. I shall await you at the Supremely Pure Eight-Prospect Palace in the Region of Non-Existence."

"Some of the magic drug still remains. Divide it between you and partake thereof, my two disciples, for to-day you must accompany me on my long flight upward." At noontide the whole host of hsien formed round him a guard of honor, and to the strains of celestial music escorted him to the topmost peak of the Tower-in-the-Clouds Mountain. Thus at the age of 123 the Saintly One ascended to heaven in broad daylight. L.H.C. (H.C.)

CHAO SHENG

One day Chang Tao-ling said to his disciples; "The great secret of the elixir I have imparted to Wang Ch'ang alone, but by and by another man will come hither from the east, who will also acquire the secret. He will arrive in daylight on the 7th of the 1st moon." And he gave an exact description of his appearance and stature. On the day named, the prediction was fulfilled by the arrival of Chao Sheng. Chang Tao-ling proceeded to subject him to seven trials:

(I) When he arrived at the Master's door, he was not admitted, but kept standing there, exposed to the insults and abuse of underlings. This he bore for over forty days and nights, during which he slept in the open air, until at last he was allowed to enter.

(2) He was sent to watch millet fields in the country and keep off wild beasts. In the evening an extraordinarily beautiful damsel appeared, with a concocted tale of having come a long journey, and lost her way. She passed the night in a bed beside Chao Sheng's, and the next day she still stayed on, pleading sore feet. Thus she remained dallying for several days, but Chao Sheng was not to be tempted from the path of rectitude.

(3) Chao Sheng was walking along the road, when he came upon thirty slabs of gold lying unguarded, but he passed on and did not pick them up.

(4) When he was sent into the hills to gather firewood, three tigers sprang out upon him and fixed their teeth in his garments, but without injuring him. Chao Sheng showed no fear, and did not so much as change color, but said to the tigers: "I am only a poor Taoist who has done no wrong; else I had not come from a distance of a thousand *li* to serve the Divine Master and learn the secret of immortality. What is it you want? You must have been sent by mountain spirits to make trial of me." After a little while, the tigers got up and made off.

(5) Another time, Chao Sheng bought some dozen rolls of silk in the market; but after he had paid for them, the silk merchant falsely accused him, saying that he had not received the money. Chao Sheng took the clothes off his back and completed the purchase with these, showing no trace of irritation.

(6) Whilst he was keeping watch over a field of grain, a man came up, prostrated himself, and begged for food. His clothes were in tatters, his face was begrimed with dirt, his body covered with purulent sores, and there came from him an abominable smell. Chao Sheng showed every sign of pity and concern: he took off his own garments to clothe him, set food before him from his private store, and made him a present of some rice to boot.

(7) The last ordeal to which Chao Sheng was subjected came when Tao-ling led his disciples to the edge of an almost vertical precipice at the very summit of the Tower-in-the--Clouds mountain. At some distance below they spied a peach tree growing horizontally out of the face of the cliff, like a man's arm. Underneath it yawned a seemingly bottomless abyss. Peaches of unusual size weighed down the branches of the tree.

Turning to his disciples, Tao-ling pointed to the peach-tree and said: "To whichever of you succeeds in plucking peaches from that tree I will impart the most important mysteries of Tao." Thereupon they all crawled to the edge and looked over, but hastily retreated again with trembling limbs and bathed in sweat, declaring that it was impossible. Chao Sheng alone came forward and said: "Under the protection of a divine being, what danger is there to fear? Our Holy Master is here, and assuredly he will not let me be dashed to pieces. If the Master bids us, there must be some way of getting those peaches." So saying, he leapt down and alighted safely on the tree, where he hastened to pluck peaches right and left, stuffing them into the bosom of his robe. The cliff, however, was so sheer and precipitous that it offered no foothold, and he was unable to get back. So he threw the peaches up one by one--two hundred and two in all--and Tao-ling caught them in the air and distributed them among his disciples until each had one. Tao-ling ate one, and kept the last for Chao Sheng. Then he stretched out his hand to help the latter climb up, while the others looked on. To the amazement of all, his arm grew out to a length of thirty feet, and in a moment the disciple was pulled up again. S.H.C.

WEI PO-YANG

Wei Po-yang, a native of Wu, had no wish for an official career, but felt an instinctive love for Tao and its mysteries; so he retired into the hills and occupied himself with concocting the divine elixir.

Two of the three disciples whom he had at that time he knew to be lacking in faith and singleness of heart; so, when he had some of the elixir prepared, he said in order to test them: "The drug of immortality is made, but it would be as well to try its effect first upon a dog. If no harm befalls the beast, we can take some ourselves; but if the dog dies, then it is not for us."

Po-yang then gave the dog a dose, and immediately it fell dead. "Ah," said he, "the drug must have been wrongly compounded owing to failure on my part to understand the divine instructions. Whoever took it would, I fear, share the fate of the dog. What are we to do?" The disciples asked: "will not then our Master swallow the elixir?" To which Po-yang replied: "I have renounced all worldly interests, and have abandoned my family to come here. Were I to fail in my efforts to become a hsien, I should be ashamed to return home. In that case I would as soon be dead as alive, so I certainly shall take it."

With these words he swallowed the potion, but on the instant that it entered his mouth he fell down lifeless. Seeing which, one of the disciples declared: "Our Preceptor is no ordinary mortal. There must be some mystical reason for his dying after taking the elixir." And then, swallowing some himself, he also fell lifeless. The other two disciples now held a consultation, and agreed that it would be better to refrain from taking a drug that brought but death, though designed to confer immortality. So they set off from their mountain retreat to make- arrangements for the funeral of their Master and dead companion.

As soon as they were gone, Po-yang rose up and set to work refining the drug until he got it perfect. Then he poured some into the mouths of his dead disciple and dog, and in a very short time they too came to life again. This done, he and the disciple went off, together with the dog, all having become hsien. On their way over the hills they met a wood-cutter, and handed him a letter to be delivered to the other two disciples, thanking them for the trouble they had taken in arranging the funeral. L.H.C. (H.C.)

WANG CHEN

Wang Chen was a native of Shang-tang [in Shansi]. At the age of seventy-nine he began to study Tao practicing the art of womb-breathing and abstaining from food for more than thirty years. His appearance was youthful, his complexion fine. He could walk as fast as a galloping horse, and his muscular power was equal to the combined strength of several men. Wu Ti of the Wei dynasty [i.e. Ts'ao Ts'ao] having heard of his fame, summoned him to an interview and found that he looked like a man of thirty or thereabouts; but suspecting trickery, he had searching inquiries made in his village, and obtained the same account from many different persons who had known Wang Cheng from their boyhood. It was agreed that he was at that time four hundred years old. Wu Ti was then convinced that he was a man of Tao and paid him much honor and respect. ... His outward appearance still continued impervious to age, until at last he ascended Mount Nu-chi and left the world to become a hsien. S.H.C.

Those who have acquired the art of womb-breathing are able to inhale and exhale the air independently of the nose and mouth, like the foetus in the womb.... When you are beginning to learn how to control your breath, you take in the air through the nose and hold it while you count your heart-beats. When you have counted 120, let the air out very gently through the mouth. During this process, care should be taken, that the passage of the air either way is quite inaudible to yourself, and more should go in than comes out.

A good test is to place a piece of swan's down at the aperture of the nostrils, and see that it does not stir when the breath is expelled. Practice will enable the number of heart-beats to be gradually increased, until at last you can hold your breath while you count a thousand. When this number is reached, the aged become rejuvenated, getting steadily younger day by day. This breathing exercise should be performed only in a period of "live air", not in a period of "dead air" ... A day and a night are divided into twelve periods of two hours each: the six periods from midnight to midday are "live air" periods, and the six from midday to midnight are "dead air" periods. Breathing exercises performed in a "dead air" period are useless.

"Womb-eating" has an analogous meaning, namely, being nourished, like the foetus, otherwise than by ordinary food and drink. In exercising the breath it is most essential that much food be not eaten; for raw vegetables, fat meat, and the like, cause the breath to become strong and hard to retain. Anger should also be avoided, because if one gets angry the breath is disturbed and wil1 not flow in abundance, or else it may set up a cough. Thus there are very few who are able to perform these exercises. My great-uncle Ko Hsuan, whenever he was thoroughly intoxicated or the weather was very hot, used to lie down at the bottom of a deep pool and only emerge after a day had passed--a feat which was only rendered possible by his faculty of retaining the breath and of womb-respiration. P.P.T.

HUA T'O

The Master Hua T'o was temperamentally inclined to peaceful life and deeply interested in medical lore. He often visited famous mountains and their secret grottos, and met with many adventures. One day he was resting, overcome with wine, at the mouth of an old cave on Mount Kung-i, when he caught the sound of voices discussing methods of curing disease. Much astonished he crept further into the cave and continued to listen, unobserved. After a while, he heard some one say, "The youth named Hua is nearby. We might impart our secrets to him." To which another replied: "Better not. The young fellow is covetous by nature, and shows no compassion for his fellow-creatures."

These words startled our hero even more, and leaping to his feet, he hurried into the cave. There he saw two old men wearing garments of bark and hats made of straw. Quickly making an obeisance to each, he said: "Worthy sirs, I have just heard your discourse on the art of medicine, and became so rapt in it that I thought no more of turning homewards. It has long been my ambition to alleviate human suffering, and I grieve because I have not yet found the right method, nor succeeded in achieving my aim by my own unaided efforts. Hoping that you will take into consideration my doltish sincerity, I beg of you to enlighten my understanding, and will remember your kindness to the end of my days."

The old man sitting in the senior's place replied: "We do not begrudge the secrets of our art, but we fear lest some day they may be a source of trouble to you. If you make no account of vicissitudes of fortune, and are indifferent to poverty or wealth, high rank or humble station; if money-making is not your chief aim, if you dread not toil and fatigue, if it is your urgent desire to bring comfort to old age and sympathy to the young, then it is in our power to remove the cause of your failure." Hua T'o thanked them with a humble obeisance, and said: "These sage and saintly words shall be treasured up in my heart and observed to the letter."

The old men smiled, and pointing to a recess on the east side, said: "You will find there a volume lying on a stone couch. Take it, and depart quickly from our dwelling. Guard this work with all secrecy, and show it not to the common herd." Having got hold of the book, Hua T'o looked round, but the old men had already disappeared. In some alarm, he quitted the cave, and suddenly it became lost to view. Clouds blew up, a deluge of rain fell, and the grotto in the rock collapsed in ruin.

When he came to examine the medical work, he found in it many strange and curious disquisitions. And from that time forth his every experiment was attended with marvellous success. But before he had reached the age of sixty, the warnings he had received from the old men were fulfilled, for he was put to death by the Emperor of Wei (i.e. Ts'ao Ts'ao). T.S.C.C.

Hua T'o excelled in the knowledge of drugs, and in dispensing medicine he limited his choice to a few kinds. He was able to estimate the fraction of a grain without having recourse to scales or measures. In his practice, the application of acupuncture and cautery was restricted to a few spots of the body. If an internal malady developed itself which could not be reached by the needle or by drugs, he first made the patient swallow "hemp-bubble-powder" mixed with wine, and as soon as intoxication and unconsciousness supervened, he made an incision in the belly or the back and cut out any morbid growth. If the stomach or intestine was the part affected, he thoroughly cleansed those organs after the use ,of the knife, and removed the contaminating matter which had caused the infection. He would then stitch up the wound, and apply a marvellous ointment which caused it to heal in four or five days, and within a month the patient was completely restored to health.

To one Wu P'u, who studied under him, Hua T'o gave the following advice: "The human body," he said, " requires toil and exertion, only it must not be carried to excess. It is exercise that enables food to be properly digested, makes the blood circulate through the veins, and prevents the onset of disease, just as the hinge of a door, being constantly in motion, will never get rusty. It is on this account that the hsien of old practiced all sorts of gymnastics--swinging about like a bear, turning their heads round like an owl, stretching their bodies and exercising their joints--in their efforts to check the advance of old age. One of the secrets of my art is called the 'Five-Animal Antics', based on the natural movements of a tiger, a deer, a bear, an ape, and a bird. For banishing disease and at the same time strengthening the leg and feet, physical exercises are essential. If your body is not in good condition, get up and do one of these animal gymnastics: it will cause a pleasant perspiration. Then dust yourself with powder, and you will experience a sensation of lightness and well-being, and have an appetite for food."

P'u put these precepts into practice, and at the age of over ninety his sight was clear, his 'hearing keen, and his teeth perfectly sound. H.H.S.

When Kuan Yu was attacking Fan, he was struck by an arrow which pierced his left arm. Afterwards, although the wound healed, whenever the weather was cloudy or rainy, the bone always ached. The physician Hua T'o said: "Poison from the arrow-head has entered the bone. An incision must be made in the arm, and the bone scraped in order to get rid of the poison. Then only will the pain cease." Kuan Yu bade him perform the operation, although he happened to be entertaining guests at the time, and was drinking wine in their company. Blood streamed from the wound and filled a bowl to the brim, whereat those present were amazed and alarmed; but Kuan Yu went on carving the meat and pouring out wine, laughing and talking just as usual. This made Hua T'o to exclaim: "Really, one would take this man for a divine being! " K.T.S.C.

Hua T'o's fame came to the ears of Ts'ao Ts'ao, who summoned him to his Court and kept him constantly in attendance. He suffered from persistent headache and giddiness, which T'o was able to cure immediately by means of acupuncture.... Now, Hua T'o was a bad-tempered man and difficult to please; he was ashamed of practicing medicine as a profession, and moreover, being separated from his family, he was bent on returning home. So he approached Ts'ao Ts'ao and asked permission to go back in order to fetch some prescriptions. Subsequently he gave out that his wife was ill, and though he often promised to return to Court, always failed to do so. Ts'ao sent him repeated messages, and also instructed the prefect and district magistrate to see that he was sent back; but T'o, feeling confident of being able to tire him out, still refused to come. Ts'ao grew very angry, and sent some one to inquire into the matter, through whom he learnt that the wife was only feigning illness. Thereupon he had T'o arrested and thrown into prison: he was put on his trial and condemned to die by swallowing poison. Somebody pleaded for him, saying: "T'o is really a skilled physician, and one on whom human lives depend. He ought to be granted a free pardon." Ts'ao rejected this advice, however, and finally put him to death. When his end was approaching, T'o brought out a roll of manuscript and offered it to the gaoler, saying: "This will tell you how to bring a man to life again." But the gaoler, fearing punishment, dated not accept the gift. T'o did not press him, but procured fire and burned the manuscript. H.H.S.

Ten days later, Hua T'o died in prison. Wu bought a coffin and had him decently buried, after which he resigned his post and hurried home to study the contents of the black bag. But when he arrived, he found his wife in the very act of burning the precious papers. Horrified at the sight, he hastily snatched the bundle out of the fire, but only a couple of sheets remained intact. In his anger he began cursing his wife, but she retorted: "Even if you were to become as great a genius as Hua T'o himself, it would only lead to your ending your days in prison, and what would be the good of that? "Wu sighed deeply, and said no more. Thus it happened that the writings in the black bag were never given to the world. The fragments that have been published, contained in the two unburnt sheets, deal only with small matters such as the methods of castrating fowls and pigs. S.K.C.Y.I.

TSO TZ'U

Tso Tz'u, styled Yuan-fang, was a native of Lu-chiang [in Anhwei]. While yet a boy, he possessed supernatural powers. Once when he was at a banquet given by Ts'ao Kung, the latter looked smilingly round at his assembled guests and said: "I have made but poor provision of delicacies for this noble company today. What we lack are some perch from the Wu-sung River with which to make a mince." Said Fang: "That is easily obtainable"; and, calling for a bronze bowl full of water, he began angling in it with a bamboo rod. After a little while he pulled out a perch, whereupon Ts'ao Kung clapped his hands vigorously, and the whole company was much astonished. "One fish," said Kung, "won't go round. It would be nice to have two." So Fang cast his line again, and soon drew up another fish. Both were over three feet long, and deliciously fresh. Kung had them minced up before his eyes, and handed round the dainty to his guests sitting at table. "Now that we have got our perch," he said, "it is a pity that we have no raw ginger from Shu to go with them."--"That too can be procured," said Fang. Suspicious lest he should buy some in the vicinity, Ts'ao Kung then said: "Some time ago I sent a man to Shu in order to buy brocade. Please instruct your messenger to tell my agent to purchase two extra lengths of it." Fang's messenger departed, and in a twinkling was back again with the raw ginger. "I saw your agent, Sir," he said to Ts'ao' Kung, "in a brocade shop, and gave him your order." More than a year afterwards Kung's agent returned, and sure enough he had got the two extra lengths. On being questioned, he said that the year before, on such and such a day of such and such a month, he had met a man in a shop who acquainted him with Kung's order.

On a later occasion Ts'ao Kung, accompanied by some hundred scholars, went for an excursion not far outside the city. Fang provided a single jar of wine and a single piece of dried meat. Tilting the jar with his own hands, he poured out wine for all the assembled guests, not one of whom but ate and drank to repletion. Kung thought this very strange, and caused an investigation to be made. On sending round to inspect the wine-shops, he found that the day before they had all been cleared of their stocks of wine and meat. This angered him, and he secretly determined to put Fang to death. The latter was just about to be arrested as he was sitting in Ts'ao Kung's private apartment, when he walked straight into a wall and incontinently vanished. Then Kung hired a number of men to capture him. One of these saw him in the market-place, and was on the point of seizing him when suddenly all the people there were transformed into his exact likeness, so that no one could tell which was really him.

Later on, some of them met Fang on the brow of the Yang--Ch'eng Hill, and again pursued him, whereupon he ran amongst a flock of sheep.

Kung, realizing that he was not to be caught in this way, told his men to go among the sheep and make the following announcement: "Ts'ao Kung does not want to put you to death. He has only been making trial of your magical arts; and now that they have stood the test, his desire is simply to have an interview with you." Then suddenly one old ram, bending its two forelegs, stood erect like a man and began to speak, saying: "What a fluster you're in!" Ts'ao Kung's men cried out: "That ram is the one we want," and all made a dash for him. But lo! the whole flock, numbering several hundreds, now turned into rams, all bending their forelegs, standing erect and calling out: "What a fluster you're in!" The result was that no one knew which of them to capture.

Lao Tzu said: "The ills that afflict me are due to my being encumbered with a body. Once I succeed in freeing myself from my body, what ill can befall me?"

Those who are of Lao Tzu's persuasion may be said to have the power of freeing themselves from their bodies. How can they fail to keep misfortune at a distance? S.S.C.

FEI CH'ANG-FANG

Fei Ch'ang-fang was a native of Ju-nan [in Honan], where he was made a market inspector. There was an aged man who used to sell drugs in the market. He had a gourd hanging over his stall, and as soon as business was over for the day, he used to leap into the gourd. None of the people in the marketplace saw what happened except Ch'ang-fang, who observed it from the upper storey of his dwelling, and marvelled thereat. This caused him to go and pay his respects to the old fellow, who said to him: "Sir, come again to-morrow." So Ch'ang-fang did go early the next morning, and then the old man and he entered the gourd together. There he beheld a magnificent hall, spacious and beautiful, where fine wines and toothsome delicacies were spread out in lavish profusion. Together they drank their fill, and then emerged from the gourd. The old man impressed upon him the need for secrecy concerning their adventure.

Afterwards he came up to see Ch'ang-fang in his chamber, and said: "I am really a hsien, but as punishment for an offence I was banished hither. Having now expiated my fault, I am about to quit this world. Would it not be possible for you to accompany me? Downstairs there is a small flagon of wine with which we might drink to each other before parting." In order to bring it up, Ch'ang-fang sent as many as ten men, yet they were unable to lift it. The old man laughed, and proceeded to carry it upstairs on one finger. Though the vessel appeared to hold little more than a pint, the two went on drinking for the rest of the day without emptying it.

Ch'ang-fang had a heartfelt longing to become a seeker after Tao, but the thought of his family caused him anxiety. The old man knew what was in his mind and cutting a piece of green bamboo, told him to hang it up behind his cottage. Now, to the eyes of his relatives this appeared to be not a bamboo but the corpse of Ch'ang-fang himself, and they thought he must have hanged himself.

Shocked by the sight, old and young alike bewailed him, and in due course prepared his body for burial. All the while Ch'ang-fang was standing nearby, yet he was quite invisible to any of them.

And thus it came about that Ch'ang-fang accompanied the old man into the mountains. They had to force their way through thorny undergrowth, and were surrounded by prowling tigers; yet, though he was left behind in a solitary place by his companion, he showed no sign of fear. Furthermore, the old man made Ch'ang-fang lie down in an empty cave, where with a rotten old rope he hung a boulder ten thousand pounds in weight just over his head. Then a number of snakes appeared and eagerly made for the rope in order to gnaw it through, yet Ch'ang-fang did not stir. On his return, the old man clapped him on the back and said; "I see that you are teachable." Next he told him to eat some ordure which contained three worms and had an evil odour of extraordinary pungency. Ch'ang-fang was overcome by feelings of disgust, whereupon the old man said: "You were near to the attainment of Tao, and it is a pity that you have broken down at this point."

Ch'ang-fang, then, had no alternative but to take his leave and return home. The old man presented him with a bamboo staff, saying: "Astride this, no matter where you are going, you will be able to get there in a moment of time. When you reach home, take the staff and throw it into the Bean Pool."

Riding on this staff, Ch'ang-fang flew back in a second. He was under the impression that he had been away from home only ten days, but in reality it was over ten years. Without delay he threw his staff into the pool, and as he watched he saw it transformed into a dragon.

His family declared that he had died long ago, and were much taken aback by his story, which they refused to believe. Ch'ang-fang said: "What you buried long ago was only a bamboo stick." Thereupon they dug up the grave and broke open the coffin, and, sure enough, found the stick still inside. L.H.C. (H.C.)

Fei Ch'ang-fang possessed the extraordinary power of contracting the veins of the earth, so that a stretch of a thousand *li* came within the limits of vision; and then, relaxing the spell, he would make it expand once more to its normal extent. S.H.C.

CHI TZU-HSUN

Chi Tzu-hsun came from nobody knows where; but in the *chien-an* period (A.D. 196-219) he was living at Wan-kou in Chi-yin [the modern Ts'ao-chou in Shantung]. He was a past-master in magic. On one occasion he was holding a neighbor's infant son in his arms, when he let the child slip from his grasp, so that it fell to the ground and was killed. The parents set up a woeful clamour, and their grief and resentment were painful to witness. Yet Tzu-hsun merely apologized for the accident: not another word did he say. The funeral took place in due course, and about a month later Tzu-hsun presented himself at the parents' house with the child in his arms. Both were very frightened and cried: "The quick and the dead travel along different roads. Although we treasure the memory of our son, we would entreat you not to tantalize us by bringing him again before our eyes."

Meanwhile, however, the child had recognized his father and mother, and showing every sign of delight, was trying to get to them. Instinctively the mother took the little one into her arms, and found it was really her son, alive and in the flesh. Great indeed was her joy, but having still some lingering doubts, she caused the grave to be opened secretly in order to see if the corpse was there. On finding nothing in the coffin except some articles of clothing, she was at last convinced.

After this event Tzu-hsun's renown spread far and wide, and all the high officials at the capital paid assiduous court to him. Some time afterwards, accompanied by his friends, he drove in a donkey-carriage on a visit to the country of Hsu [in Honan], and having reached Jung-yang, put up at a hostelry there. The donkey, however, which he had been driving, suddenly fell down dead, and crawling maggots appeared in the carcass. The landlord hurriedly brought the news to Tzu-hsun, who merely remarked: "Is that so?" and quietly sat down to dinner. When he had finished, he sauntered out and gave the donkey a tap with his stick, whereupon it sprang to its feet and resumed the journey.

In a later generation he was seen at Pa-ch'eng, east of Ch'ang-an, engaged with an old man in polishing a bronze statue. He said to his companion: "I happen to have witnessed the actual casting of this bronze nearly five hundred years ago." On looking round and seeing that he was observed, he made off, still driving the same old donkey-carriage as of yore. Those who saw him called out: "Master Chi, tarry with us a little! " and began following in the same direction; but though he seemed to be travelling at quite a slow pace, they found that a galloping horse could not overtake him, and gave up the pursuit. H.H.S.

The nobles of the capital, having heard of these wonders, were all very anxious to meet Tzu-hsun, but could find no pretext to gain his company. Now, there was a young advanced student whose family lived near Tzu-hsun. So the nobles formed a plan, and having called the student to them, said: "You are studying with toilsome industry in the hope of compassing wealth and honors. All you have to do is to get Tzu-hsun to come hither, and we will see that you obtain these things without effort." The young man agreed to the proposal, and went home to enter Tzu-hsun's service, sprinkling and sweeping, and attending to his personal wants for many months. Tzu-hsun knew what was in his mind and said: "My young friend, you must be studying for the attainment of Tao, else how could you labor thus?" The other still dissembled his motives, until Tzu-hsun said: "Why don't you tell me the truth instead of keeping up these hollow pretences? I know what is at the back of your mind. The nobles wish to meet me. Well, I won't grudge the trouble of a journey if it leads to your obtaining a good appointment. Go back to the capital, and on such-and-such a day I will come."

The youth, much delighted, took his leave, and on arriving at the capital told the nobles all that his master had said.

When the appointed day came, the latter had not yet started on his journey, so the young man's parents came to make inquiries. "Ah," said Tzu-hsun, "you are afraid that I have forgotten my promise, and will cause your son to break faith with the nobles, thus forfeiting his official post. I am just having a meal, after which I will start without delay." In half a day he covered the two thousand *li* to the capital, where he was at once met by the youth with respectful salutations. When he asked who it was that wished to see him, the youth replied: "A great many persons, Sir, and they deem it no hardship to travel withersoever you may happen to be."--" A thousand *li* do not fatigue me," replied Tzu-hsun, "so how can I grudge a matter of a few paces? Tell those who want to see me to stay at home, and to-morrow I will pay a visit to each man's house." The youth reported these words to the nobles, and they all refrained from going abroad, but had their houses swept and garnished.

When the time came, Tzu-hsun duly appeared: in every one of the twenty-three homes there was a Tzu-hsun! Each of the courtiers believed that his own particular house had been visited first; but the next morning, when they went to Court and asked each other at what hour Tzu-hsun had been to their respective homes, it turned out that all the twenty-three had received him at exactly the same time. He had been seen by all dressed in the same clothes and presenting the same general appearance, only the words he had used varied according to the conversation of each particular host. The whole capital was struck with wonder and amazement at such a miraculous feat ....

Tzu-hsun arrived at the house of one Master Ch'en and said: "To-morrow at noon I must depart." Ch'en inquired whether his journey would be long or short, to which he replied: "I shall return no more." Ch' en provided him with a single garment made of summer cloth, and when the hour came Tzu-hsun simply died. He lay rigid, with hands and feet crossed like pieces of bent iron, so that it was impossible to straighten them. A mysterious blend of the five perfume arose from the corpse and penetrated into the neighboring streets.

The body was now placed in the coffin, but before it had been carried out for burial a sucking noise was heard inside the coffin, followed by a thunder-clap and a dazzling flash which lighted up the whole house. The mourners flung themselves on the ground, and when after sometime they ventured to look up they found that the lid of the coffin had been split into pieces and tossed into the air, while the coffin itself was empty except for a single shoe. A few minutes later, a cavalcade with flutes and drums was heard passing along the highway: it made straight for the east and vanished.

Tzu-hsun was never seen again; but for a hundred days and more after his departure a fragrant perfume hung about the main road for a distance of some thirty *li*. S.H.C.

8. THE THREE KINGDOMS (A.D. 221-277)

KUAN LU

KUAN LU, also called Kung-ming, was a native of P'ing-yuan [in Shantung]. His features were coarse and ugly, and his manners lacking in dignity. Much addicted to wine and good cheer, and fond of his joke, he would only associate with congenial spirits. Hence he was an object of affection to many, though not regarded with particular veneration. At the age of eight or nine he was very fond of gazing at the stars, and was always asking what their names were. At night he would not go to sleep, and his parents found it impossible to keep him from his favorite occupation. "Although I am only a little boy," he said, "I do love looking at the patterns in the sky." He also used to say: "Even barn-door fowls and wild herons know about the seasons: how much more should man!" When playing at mud-pies with the urchins of the neighborhood, he would draw pictures of the sun, moon, and stars on the ground. All his sayings and repartees were highly original, and his seniors were unable to get the better of him in argument. Everyone knew he was destined to be a man of extraordinary talent...

The magistrate of Hsin-tu had a wife and daughter who were afflicted with nervous terrors which developed into a serious malady. He got Kuan Lu to investigate the cause by means of stalk-divination, and the latter said: "On the west side of your house two dead men are buried, one with a spear in his hand, the other holding a bow and arrow. Their heads lie [86] just inside the wall of the house, and their feet are outside. The man with the spear is the cause of the severe headaches from which your two patients suffer, while the man with the bow and arrow is responsible for the pain in the region of the heart which prevents them from eating and drinking. During the daytime these spirits are roaming about, but when night comes they are a plague to human beings, causing nervous terrors." The skeletons were immediately dug up and removed, whereupon both patients recovered ....

Hsii Chi-lung, magistrate of Ch'ing-ho, once took thirteen different articles which he placed in a box, and then asked Kuan Lu to guess what they were: "There are thirteen different things in here," replied the latter, "jumbled all together. The first is a hen's egg; the second is the chrysalis of a silk-worm "--and so he went on, naming each article in turn. His only mistake was when he said a fine-toothed comb instead of a large-toothed one.

Kuan Lu was accompanying the army of Wei on its march to the west when he came to the tomb of Wu-ch'iu Chien. Seized with a fit of melancholy, he leant against a tree and began to chant a doleful ditty. Someone asked him why he did so, whereupon he said: "This is a fine grove of trees, but it does not appear likely to last long; this is a beautiful monument, but it will not. be preserved for posterity. The Black Warrior hides his head, the Green Dragon has no feet, the White Tiger is holding a corpse in his jaws, the Red Bird is wailing and lamenting.

The four signs of danger are all present: this means that his whole clan is doomed to extinction." Two years had not passed before this prophecy was fulfilled ....

In the second year of Cheng-yuan [A.D. 255] Kuan Lu's younger brother Ch'en said to him: "The Commander-in-Chief has taken you into great favor: are you not looking forward to wealth and honors?" But Kuan Lu sighed deeply and replied: "I know the portion allotted to me. Heaven has bestowed on me intellectual gifts, but has not granted me length of years .... I am not fated to rule over the living, but am going to Mount T'ai to rule over the spirits of the dead." Ch'en wanted to know the grounds of his misgiving, and Kuan Lu said: "There is no bone of life in my forehead, no essence of stability in my eyes, no beam and pillar to my nose. My back, my belly, and the sole of my foot all lack the marks of longevity. Moreover, I was born in the night during an eclipse of the moon. Heaven has its immutable laws which it is impossible to escape. First and last, I have predicted the death of more than a hundred persons, and have never made a mistake."

In the 8th moon of the same year Kuan Lu was appointed an Assistant-Governor, and in the 2nd moon of the following year he died at the age of forty-eight. S.K.C.

Kuan Lu was travelling to his native place when he saw a youth who was cutting wheat in a field. He heaved a deep sigh as he passed him, which made the youth inquire the cause of his mclancholy.--" What is your name?" asked Kuan Lu. On being told that it was Chao Yen, he said: "I was only sad to think that your span of years would not exceed twenty." When pressed further, he added: "Our destinies are controlled by Heaven, and I can do nothing to save you." The youth [88]
ran home and told his father, and together they caught up Kuan Lu before he had gone far along the road. In response to their entreaties that he would rescue the son from such an untimely fate, Kuan Lu said: "His destiny is not in my hands, but I will do my best for you. Go home and prepare a flagon of wine and a joint of venison, then await my arrival." They followed these instructions, and on the morrow Kuan Lu appeared in due course. "South of the spot," he said, "where you were cutting wheat yesterday, there is a large mulberry tree. Under this tree you will find two men playing a game of *wei-ch'i*.

Go up to them, and place these viands before them, replenishing their cups as soon as they are empty. If they question you, be careful not to say a word, but only bow. This perchance may save you. I will remain here until you return."

Chao Yen did as he was bid: he found the two men playing wei-ch'i, and so absorbed were they in the game that they finished the wine and venison without noticing him. At last the game came to an end, and the man who was sitting on the north side raised his head. When he saw Chao Yen waiting on them, he cried out in anger: "What do you mean by coming here?" The youth, however, only bowed and made no reply. Thereupon the man on the south side said to his companion: "I am afraid we look rather silly. Here we have been drinking all this man's wine, and eating up his venison. Ought we not to show him some gratitude? "--" That is all very well," replied the other; "but the warrant is already drawn up and cannot be altered now."--" May I have a look at it? " said his companion; and, taking the document, he saw that the length of life therein assigned to Chao Yen was some nineteen years. "Why, there is no difficulty here," he cried; "the figures only need transposing."

And, making a flick with his pen, he said to the youth: " We hereby guarantee that you will live until the age of ninety-one."

At these words, Chao Yen was unable to contain himself for joy: making a low obeisance, he hurried home, where Kuan Lu congratulated him on the welcome addition to his years.--" The man sitting on the south side," he said, "was the Spirit of the Southern Dipper [a constellation consisting of six stars], and the man on the north, the Spirit of the Northern Dipper [the seven stars known to us as the Great Bear]: they preside over birth and death respectively. Every person born into the world passes from the domain of the former into that of the latter; and all prayers for longevity have accordingly to be submitted to the Spirit of the Northern Dipper." The grateful parent wished to load Kuan Lu with rich presents, but he refused to take anything. S.S.C.

CHIAO HSIEN

Chiao Hsien was a native of Ho-tung [Shansi]. At the age of 170 he was in the habit of eating white stones after boiling them thoroughly like yams, and used to distribute them to others. Every day he went into the mountains to cut fuel which he gave away to the headman and other villagers in turn, after which he began afresh. Carrying the fuel on his back, he would deposit it outside each man's door. Anyone who happened to see him would spread a mat and invite him in to partake of a meal. Chiao Hsien would then sit down but say not a word to his host. If he saw no one when he came with his fuel, he would put it down silently at the door and go away. So it went on year after year.

When the House of Wei established their dynasty, he was dwelling on the bank of the Yellow River, having built himself a thatched hut in which he lived quite alone. He had no proper bed, but sat on a straw mattress. His body was dirty, as if he had been soused in liquid mud. Sometimes he would go several days without eating. In walking he did not keep to the path. He shunned the company of women. When his clothes wore out he would sell some firewood in order to buy old garments to replace them. Winter and summer alike, he wore clothing of a single thickness.

The Governor Tung Ching went to pay him a visit, but Hsien refused to speak to him. This only heightened Ching's opinion of his worth. Eventually his hut was caught in a forest fire, and men who came to look for Hsien found him sitting upright and motionless under the roof. When the fire had burnt itself out and the hut lay in ashes, Hsien got up quite calmly, and then it appeared that his clothes were not even singed.

After he had made himself another hut, there suddenly came a great snowfall which wrecked a large number of houses. Hsien's hut collapsed, and a party of rescuers, seeing no trace of him, feared that he must have frozen to death. But on digging their way into the hut they found him fast asleep under the snow, with a ruddy face and breathing freely, just like one lying drunk in the height of summer.

People recognized that he was no ordinary being, and many wished to learn from him about Tao; but Hsien declared that there was no Tao in him. Thus he continued, now old and now young, for more than two hundred years. At last he parted from his fellow men and went no one knows whither. Those who had questioned him got not a single word to appease their curiosity. S.H.C.

Somebody having asked Huang-fu Mi what kind of man Chiao Hsien was, he replied: "I am not able fully to under-stand him, but can speak from superficial observation only. What the world in general desires is honor and sensual gratification. Clothes are required by the human form, shelter is necessary for our bodies, the mouth cannot do without speech, the heart cannot endure the utter lack of kith and kin. Yet Chiao Hsien renounces honor and the pleasures of the senses, he does without clothes, without house, without kindred. He keeps his mouth shut and speaks not, he makes the universe his roof-tree, he is in mystic unity with the antecedents of supreme Tao, he transcends the world of phenomena and enters into the seclusion of Primordial Stillness. No man is able to fathom his thoughts; the breadth of the Four Seas cannot encompass his mind .... Danger and stress cause him no qualm, honors and affections do not entangle his spirit. He lets not his ears and eyes be defiled by sights and sounds. He has planted his foot in the domain where no hurt is, and has established himself in the realm of independence. His length of years, exceeding those of the centenarian, cannot be reckoned even by his oldest acquaintance. He has been one and the same ever since the time of the Emperor Fu Hsi. K.S.C.

9. DIVISION INTO NORTH AND SOUTH

WU MENG

Wu MENG was a native of Pu-yang [in Hunan] and served as an official in the Kingdom of Wu. By disposition he was an extraordinarily filial son.

He fell. in with the great adept Ting I, who presented him with a number of divine prescriptions, besides which he acquired all manner of secret arts, celestial charms, and feats of Taoist magic. Once when a storm was raging, he wrote out a charm and threw it on the roof, where a black crow seized it in its beak and flew away. The wind instantly dropped. Asked why he had done this, he replied that a boat on the Southern Lake had been caught in the storm, and that on board was a Taoist priest who had prayed to be saved from the peril. On investigation this turned out to be true.

After Yu Ch'ing, magistrate of Hsi-an, had lain dead for three days, Meng declared that his allotted span was not yet exhausted: "I must go and lodge a complaint before God," he said. So he lay down to sleep beside the corpse, and after a few more days both he and the magistrate rose to life again.

After this, Meng returned to Yu-chang [in Kiangsi] with one of his disciples. The Yangtse River happened to be in flood, so that no one could cross. But he pointed the white feather fan in his hand across the stream, and lo! a path was opened and left dry for them, by which they crossed over in a leisurely manner. As soon as they were safely over, the water resumed its former course, much to the astonishment of the onlookers. S.S.C.

In Shu, where an epidemic was raging, Meng effected many marvellous cures with magic water. He was arrested by the rebel general Wang Tun, but escaped and reached home in his boat in a single night. His disciples noticed that the boat did not actually touch the water, but was being borne along by two dragons with eyes as big as saucers. Y.C.C.C.

In the Lu mountains [near Kiukiang] there is a bridge called the Bridge of the Three Rocks. Though some hundreds of feet long, it is not quite a foot in width, and it spans what seems to be a bottomless abyss. Taking a disciple with him, Wu Meng climbed the mountain and crossed over this bridge. They came upon an old man sitting under a cassia tree, and catching 'sweet dew liquor' in a jade goblet which he presented to Meng. A little further on they saw a small party of men preparing 'jade-fat' for him.

The disciple purloined a piece of jade, with the intention of exhibiting it to his friends later on; and immediately the bridge shrank in size to a finger's breadth. Meng made the disciple return and replace the precious stone; then, grasping him by the hand and bidding him shut his eyes, he drew him back across the bridge in safety. S.C.C.

SUN TENG

Sun Teng dwelt in a cave on the North Mountain in the prefecture of Chi [in Honan]. In summer, he made himself garments of plaited straw; in winter he covered himself only with his long hair. He was an expert in the art of whistling without a break, and he loved to read the Canon of Changes and to thrum a one-stringed lute. By temperament he was prone neither to joy nor to anger.

The high-born statesman Hsi K'ang accompanied him in his wanderings for three years, yet whenever he questioned his Master about his aims, he could get no reply. When about to leave him, Hsi K'ang said: "After all this time, Sir, have you no word for me? " Sun Teng replied: " You know what fire is, don't you? It has the natural property of giving light, but not of using that light; yet its importance depends on the use made of its light. In man, intellectual capacity is a natural gift, but not the use made of that capacity; yet his worth depends on the use he makes of it. The use of light is contingent on a supply of fuel wherewith to preserve its radiance; and the use of intellect consists in acquiring a knowledge of Pure Truth so as to keep one's life immune from harm." Hsi K'ang also asked for instruction in playing the lute, but Sun Teng would not teach him. "Your intellectual capacity is great," he said, "but your knowledge is small. It will be difficult for you to pass unscathed through the world of to-day." This prophecy was verified later on, when Hsi K'ang met his fate in the Lu An affair.

During his imprisonment he wrote a poem of self-censure containing the lines:

"Erstwhile I was abashed when I thought of Hsia Hui; And now I am conscience-stricken when I remember Sun Teng." In the end, Sun Teng rose up to heaven in broad daylight. L.H.C. (H.C.)

Sun Teng, it is said, was seen by many successive generations, but his appearance never seemed to change. He used to beg for cash in the market-place, and then distribute them to the poor, though he himself had no other means of subsistence and was never seen eating. Yang Chun, who was at that time Grand Tutor, sent somebody to interrogate him, but Sun Teng made no reply. Once Yang Chun presented him with a cloth robe, which he accepted; but as soon as he got outside the gate, he borrowed a knife and slashed it in various places, threw it down on the threshold, and finally cut it into pieces. Everybody thought that he was mad, but afterwards it was realized that he was enacting in advance the impending slaughter and mutilation of Yang Chun himself. The latter now ordered his detention, whereupon Sun Teng lay down and died. Yang Chun provided a coffin and buried him at the Swaying Bridge, but a few days later he was seen alive .... S.H.C.

KO HUNG

Ko Hung was a native of Chu-jung in Tan-yang [in Kiangsu]. He was a studious lad, and his family being poor, he worked as a wood-cutter in order to provide himself with pens and paper. Much of the night he would spend in writing and in reciting what he had learnt; thus he soon acquired some reputation as a scholar. Being of a contented disposition, he had no great craving for pleasure; a simple fellow, awkward of speech, he hankered not after money or distinction. When the doors were closed at night, he swept the floor and never sought the company, of his fellows. Sometimes, when on the quest for a book or the meaning of a certain passage, he would think nothing of travelling immense distances over rugged and difficult country in order to get what he wanted. He was a great reader of old books, being especially interested in the secrets of hsienship and the physical exercises and trainng involved therein. When Shih Ping started his rebellion in the T'ai-an period (A.D. 302-3), Hung received a special commission as captain, attacked Shih Ping's lieutenant and defeated him. For this service he was promoted to the post of "Wave-quelling General."

After the rising had been suppressed, he became military adviser to the Governor of Canton, and continued to stay in the south for many years, disregarding all the summonses he received from the capital. At last he returned home, and was rewarded with the title of Marquis.

Feeling the weight of years, he was now anxious to compound the elixir so as to secure immortality; and having heard that cinnabar was produced in Chiao-chih [part of Annam], he begged for an appointment in that neighborhood. To this the Emperor objected that Hung's official standing was too high for such a post. But when Hung explained that he cared not for distinction, and that the cinnabar was what attracted him, the Emperor let him have his way. Accordingly, accompanied by his son and nephew, he travelled again to Canton. Here his friend the Governor detained him, and would not hear of his continuing the journey; so Hung stopped on Mount Lo-fou, and there prepared the magic drug.

For a number of years he wandered at will among the mountains, cultivating Tao and writing ceaselessly, until at last he passed away as though he were falling asleep. He was 81 years old, yet his complexion was that of a new-born babe, and his whole body, too, was soft and supple. When they raised the corpse to put it in the coffin, it was as light as an empty suit of clothes. The general belief was that he had merely been released from the flesh and become a hsien. C.S.

I was of a rustic habit, slow-witted and stammering. My exterior was clumsy and unprepossessing, my dress shabby and dirty, but this caused me no shame. Conservative in my taste, I steadfastly refused to follow the dictates of fickle fashion, whether it was the mode to wear broad collars and expansive girdles, or tight waists and long sleeves, or flowing skirts that swept the ground, or short ones that did not cover the feet. In speech I was truthful, and eschewed all jesting and raillery. Unless I found a congenial spirit, I would always remain silent. Hence the people of my district spoke of me as the Simple Scholar, a nickname which I adopted for my book.

My constitution was feeble, and I was often ill. I was too poor to afford a horse and carriage, yet not strong enough to go everywhere on foot; besides, the exercise of walking was naturally distasteful to me. Hence I kept mucli to myself, and lived in solitude with my pen ....

I felt that I was at the parting of the ways: unless I renounced the world and its affairs, how could I devote myself to stillness and mysticism? Yet I could not entirely abandon the life of a scholar. As I said to myself with a sigh: "Tao is not confined to the mountains and forests. The reason why the ancient devotees of Tao retired thither was that they wished to get away from the noise and clamour which might have disturbed the tranquillity of their souls." ...

At the age of fifteen or sixteen I had written verses and various other things which at the time seemed to me worthy of publication. But on looking at them again a few years later, I found much in them to displease me, and I rejected the whole of this early work. When I was something over twenty, I came to the conclusion that these minor writings were dissipating my energy, and that it would be better to concentrate on a single philosophical work. So I made a preliminary sketch of my Pao P'o Tzu. But then came the rebellion; and during my wandering life and my exile in the south, parts of the work were lost. More than ten years passed before I was able to complete the book in its final form, the esoteric part in 20 rolls, the exoteric in 50 rolls. This was in the chien-wu period (A.D. 317). The esoteric chapters treat of hsien and the drugs necessary for hsienship; of demons and magical transformations; of the conservation of vitality and the attainment of longevity; of the exorcising of evil spirits and the warding off of misfortune: all appertaining to Taoism. The exoteric chapters treat of success and failure in the world of mortals, and of what is good or bad in mundane affairs: philosophy of the orthodox school....

Owing to the poorness of my physique, I took little interest in sports and games. When a small boy, I was not equal to my companions in throwing the tile or in boxing. I never engaged in cock or duck fights, nor attended dog or horse racing.

If I see people playing games and gambling, I take no notice of them; and if somebody drags me off to watch them, it makes no impression whatever on my mind, and I fall into a sort of daydream. Thus it is that even at the present day I do not know how many squares there are on a chess-board, nor the names of the notches on dice. In general, it may be said that such trivial accomplishments tend only to confuse the mind and interfere with every sort of useful activity. They go by the name of pleasure, but in reality they give rise to sorrow, shamelessness, and the spirit of contention, besides causing material losses and leading to quarrels and resentment.... When I began writing this autobiography, some one criticized me for doing so, and asked why I should have any misgivings as to the verdict of posterity. To this I replied that man's life was fleeting and insecure, and my own position singularly unstable. I had been in conflict with the age, had no influence or friends at Court. No history had sounded my praises, nor had my fame been perpetuated by inscriptions on bronze. Although this autobiography might not advantage me in my own lifetime, yet it would serve to hand my memory down to future times. P.P.T.

KUO P'O

Kuo P'o was a classical scholar of wide learning and eminent talents, though halting in conversation, and his poems were the best of all those produced in the period following the civil war of the Three Kingdoms. He was interested in the archaic script and out-of-the-way characters, and was a marvellous adept at sorcery and divination.

When troubles broke out in the country north of the Yellow River, P'o threw his divining slips in order to forecast future developments. "Alas!" he sighed, "the black-haired people are about to be submerged by an alien race, and I fear our native homesteads will be turned into barbarian wastes."

Thereupon he secretly collected his friends and relations, and travelled about in all directions to dozens of families, urging them to flee the country and betake themselves to the south-east. Kuo P'o now proceeded to Lu-chiang [in Anhwei], where Hu Meng-k'ang was governor. At that time the district between the Huai and the Yangtse was enjoying perfect peace, and Meng-k'ang, lulled into a sense of security, had no mind to retreat south of the great river. P'o had recourse to divination, and obtained in response the single word "Ruin", but Meng-k'ang still refused to be convinced. In urging the people to pack up and go, P'o was actuated to some extent by a passion for one of his host's servant-girls. Finding no other means of getting hold of her, he took three peck-measures of small beans and scattered them in a circle about his host's dwelling. Early the next morning the latter saw several thousand men in scarlet surrounding the place, who however vanished when he approached to examine them more closely. Much disturbed by this vision, he begged P'o to consult the mystic diagrams on his behalf. P'o did so, and told him that he ought not to keep that particular girl in his household: "You should have her conveyed," he said, "twenty li away from here towards the south-east, and there put her up for sale; but be careful not to haggle over the price. Thus you may get rid of this uncanny manifestation." The other did as he was told, and P'o secretly commissioned a man to buy the girl for him at a low price. Then he wrote out a charm and threw it into the well, whereupon all the men in scarlet appeared with their hands bound behind their backs, and making for the well, jumped into it one after another. P'o's host was overjoyed, and P'o himself went off with the girl. Only a month or two ater Lu-chiang fell into the hands of the Tartars ....

The Emperor's chief minister, Wang Tao, had a high opinion of Kuo P'o, and retained him as military adviser on his own staff. Once, when he had bidden him consult the diagrams, P'o replied: "Your Excellency is in danger of being struck by lightning. Order your men to drive some distance to the west, and fetch a cypress tree. Have this cut down to the length of your body, and keep it in the apartment where you are accustomed to sleep. In this way the mischief will be averted." Wang Tao acted on this advice; and, indeed, a few days later a thunderbolt fell, smashing the cypress log to atoms ....

Afterwards Kuo P'o entered the service of Wang Tun, then plotting rebellion, who asked him to consult his divining slips as to the outcome. P'o returned the answer: "No success." This confirmed Tun in his suspicion that P'o had had dealings with his enemies; and having been told that the diagrams were also unfavorable, he went on to inquire how long he was going to live. P'o replied: "My previous reading of the diagrams, Sir, makes it clear that if you embark on this enterprise, disaster will overtake you ere long; but if you remain quietly at Wu-ch'ang, your length of years will be beyond computation." This made, Tun very angry: "Now tell me, please," he said, "how long your own life will last."--"My allotted span," replied P'o, "comes to an end this very day." In a rage, Tun had him arrested and taken out to the South Hill for execution. Kuo P'o was then forty-nine years of age. C.S.

PAO CHING

"Long have you been yearning for Tao. I will initiate you into the secret of hsienship. All those who are not conceived as hsien in their mother's womb can only attain to hsienship by release from the flesh. The better way of obtaining release from the flesh is by means of a sword; the inferior method is by means of bamboo or wood. Dipping your brush into the divine elixir, you write on the sword blade the charm of the Supreme Mystic Yin Sheng, and in a little while the sword is transformed into the shape and appearance of the person who is being translated, and lies quietly on the bed while the real man disappears. But the people of the house see only a corpse, and do not see the sword." L.H.C.C.

WANG CHIH

Wang Chih was a native of Ch'u-chou [in Chekiang]. He entered a mountain forest to fell trees, and came to a rock cavern in which he found a few old men playing wei-ch'i. Putting down his axe, he stood and watched them. One of the party took up something that looked like a date-stone and handed it to Chih, telling him to suck its juice, when he would find himself immune from hunger and thirst. Then he said to him: "You have been here a good while: you had better go home." Wang Chih picked up his axe, but found that its handle had crumbled away into dust. Quickly he returned to his home, and discovered that several centuries had elapsed! All his relatives and friends had long since disappeared, so he went back to the mountains and finally attained Tao. From time to time he was seen, still alive, by his fellow men. L.H.C. (H.C.)

T'AO HUNG-CHING

T'ao Hung-ching was a native of Tan-yang [near Chinkiang on the Yangtse]. While yet a boy, he evinced an exceptionally strong character. At the age of ten, having acquired a copy of Ko Hung's *Shen Hsien Chuan*, he set himself to study the work night and day, and was fired with the ambition to cultivate his own spiritual nature. He read a vast number of other books, and was much ashamed if there was anything he did not know. Before he reached manhood he was made a minister by Kao Ti of the Ch'i dynasty, and appointed tutor to the Imperial Princes. Exemption from attendance at Court was granted to him, and although he held this high position, he kept himself in strict seclusion, having no intercourse with the outer world. In the 10th year of the *yung ming* period (A.D. 492) he petitioned the Throne to be allowed to resign his office and emoluments, and permission to do so was granted him by the Emperor, who bestowed on him a bale of silk and also instructed the authorities to provide him with five pounds of *fu-ling* and two pints of white honey every month, in order to facilitate his dietetic experiments.

He now settled on the Mao mountain, beneath which, as he often maintained, was to be found the eighth cave-palace, one of the Ten

Greater Celestial Domains, which was 150 li in circumference. Some years later he erected a three-storeyed building, of which he himself occupied the top floor and his disciples the middle floor, while guests were admitted to the ground floor only. He loved the sound of wind in the pines, and had all his courtyards planted with those trees. Occasionally he would wander alone amongst rocks and springs, and everyone who saw him took him for a hsien.

He also constructed a celestial globe, or planetarium, which was about three feet high. The earth was in the middle and remained stationary while the heavens revolved about it. The 28 Stellar Mansions thus fulfilled their periods, and the Seven Bright Ones (sun, moon, and five planets) pursued their courses. The stars were luminous in the dark and faded in the light. The globe was kept constantly revolving by a mechanical device, and the whole thing agreed with the actual motion of the heavens.

When he had received the divine charms and secret formulas from a friend, Hung-ching felt convinced that the elixir could be prepared, only it distressed him that he had none of the necessary drugs. The Emperor, however, gave him pure gold, cinnabar, copperas, realgar, and other minerals, with which he succeeded in compounding a "flying elixir". It looked like hoar-frost or snow, and when he swallowed some it made his body lighter. The Emperor also took it with good results, and his esteem for Hung-ching increased. He frequently sent him presents with invitations to accept office at Court, which, however, Hung-ching declined. He merely drew a picture of two oxen, one of which was disporting itself in a meadow, while the other was wearing a golden headstall, and being led by a man who whipped it to make it go. The Emperor laughed and said: "Our friend is not to be won over." On all important matters of State, however, he was invariably consulted, whence he acquired the sobriquet of "Minister in the Mountains" . One of Hung-ching's disciples, named Huan K'ai, having attained Tao, was about to ascend on high. His master said to him: "I too have cultivated Tao and practiced its teachings with extreme dilligence. Surely there must be some fault in me that I am still kept lingering here on earth." Accordingly, he commissioned K'ai to make inquiries, and after the latter had ascended to heaven, he returned and told Hung-ching, saying: "O Master! Your secret merit has been abundantly manifested; only in the preparation of your *Materia Medica,* you have made extensive use of gadflies, leeches, and the like, so that, while deserving well of human beings, you have done injury to other living creatures. On this account twelve years must pass before you can emerge from the husk of your mortality and brush away the dust of this world, to become Supervisor of the Watery Element at the capital of P'eng-lai." Hung-ching then atoned for his fault by preparing a new edition of his *Materia Medica,* in which he was able to substitute vegetable drugs for those made from living creatures.

One day, although free from illness, he felt that his hour was at hand, and after composing a poem announcing his departure, he died at the age of eighty-five; but his complexion remained unaltered, his limbs were as supple as ever, and a fragrant perfume hovered over the mountain for days together. L.H.C.C.

T'ao Hung-ching once dreamed that a spirit appeared to him and said: "The hills are behind you, the sea in front, a golden box and a jade coffer on either hand: in this place you may keep your cinnabar." Accordingly he buried his cinnabar there; and every night after that the local fishermen used to descry the light of flames.

At the beginning of the shao-hsing period (A.D. 1131) a villager, when digging up the soil, found three porcelain boxes of different sizes, containing a reddish-brown mineral like rusty iron. One who lived nearby, Lu Chih by name, got possession of the find and kept it for six months. Then a wandering Taoist, called the Hermit of Mount Mao, appeared on the scene. Lu was much charmed by his conversation, and showed him the cinnabar, at which he expressed his astonishment. It was late in the night before they sought their beds, and when morning came, both the stranger and the cinnabar had disappeared. N.H.H.C.

10. T'ANG DYNASTY (A.D. 618-907)

YEH FA-SHAN

HIS ancestors for three generations had been Taoists, and were skilled in the arts of divination and the preservation of vitality. Secret charms were imparted to him as a boy, which gave him the power of holding spirits in subjection. The Emperor Kao Tsung heard of his fame, and invited him to come to the capital. Here he wanted to confer on him rank and office, but Fa-shan steadfastly declined them, and asked only to be a Taoist. Accordingly, he was installed in a temple attached to the Palace and treated very liberally. On one occasion Fa-shan was sacrificing before an altar which he had erected in the Ling-k'ung Temple, while a crowd of men and women watched the proceedings. Suddenly thirty or forty persons threw themselves into the flames. The onlookers were horrified, and hastened to pull them back to safety. But Fa-shan smiled and said: "These people were all possessed by disease-demons, which have been detected by my magic art." Inquiry proved this to be true, and the sufferers went away cured. C.T.S.

The Feast of Lanterns, on the 15th night of the 1st moon, was being celebrated in the grounds of the Palace with lavish profusion. The Imperial Artificer had designed a twclve-storeyed belvedere, 150 feet in height, made of colored silk and hung with blue and gold ornaments, jade and other precious stones, which tinkled harmoniously in the lightest breeze. The lanterns, made in the shape of prancing dragons, phoenixes, tigers and leopards, showed a degree of inventive skill hardly attainable by man.

Yeh Fa-shan, hurriedly summoned by the Emperor to behold the spectacle, admired it greatly: "Only the display at Liang-chou [in Kansu] can compare with it," he said. "Why, have you been there so lately?" asked the Emperor. "I had just come from there," replied Fa-shan, "when I received your Majesty's summons." The Emperor was puzzled by this, and said: "If wanted to go there now, could I do so?" —-"With the greatest of ease," replied Fa-shan; and he bade the Emperor shut his eyes, recommending him not to take a peep, as otherwise he might be terrified by what he saw. The Emperor followed his advice, and with one bound they found themselves flying through the upper air. When their feet touched earth again, Fa-shan said: "Now you may gaze your fill." And they beheld row upon row of lanterns extending for miles in continuous array amid tightly packed horses and chariots and vast crowds of sightseers. The Emperor expressed his wonder at the scene, and after a while Fa-shan said: "Now we have enjoyed the spectacle, we must go back." So once again the Emperor shut his eyes and rose up with his companion into the void. In an instant they were back in their original position at the foot of the belvedere, where songs and music were still in progress ....

The Tibetans sent an envoy to Hsuan Tsung with a richly carved box which he was entreated to open himself, so that no one else should discover the wonderful secret within. The other courtiers remained silent, but Fa-shan, scenting mischief, persuaded the Emperor not to open the box himself, but to make the envoy do so. And no sooner had the lid been raised than a hidden cross-bow came into action and shot the envoy dead ....

Chang Yueh, Duke of Wei, visited Fa-shan at his temple, and wine was served. As there was no other guest, the Master mentioned that there lived on the premises a certain retired scholar Ch'u, who had long been a recluse, with an impediment in his speech, but a great wine-bibber. At the Duke's request he was brought in, and turned out to be a squat figure hardly three feet high, with a waist of enormous girth. His salutations were clumsily performed, after which he addressed himself exclusively to the liquor. Bowl after bowl was emptied, yet his face remained quite expressionless. When the Duke was about to take his leave, the Master suddenly began to brandish his sword and abuse Mr. Ch'u, shouting: "Far from engaging in lofty conversation or profitable discourse, you have done nothing but immerse yourself in wine like a sot. What good is that?" With these words he cut off his head, and lo! it was only a large wine-cask ....

Fa-shan had arranged to make a sea-trip to Kua-chou [in Chekiang], and the boatmen were waiting for him when they saw two old men, one dressed in yellow and the other in white, who settled down on the shore and decided to while away the time with a game of wei-ch'i. So they made a beckoning gesture in the air, and an imp emerged from the water, his clothes showing no trace of wet. He was told to bring a chess-board and wine, and they sat down to their game after having agreed that "the winner should eat the Taoist who was coming on the morrow from the north". They laughed heartily at this gibe, and began putting down their pips. After a while the man in white exclaimed: "You have lost, my dear Sir! Though he is a succulent morsel, I hope you won't poach on my preserves!" Then they strolled out a long distance over the water and sank beneath the surface.

The boatmen, realizing that mischief was intended to Fa-shan, felt very uneasy, and when the Household Officer came along, informed him of what had passed. He too was much alarmed, and told Fa-shan what he had heard. But the latter only smiled and said: "Indeed! Happily there is no cause for anxiety" The boat had no sooner put off than a fierce storm arose, obscuring the light day. The other people on board grew pale with fear, but Fa-shan said quietly to his attendants: "Take my black charm and throw it over the bows." Directly this was done, the waves subsided and all was still, and they soon accomplished their voyage. Fa-shan then told the boatmen that they would find a huge fish somewhere within a radius of ten *li*. And, sure enough, a white fish over a hundred feet long and thirty spans in girth was discovered lying stark and stranded on a sand-bank. They chopped it up into slices, and it provided several months' food for the neighboring hamlets. T.P.K.C.

At noon on the 3rd day of the 6th moon, the Holy Man turned his sword into the semblance of a corpse. A cloud chariot drove up to his door, strains of celestial music filled the house, a rainbow cloud enveloped him, exquisite perfumes spread abroad, and he departed with his cortege. During the whole of that day, a column of blue smoke was seen by the citizens rising straight up to heaven from the courtyard of the temple. T.Y.C.J.C.

LO KUNG-YUAN

Lo Kung-yuan was a native of O-chou [Wu-ch'ang]. The prefect of that place gave a feast in celebration of spring, and spectators poured into the city. Among them was a man dressed in white, over ten feet in height, and very strange in his appearance. He came along with the crowd, and the gate-keepers all wondered at him. Just then a youth passed by, and shouted angrily to the stranger: "Hi! you there: why have you left the place where you belong, and come to frighten these officials? Get out as fast as you can!" Thereupon the man picked up his skirts and ran away. But the police runners took the youth into custody, and having brought him into the banqueting hall, informed the prefect of the affair. The latter asked what his name was, and he replied: "My surname is Lo, my personal name is Kung-yuan. Ever since I was a child I have been interested in Taoist arts. I just happened to catch sight of the Keeper of the River Dragons, who had come ashore to see the fun, and I sent him about his business." The prefect did not believe this story, and said: "You will have to show him to me in his proper shape." – "Very well," was the reply, "if you will kindly wait until tomorrow."

When the time came, the youth dug a small pit by the river bank, just one foot deep, and about ten feet away from the water's edge. This is filled with water. While the prefect and other citizens were looking doubtfully at these preparations, a white fish, five or six inches long, came swimming down with the current and leapt into the pool. It gradually increased in size, and a thin column of blue smoke began to rise out of the water. Very soon a dark haze filled the sky, making it hard to distinguish one object from another. Kung-yuan then said: "Let us adjourn to the Court house." But before they had got there, lightning flashed, and a deluge of rain followed. When this had abated, they saw a huge white dragon in the middle of the river, with its head touching the clouds. A moment later it had vanished.

Now it happened that Hsuan Tsung was passionately fond of hsien magic, so the prefect sent Kung-yuan to the Court, together with a memorial recounting the miracle. The Emperor was playing wei-ch'i with Chang Kuo and Yeh Fa-shan. When these two saw the newcomer, they burst out laughing and said: "What on earth can this village lad have to teach us?" Each then took a handful of *wei-ch'i* pips and asked him: "What have we got in our closed fists?" Kung-yuan replied: "Nothing at all." They opened their hands, and sure enough they were empty, all the pips being held by Kung-yuan! The Emperor was dumbfounded, and directed that he should be seated in the same order of seniority as Chang and Yeh.

There was a certain fruit known as 'sun-ripened berries' which was then for the first time being brought to the Court from the distant province of Chien-nan. It was fetched by the magic arts of Chang and Yeh, and used to arrive every day just after noon. On this day, however, night came without the fruit. The two magicians looked at each other and said: "Can this be the work of Master Lo?" It was cold weather, and they were sitting round the stove. Kung-yuan, who had previously stuck a chopstick in the fire, now laughed and drew it out. Soon afterwards the fruit arrived. Yeh questioned the bearer as to the delay, and he said: "When I was just about to reach the capital, blazing fire filled the heavens, and there was no way for me to pass. A few moments ago the fire died away, and I was able to get through." Thenceforward, everyone treated Kung-yuan with the utmost deference. T.P.K.C.

Hsuan Tsung took lessons from Kung-yuan in the art of making himself invisible, but could not get the latter to disclose the whole secret, so that either a piece of his robes or a corner of his hat could always be seen. He inquired the reason, and Kung-Yuan replied: "Your Majesty is unable to cast away the Empire like an old shoe, and is only making a game of Tao. Were you complete master of all my magical arts, the bearers of the Imperial seal would be oppressed with the weight of your intellect." This made Hsuan Tsung very angry, and he began cursing his teacher; whereupon Kung-yuan quickly passed into the substance of one of the pillars in the hall, from which coign of vantage he remonstrated with the Emperor on his lack of courtesy. More furious still, the Emperor ordered the pillar to be removed, but when it had been cut away, a loud voice was still heard issuing from the stone pedestal. This also was removed, and on examination was found to be transparent, the form of Kung-yuan, little more than an inch high, being clearly visible within. The pedestal was then smashed to pieces, but in each of the fragments a tiny figure still remained. Thoroughly alarmed, the Emperor now offered an apology, and the figures disappeared. L.H.C.C.

Some time afterwards, an Imperial envoy was making his way to Shu when he met Kung-Yuan face to face. Taking a sealed envelope from his sleeve, the latter said: "Pray give this to his Majesty, and say it comes from one Wei Ssu-yen. He will understand." On reading the letter, Hsuan Tsung was quite disconcerted; but no sooner had the envoy left the presence than Kung-yuan himself appeared. "Why have you changed your name?" asked the Emperor. "Your Majesty removed my head," was the reply, "so I made the same alteration in my name."
The three characters used for writing "Wei Ssu-yen" are the same as those for "Lo Kung-yuan" *minus* their tops. The Emperor humbly admitted his fault and wanted to make amends; but Kung-yuan assured him that the whole affair was merely a joke. "One who has attained hsienship," he said, "is immune from all calamity. Heaven and Earth might be engulfed, and still he would remain unscathed; how much less could he be injured by ordinary weapons?" T.P.K.C.

MA HSIANG

Ma Hsiang, better known as Ma Tzu-jan ["Ma the Natural Man"], was a native of Hangchow, and became a petty official in that district.

The Minister Ma Chih was so impressed with his personality that he said to him: "By a happy chance, we bear the same surname. Let us enter into a bond of brotherhood." Meeting him again at a banquet, Ma Chih asked to be shown some minor feats of magic. So Hsiang placed a porcelain bowl on his mat, filled it with earth, and sowed a melon seed. In a few moments a melon plant was spreading in every direction, and put forth flowers and fruit. These were picked and handed to the assembled guests, who pronounced them to be delicious, and much superior to ordinary melons in flavor. He went on to extract a great number of cons from all parts of his person right down to his stockings.

They were thrown on the floor, and all appeared to be good copper cash. Then he swept them together into a well, and uttered a cry, whereupon they all came flying out one by one. They were picked up by the company, but after a while they disappeared again. Ma Chih having happened to remark that the city was infested with rats, Hsiang wrote out a charm, and got someone to stick it up on the south wall. Then he drummed on a bowl with a pair of chopsticks, and gave a long whistle. At once an army of rats appeared, scuttled up under the charm, and stopped there cowering. Hsiang commanded one of the rats, larger than the rest, to approach the dais on which he sat, and addressed it thus: "You diminutive creatures of the furry tribe, Heaven supplies you with food in the shape of grain. Why must you burrow your way through walls and gnaw holes in our dwelling-houses, making yourselves day and night a nuisance to his Excellency? Being tender-hearted, I cannot bring myself to exterminate you utterly, but your leader must in return conduct his hordes away from this town." The large rat then retired, and all the others came forward to make a sort of prostration, as though in contrition for their guilt. This done, they re-formed their ranks and passed out of the city gates in an unending stream. From that time onward the city has been entirely free from rats.

Later on, Ma Hsiang journeyed south with two Taoist companions, Wang Chih-wei and Wang Yen-sou, and came to a Buddhist monastery where three hundred monks were having a meal. Seeing that Hsiang and the others were just ordinary unescorted wayfarers, they remained squatting and eating their food without troubling to make any polite salutations. They let them have a little rice, but Hsiang refused to touch it, and hurried his companions away to an inn situated at some distance from the monastery.

In the middle of the night voices were heard outside inquiring for three Taoists, and the landlord hastened to tell them that the men they sought were still under his roof This news appeared to fill the inquirers with great joy, and they begged to be allowed to see them without delay. When they were admitted, they turned out to be two of the monks. After making humble obeisance, they exclaimed in piteous accents: "Our brethren of the monastery did not recognize you yesterday as men of Tao, and failed to receive you with proper respect, thereby drawing down severe punishment on their heads. Since then, none of the three hundred have been able to rise from their seats. We two alone were not seated, as we were engaged in work at the time, and that is how we were able to follow you hither in order to beg the release of our brethren."

Hsiang did not reply to this appeal, but continued to slumber, while the other two only laughed. But the monks renewed their supplications with such earnestness that at last Hsiang said: "In future, don't behave so rudely to strangers. Go home again, and when you enter the monastery you will find that your companions are able to rise from their seats." The two did as they were bid, and it fell out just as Hsiang had promised ....

The three friends continued their journey and put up for the night at another inn. The accommodation here was small, and the place was already crowded, so the innkeeper said jestingly: "There is no room left, but you Taoists can sleep on a wall, and I give you full permission to do that." Darkness was rapidly coming on, and both Chih-wei and Yen-sou were strongly in favor of staying there for the night, so Hsiang said to them: "Do you sleep in the common room, and I will look after myself." So saying, he sprang lightly up on to one of the roof-beams, and hanging from it by one leg, went to sleep upside down.

The innkeeper, happening to get up in the night, saw him in this posture by the light of his candle, and was struck dumb with amazement. But Hsiang said: "If I can make a beam do, what prevents me from trying the wall?" And in a trice he had passed into the wall itself, where he remained for a long time. Mine host was now full of apologies, and ushered the other two into his private apartments, where he provided them each with a clean and comfortable bed. The next morning he tried to persuade Hsiang to make a longer stay, but the latter suddenly vanished; and Chih-wei and

Yen-sou, having proceeded several li in search of him, found him eventually waiting for them by the roadside. H.H.C.

Ma Hsiang had all the outward appearance of a lunatic. He was in the habit of buying wine on credit from a wine-shop in the street of the White Pagoda. One day, when flushed with liquor, he said to the owner of the establishment: "Now that I have achieved hsien-ship, I cannot bear to haggle over the price of the wine that I owe you for." And, producing the philosopher's stone from his satchel, he proceeded to turn all the wine-vendor's iron vessels into glistening gold! C.H.F.C.

We may fitly conclude with some stanzas attributed to Ma Hsiang. They sum up the philosophic creed of this eccentric hsien.

In days gone by I followed Wei Po-yang as my Master,
And spent half my time lying tipsy on a gilded couch.
He chid me harshly for slothful ways,
And back into the world I went, still a frenzied lover of wine.

Before I awakened to the Truth, I enjoyed no interval of repose;
But now I have shaken off all cares with the dust of mortality.
Let us sing the praises of good wine, precious as jade-juice,
And cease hankering after the charms of female face and form.

With smiles we disguise the bitterness in our heart,
And our hair turns white with the anguish of separation.
Happily, a refuge awaits me in cloud-land:
The illimitable green hills shall be mine!

Wherefore refine cinnabar in order to preserve our youth?
Noise is not in the market-place, not quiet on the mountain tops.
To those in quest of life-prolonging drugs I say:
"The great secret is to take things with an impassive mind." S.H.T.K.

11. THE EIGHT IMMORTALS

About the "Eight Immortals", that figure so frequently in Chinese works of art, much has already been written, but a few words on each of them may not come amiss. Many such groups of eight have been famous in the past, the most ancient, so far as we know, being the Eight Worthies who visited Liu An. The present group was apparently not heard of until the thirteenth century, though most of its members are assigned to the T'ang period. "Nine Immortals" are also mentioned in a manuscript of the seventh century, and their cult appears to have been widespread. One of the nine, having the sight of one eye, acted as leader to the other eight, who were all totally blind. They begged in the street as they went along, and used to perform feats of magic.

Chung-li Ch'uan, the earliest in point of time, seems to have been chiefly responsible for the formation of the group. Tradition makes him a Han general, but there is no real evidence to show that he was an historical personage; and, considering his popular renown, he has but few striking exploits to his credit. His birth was accompanied by strange phenomena, and several physical peculiarities are recorded. All his life he was a wanderer, and he was converted to Tao by an aged man whom he met in a remote village. Towards the end of his career he fell in with the Taoist adept T'ao Hung-ching, and received from him "a pinch of the Great Monad" (a mysterious cosmic entity existing before the evolution of material things), a fire-charm, and some of the spiritual elixir.

Artists depict him as a fat, bearded old man, scantily clad, and carrying a feathered fan, with fly-whisk attached, or sometimes a two-edged sword.

Chang Kuo was a hermit whose origin is unknown. It was his custom to ride a white donkey, on which he could cover immense distances in a single day. When he stopped to rest, he would fold the animal up like paper, and put it away in his cap-box. Then, when he was ready to start again, he sprayed water over it from his mouth, and changed it back into a donkey. He is said to have been invited to Court by more than one of the early T'ang emperors, but did not respond until the reign of Ming Huang, who treated him with great respect. On receiving another summons, however, he immediately lay down and died. He was buried in the usual way by his disciples, but subsequently, when the coffin was opened, it was found to be quite empty. Pictures of Chang Kuo show him seated on his donkey and holding a musical instrument called a fish-drum, which looks like a golf-bag with two clubs (really castanets) protruding from it.

Lu Yen (or familiarly, Lu Tung-pin), also of the T'ang dynasty, is probably the most popular member of the group. Though he is said to have failed twice for the doctor's degree, he is widely worshipped as a patron saint of literature. He became the pupil of an old Taoist encountered by chance, who was no other than Chung-li Ch'uan, and during a period of probation before he became a hsien he had to undergo a series of ten ordeals. The last of these was the hostile approach of a host of demons in terrifying shapes, which left him completely undismayed. Once he fell asleep while a meal of yellow millet was cooking, and dreamt of events extending over the best part of a lifetime; yet on awaking he found the millet still uncooked.

His emblem is the magic two-edged sword which conferred the gift of invisibility, and enabled him to overcome evil spirits.

A picture of Lu Tung-pin, reproduced from a painting on silk through the courtesy of Professor W. Perceval Yetts, will be found on the cover of this book.

Ts'ao Kuo-chiu is said, on dubious authority, to have been the younger brother of a Sung empress in the eleventh century, "a handsome youth of peaceful disposition". One day, in the course of their wanderings, Chung-li Ch'uan and Lu Tung-pin came to his dwelling-place, and asked to be told the object of his spiritual meditations. "Tao alone," he replied, "is the object which I have in view." – "And where is Toa?" [sic] asked the two hsien. Kuo-chiu pointed up to heaven.--"Where then is heaven?"--Kuo-chiu pointed to his heart. Chung-li Ch'uan smiled and said: "The heart is one with heaven, and heaven is one with Tao? Nay, then you have a true understanding of the essential constitution of things." And accordingly they admitted him to the company of immortals.

Ts'ao Kuo-chiu is usually represented as a bearded grandee in Court attire. His distinctive attribute is, somewhat incongruously, a pair of clapper castanets.

Li T'ieh-kuai, that is, "Li with the Iron Staff", is depicted as a lame and repulsive-looking beggar, though originally he was a handsome, well-built man. This is how the transformation came about. When he was setting off to meet Lao Tzu on one of the sacred mountains, he told a disciple that only the spiritual part of him was making the journey, while his body would remain behind. If the spirit should not return within seven days, the body might be burnt. Now, the disciple was anxious to visit his sick brother, so he left on the sixth day, after burning the body. Consequently, when the Master's spirit returned on the following day, it had nowhere to go, until at last it entered and re-animated the corpse of a beggar who had died of starvation. Thereafter Li T'ieh-kuai walked the earth in the guise of a cripple, clad in rags and tatters.

In pictures he is seen hobbling along with the aid of a staff. Out of a bottle-gourd in his hand there rises a mysterious vapour, in which appears an emblem of his spiritual self.

Han Hsiang Tzu was a nephew of the great T'ang poet Han Yu. At birth he had all the marks of a future hsien. Of an eccentric disposition, he hated all the pomps and vanities of the world, and delighted in stillness and obscurity. His mind was absorbed in the art of alchemy and the pursuit of the elixir. When urged by his uncle to apply himself to study, he replied: "The object of my study is different from yours." He was instructed by Chung-li Ch'uan and Lu Tung-pin in their system of Tao, and followed them on their wanderings. Coming to a peach-tree, he climbed up to pluck the fruit of immortality, but was thrown to the ground by the snapping of a branch and was killed. At the very same moment he was transfigured and became a hsien. Afterwards, in the guise of a Taoist priest, he tried to convert his uncle, who was a strong Confucianist, and succeeded at least in convincing him that he was no charlatan.

His attribute is a flute, besides which he is often to be seen with a pair of long castanets and an alchemist's crucible.

Lan Ts'ai-ho is portrayed as a ragged, unkempt, good-looking youth, sometimes even as a girl. All accounts of this hsien are purely legendary, but he is said to have gone about with one foot bare, singing crazy songs which he improvised as he went along. In summer he stuffed his gown with cotton-wool, while in winter he would sleep in the snow, with vapour rising from his body like steam. When drunk, he used to sing and caper, and was followed by crowds of people who did not know what to make of his antics. The cash which he received as alms he would thread on a string and trail behind him as he walked. If any were lost, he would pay no heed. He used to give his money to the poor, or spend it in wine-taverns. It was from a wine-tavern that he eventually soared up to the sky on the back of a crane. This strange being is generally shown with a basket full of flowers and plants associated with longevity, such as chrysanthemums, plum-blossoms, sprigs of pine and bamboo, etc.

Ho Hsien Ku is the only undoubted female hsien belonging to the group. At the age of fourteen or fifteen she dreamt that she was visited by a divinity who advised her to eat powdered mica in order to etherealize her body. She also met a stranger who gave her a peach, and on returning home she found that she had been absent not for one day, as she had supposed, but for a whole month; yet she was not one whit the worse for going all that time without food. Having made a vow of chastity, she withdrew into the mountains, where she would flit to and fro like a bird. Towards the beginning of the eighth century she is said to have ascended on high in broad daylight. Ho Hsien Ku's special emblem is a bamboo ladle, for which the following explanation is given: she had a stepmother who treated her harshly and kept her toiling all day long over menial domestic duties. Despite this, she behaved with such exemplary patience the Lu Tung-pin was moved to come and rescue her from her miserable drudgery. He found her busy in the kitchen, and as he bore her upwards the ladle she was using still remained in her hand.

Made in the USA
Monee, IL
18 October 2026

66035038R00208